NEW FORCES IN WORLD POLITICS

Seyom Brown

NEW FORCES IN WORLD POLITICS

The Brookings Institution
Washington, D.C.

THE BROOKINGS INSTITUTION is an independent organization devoted to nonpartisan research, education, and publication in economics, government, foreign policy, and the social sciences generally. Its principal purposes are to aid in the development of sound public policies and to promote public understanding of issues of national importance.

The Institution was founded on December 8, 1927, to merge the activities of the Institute for Government Research, founded in 1916, the Institute of Economics, founded in 1922, and the Robert Brookings Graduate School of Economics and Government, founded in 1924.

The Board of Trustees is responsible for the general administration of the Institution, while the immediate direction of the policies, program, and staff is vested in the President, assisted by an advisory committee of the officers and staff. The by-laws of the Institution state, "It is the function of the Trustees to make possible the conduct of scientific research, and publication, under the most favorable conditions, and to safeguard the independence of the research staff in the pursuit of their studies and in the publication of the results of such studies. It is not a part of their function to determine, control, or influence the conduct of particular investigations or the conclusions reached."

The President bears final responsibility for the decision to publish a manuscript as a Brookings book or staff paper. In reaching his judgment on the competence, accuracy, and objectivity of each study, the President is advised by the director of the appropriate research program and weighs the views of a panel of expert outside readers who report to him in confidence on the quality of the work. Publication of a work signifies that it is deemed to be a competent treatment worthy of public consideration; such publication does not imply endorsement of conclusions or recommendations contained in the study.

The Institution maintains its position of neutrality on issues of public policy in order to safeguard the intellectual freedom of the staff. Hence the interpretations or conclusions in Brookings publications should be understood to be solely those of the author or authors and should not be attributed to the Institution, to its trustees, officers, or other staff members, or to the organizations that support its research.

Foreword

The era called the cold war was a period of unusually stable expectations regarding the identity of friends and adversaries—expectations that profoundly influenced the day-to-day diplomacy of military affairs, trade and investment, development assistance, and international institutions. Foreign policy analysis could reasonably be concentrated on precise evaluations of specific policy options.

With the waning of cold war attitudes, expectations underlying inherited policies and institutions, both in the United States and abroad, seem to be dissolving. An attempt to discern emerging patterns in the currents of contemporary world politics is necessarily speculative, yet informed speculation is perhaps most important—and most difficult—when traditional patterns appear to be breaking down. Neither a revision of established policies nor the nature of their possible successors can be evaluated without substantial conjecture as to the sources of pressures for change, their strength, and their likely duration.

A set of such conjectures on the emerging world political context of American foreign policy is the substance of this book. In presenting his interpretation of world political trends, the author does not presume that all reasonable men looking at the same events and asking themselves the same questions would come to the same conclusions. Rather, he offers his hypotheses in the spirit of dialogue, to stimulate others to speculate, before all the evidence is in, on the sources and long-term potentials of the current political flux, and on their significance for American policy over the near term.

The range of subjects treated has required the author to draw heavily on the insights of others, as much, owing to the scarcity of speculative writing on world politics in recent years, through conversation as through their published works. For this reason, and because this book expresses the author's own synthesis of pertinent information and ideas, the footnoted citations do not adequately convey his intellectual debts.

Of singular importance to the development of his ideas has been the opportunity to participate in a Council on Foreign Relations study group on future world order, chaired by Miriam Camps. Other members of the group are Lincoln Bloomfield, Richard N. Cooper, William Diebold, Jr., Ernest B. Haas, Stanley Hoffmann, Klaus Knorr, David W. MacEachron, Joseph S. Nye, and Eugene B. Skolnikoff. In addition to thanking members of the study group, the author gratefully acknowledges advice on both the form and substance of the manuscript given by Robert Bowie, Zbigniew Brzezinski, Edward R. Fried, Larry L. Fabian, Morton H. Halperin, Carl Kaysen, Robert E. Osgood, Henry Owen, and Marshall Shulman. Others whose advice and criticisms were valuable at various stages in the project include Philip Abelson, A. Doak Barnett, C. Fred Bergsten, Lester Brown, Ralph N. Clough, Melvin Croan, Bart Fisher, Leslie H. Gelb, John Sewell, Philip H. Trezise, and John Yochelson.

Research assistance was provided by Breck Milroy, Moses N. Nwoye, Rita O'Conner, Terese Sulikowski, and Mary Ann Woodland. The largest burden of typing and associated manuscript preparation tasks fell to Georgina Sorzano and Olive Williams. The manuscript was edited by Jane H. Carroll; the index was prepared by Patricia P. B. Wells.

The author, Seyom Brown, has been a senior fellow at the Brookings Institution since 1969. He is also an adjunct professor of foreign policy at the Johns Hopkins School of Advanced International Studies in Washington, D.C.

The study was conducted as a part of the Institution's program of Foreign Policy studies directed by Henry Owen, and was supported in part by a grant from the Ford Foundation.

Part of Chapters 6 and 11 appeared in Mr. Brown's essay, "The Changing Essence of Power," in *Foreign Affairs*, January 1973, published by the Council on Foreign Relations, and are reprinted here with the permission of the Council.

The views, opinions, and interpretations in this book are solely those of the author. They should not be attributed to other staff members, officers, or trustees of the Brookings Institution, or to the organizations that support its research.

February 1974   KERMIT GORDON
Washington, D.C.   *President*

Contents

Introduction   1

Part One: Disintegration of the Cold War Coalitions

1. **The Weakening of the Foundations**   7
   Cornerstone Premises of the Cold War Coalitions 8
   The New Fragmentation of Military Security 9
   The Slackening of Ideological Bonds 20

2. **Strains in the Anticommunist Coalition: The Rise of
   Nonmilitary Issues**   29
   Effects of the Decline in Security Concerns 29
   Growing Tensions in the Economic Realm: Multipolarity
      and Interdependence 33
   The Pull of Domestic Problems 42

3. **Cracks in the Soviet Sphere**   45
   Destalinization and Desatellization 46
   Ramifications of the Sino-Soviet Split 50
   The Future of the Socialist Commonwealth in Europe 54

4. **Spans across the Ideological Divide**   66
   Economic Ties between Russia and America 67
   Openings in the Great Wall of China 78
   Dangers and Opportunities in Europe 84

5. **North-South Tensions**   93
   Legacies of Cold War Neocolonialism 94
   The Group of Seventy-seven 103
   New Opportunities for Selective Leverage 104
   Long-Term Prospects 106

6. **The Emerging System of Multiple Coalitions**   109
   The Dominant Tendencies 109
   The Emerging International System 112

Part Two: Challenges to the Nation-State System

7. **The Impact of Technology on Community**   123
   Primacy of the Nation-State System *124*
   Incapacities of the Existing System *125*

8. **Economic Transnationalism**   144
   Economic Challenges to the Autonomy of the Nation-State *144*
   Alternative Political Responses *151*

9. **Cultural Pressures on the Nation-State**   161
   Cosmopolitanism *161*
   The Affluent Counterculture *163*
   Ethnicity *171*
   The Intersection of Countercultures *178*

Part Three: Prognosis and Prescription

10. **The Transformation of World Politics**   185
    The Evolving Polyarchy *186*
    Regionalism as an Alternative *190*
    Constructing a Political Framework for World Community *197*

11. **Policy Opportunities for the United States**   208
    Constructive Statemanship for the Last Quarter of the
       Twentieth Century *209*
    The Role of the United States *210*

    Index   217

NEW FORCES IN WORLD POLITICS

Introduction

The alignments and antagonisms of the recent past are shifting ground, and structures premised on their stability appear to be crumbling. Even the bedrock of the international system, the sovereignty of nation-states, is subject to severe erosion. In 1974 simply to portray the current instabilities in world politics would be to recount the obvious. The attempt here is to seek the underlying causes, to speculate on their force and how they could alter the political and institutional landscape, and, finally, to suggest how U.S. policies could encourage or discourage the eventual emergence of alternative patterns of world politics.

But is it possible in the midst of the flux to distinguish clearly the lasting from the ephemeral changes so as to prescribe with confidence U.S. policies consistent with the most significant forces? The answer surely is no, if exact prognosis based upon measurable trends is required. The sources of many current instabilities lie too far beneath the surface, embedded in historical strata subject only to fragmentary probes. The present contains too much movement and tension to apply precise tools of measurement. And the future, though largely determined by past events, has yet to be shaped by the decisions of men and women of this generation—decisions which will be affected by their images of, and preferences for, alternative futures as well as their understandings of the past.

One response to the elusiveness of the future is to concentrate on the more tangible present and put out of mind the long-range implications of current actions as beyond deliberate control by today's decisions anyway. Accordingly, the only sensible way to manage one's affairs is to serve those specific interests clearly within reach with capabilities readily at hand. Up to the fall of 1973 such "pragmatic marginalism" had been the typical response of world statesmen to alarmist forecasts of impending shortages in the supply of petroleum and other raw materials, as well

1

as to signs that the Arabs might use oil as a political weapon. Western commercial and political diplomacy was working to reduce immediate tangible costs and risks, on the wishful assumption that what was intangible and only problematical would not materialize in the near future.

Another response to the realization of the future's unpredictability is to try to reinforce patterns inherited from the past, assuming that the structures which have survived into the present are probably the most resilient. Since enough is not known about either the past or the future, the appearance of cracks in the plaster recommends a repair and reinforcement job rather than removal or new construction. Even if the reinforcements involve considerable current outlays, the conservative will favor incurring these costs. Moreover, he does not require certitude that, once reinforced, the old structure will in fact survive the new forces. His greatest fear is of the unwisdom of his contemporaries. He profoundly doubts their ability to foresee the future or to build survivable institutions. The safer course is to stick with what has been handed down to us, imperfect though it may be. This point of view is best represented in current world affairs by those in the noncommunist West and those in the Soviet sphere who are opposed to increasing East-West intercourse on grounds that it could dangerously erode the bipolar structure of world politics, especially in Europe, where NATO and the Warsaw Pact have been assumed to be simultaneously the major barriers to cross-bloc aggression and major instruments of discipline within each bloc.

This book offers a response to the volatility of contemporary world politics which differs importantly from that of the pragmatic marginalist *and* the conservative realist—both of whom would defer choices of fundamental social policy and institution building as far as possible into the future, to situations where crises demand choice but the options are already narrowed. The approach taken here strives to anticipate developments in science, technology, and commerce in order to channel them in accordance with the imperatives of social order and justice. Otherwise the dominant social forces are likely to be driven almost exclusively by narrow and short-range materialistic values. Only through advance speculation about the likely impact of diverse world trends upon one another, and a willingness to act upon these speculations in the face of considerable uncertainty, can effective social policy constraints be put on current forces now drastically exacerbating arms races, cutthroat competition for scarce resources, ecological damage, the world poverty gap, and the alienation of various cultures from one another.

For two decades following World War II the most powerful social policy constraints on scientific, technological, and economic developments were those dictated by the cold war. On both sides of the ideological divide, the need to protect one's society against malevolent enemies was invoked to justify the co-optation of science and technology by the state and the international transfer of resources for political purposes. The cold war provided two vast hierarchical overlays on the 300-year-old nation-state system that prior to World War II had been the major political structure for men's activities. What is now happening to international alliances and the underlying nation-state system is therefore crucial for any attempt to prescribe social policies for channeling man's expanding capacities to alter the natural universe.

In Part 1 of this book the fate of alliance structures is examined through an analysis of the sources and future force of cross-pressures on the dominant postwar coalitions. A conventional assumption in the political literature of the cold war period, as well as in policy circles, has been that a major thaw in the cold war, if and when it occurred, would lead to a worldwide strengthening of the nation-state as the structure for regulating man-to-man and man-to-nature relationships. But this assumption is now being undermined by what looks like a marked disintegration of the cold war coalitions and by growing challenges to the competence and authority of nation-state institutions. Part 2 shows that some of the social demands and movements loosened by the thawing of the cold war are having erosive impacts on the older nation-state structure of world politics. In addition, other challenges to the authority of the nation-state are strengthening some of the social forces undermining the cold war coalitions.

A central thesis of the book is that both powerful structures—the cold war coalitions and the nation-state system—are being undermined simultaneously, but at different rates, and unevenly in various segments of the globe. The weakening of both of these structures gives other bases of political community—ethnicity, religion, social class, economic function, generation—more opportunity to assert themselves and to vie for the loyalty of individuals. A companion thesis is that the resulting incoherence in the world's political structure is likely to be profoundly inadequate to the tasks of global management required to assure the healthy survival of the human species.

Part 3 draws from these prognoses the choices emerging for world statesmanship—the most basic being whether to attempt to reduce the dependence of societies upon one another or to support policies making for greater interdependence. The concluding chapter suggests how the United States can influence the emergence of those patterns of world politics most consistent with this country's capabilities and character.

PART ONE

Disintegration of the Cold War Coalitions

CHAPTER ONE

The Weakening of the Foundations

The cold war coalitions were the dominant ordering structures of international relations in the quarter century following World War II. A fresh look at their foundational weaknesses and the sources of their apparent increasing disintegration is therefore the starting point for an effort to gear U.S. foreign policy to the emerging shape of world politics.

The loosening of coalition unity and the changes in international alignment now observable are viewed from one perspective as simply a shift in the surface strata of world politics. Speculations about underlying structural erosions are regarded as unverifiable and unhelpful. The increasing conflicts of interest between the Western European countries, the United States, and Japan, the intensification of the Sino-Soviet conflict, and the fashioning by the communist countries of special relationships with various members of the anticommunist coalition are portrayed as marginal adaptations of the basic cold war pattern of amity and enmity: A certain amount of multipolarity, it is argued, was bound to develop in both camps as Europe and Asia recovered from the devastation of World War II; but fundamentally the postwar balance of power remains two-sided, and the most salient basis of international alignment is still the value conflict between the communists and the anticommunists.[1]

1. The view that the essential cold war persists and nothing crucial has really changed (except the emergence of a neo-isolationist mood in the United States) is well reflected in Walter Laqueur's recent articles: "The World of the 70's," *Commentary*, Vol. 54, No. 2 (August 1972), pp. 21–28; "From Globalism to Isolationism," *Commentary*, Vol. 54, No. 3 (September 1972), pp. 63–67; "The Cool War," *New York Times Magazine* (Sept. 17, 1972), pp. 15 ff.; and "Kissinger and the Politics of Détente," *Commentary*, Vol. 56, No. 6 (December 1973), pp. 46–52. Many sovietologists report that parallel skepticism about détente pervades the Politburo, despite General Secretary Brezhnev's public rhetoric about fundamental changes in the world situation.

But the insistence that the essence of the cold war persists also rests on many unverifiable speculations. The interdependence of variables is too complex and the pace of events too rapid to isolate with confidence the constant from the changing patterns. The 1973 Middle East crisis, for example, could be seen as evidence of either a recrudescence of the cold war or its death rattle.

While it would be reckless to base U.S. foreign policy on the assumption that the USSR has suddenly become a benign power, prudent statesmanship would seem to require some planning on the premise that the foundations of the grand cold war coalitions are being fundamentally undermined. The real situation is exasperatingly elusive, and all planning must be highly tentative, not only because of the coexistence of many contrary tendencies in contemporary world politics but also because both coalitions are shaped by the prevailing *beliefs* about them (on the part of statesmen, analysts, and lay publics) as well as by so-called objective forces.

This chapter attempts to show that the observable disintegration of the cold war coalitions is the product of deeply cutting social and material forces which may be largely irreversible. In subsequent chapters the sources and potential consequences of a continuing erosion will be examined in greater detail.

Cornerstone Premises of the Cold War Coalitions

The architects and operators of the rival cold war coalitions came to believe they were elaborating structures whose foundations had been set by the heavy hand of world history. The Russians, schooled in Marxist historical materialism, saw the two coalitions as the international expression of the inevitable worldwide conflict between the capitalists and working classes. Western political leaders, particularly the Americans, reluctantly adopted a kind of historical determinism of their own as a rationale for their virtual abandonment by the early 1950s of the liberal, cooperative world view which underlay their support of the United Nations system. While differing profoundly over basic causes and ultimate solutions to the cold war, most statesmen on both sides, by their actions and rhetoric, appeared to accept four cornerstone premises:

1. The role of the United States as leader of a broad anticommunist

coalition was inescapable, since the Soviet Union could expand into the power vacuums of Europe, Asia, and the Middle East if the nations of these areas did not have the protection of the United States.

2. The Soviet Union, even if it abandoned or postponed its professed goal of transforming the world into a system of soviets, would continue to fear imperialist wars and capitalist encirclement and therefore was bound to secure its borders in the West, East, and South. These fears would drive it to assure the absolute loyalty of regimes in Eastern Europe and wherever else on the periphery of the USSR allies could be signed on.

3. This historically determined power configuration—two rival superpowers separated by power vacuums—made inevitable a clash of vital interests in the areas between. War over any of these interests became an ever-present possibility.

4. Consequently, an advantageous global balance of military power and access to zones of potential combat would be sought by each superpower. This competition for military advantage created additional geopolitical imperatives—economic resources, manpower, and bases for military operations—for maintaining large and highly coordinated multinational coalitions.

From these perspectives, national security was so dependent on the cohesion of one's coalition that the coalition itself tended to be regarded as an end rather than a means. At the least, the strength and cohesion of the coalition was thought to be the sine qua non for the pursuit of other valued objectives.

Yet hardly had the cold war coalitions been constructed before scientific, technological, and economic developments began to contradict seriously some of the military-security assumptions on which they were based. Of equal challenge to their viability was the reflowering of national rivalries and conflicts of special interest in both camps and the cultivation, though limited and experimental, of complementary interests across coalition lines.

The New Fragmentation of Military Security

The extension of the range and destructive power of weapons and the elaborate economic base needed to sustain modern military technology seemed, from the vantage point of the later 1940s and early

1950s, to validate the prophecies of early twentieth-century Anglo-American geopoliticians concerning the requirement for an extensive and permanent coalition of the Western nations. And Stalin seemed sustained in his claim that the security of the USSR required, at a minimum, a recognized sphere of Soviet dominance covering Eastern Europe. But paradoxically the volatility of technology, which was making national security by national means obsolete during the first half of the century, began during the second half to negate the utility of even the globe-girdling security communities established by the United States and the Soviet Union. As the interior zones of the extended security communities became vulnerable to massive destruction from intercontinental missiles, the importance of forward-defense allies diminished, and allies began to question the credibility of superpower pledges of protection.

Geopolitical Legacies

American geopolitical explanations for cold war bipolarity can be traced back to Tocqueville, who in 1835 saw the United States and Russia each "marked out by the will of Heaven to sway the destinies of half the globe."[2] The pre–World War I ideas of Captain Alfred Thayer Mahan, as refined in the interwar period by Sir Halford MacKinder, postulated a fundamental contest for global ascendancy between an expansive Russian empire and the insular states—Britain, the United States, and Japan. In the 1940s American geopoliticians saw an aggressive Germany in alliance with or overpowering Russia as the most menacing heartland power. But the basic minimum strategy for the insular nations remained constant: Hold the rimlands around the vast Eurasian land mass, for if the resources and sea access of the rimland areas were absorbed by the power that also controlled the heartland, that power would dominate the world.[3]

2. Alexis de Tocqueville, *Democracy in America* (Random House, Vintage Books, 1954), Vol. 1, p. 452.

3. Alfred T. Mahan, *The Problem of Asia and Its Effects upon International Relations* (Little, Brown, 1900); Halford J. MacKinder, "The Geographical Pivot of History," *Geographical Journal*, Vol. 23 (1904), pp. 421–41; Nicholas Spykman, *The Geography of the Peace* (Harcourt Brace, 1944). This interpretation of the essential similarities among Mahan, MacKinder, and latter-day American geopoliticians finds support in Stephen B. Jones, "Global Strategic Views," *Geographical Review*, Vol. 45 (1955), pp. 492–508.

The globalist geopoliticians built on the traditional American as-sumption that United States security required, first and foremost, the prevention of major enemy colonies or bases on the North American continent. Keeping the northern portions of South America out of hos-tile hands was an essential corollary of this objective. Since access to the Caribbean was primarily by sea, the United States either had to become a powerful maritime country or accept the protection of one. This was the heart of the Monroe Doctrine, which in 1823 put U.S. interests in the Western hemisphere under the ultimate protection of the British navy. If the Monroe Doctrine implied a vital American interest in the security of Britain, then by extension was not America required to support Britain's interest in a balance of power to prevent one country from dominating Europe or Asia? At the turn of the cen-tury such an American realpolitik provided a high-statecraft justifica-tion for translating the growing missionary and economic impulses for an expanded world role into support for a powerful and globally mobile U.S. navy, especially in the context of the rising German chal-lenge to British maritime supremacy. America's entry into World War I, it will be recalled, was rallied by the call to preserve the "freedom of the seas."[4]

These analyses and prescriptions of traditional Anglo-American geo-politics seemed to be confirmed by the imperial thrust of Russian for-eign policy since Peter the Great. The straits connecting the Black Sea and the Mediterranean, the approaches to the Gulf of Finland and the Baltic, national groups along the invasion routes from the West, the Oriental populations of Sinkiang and Mongolia, the northern Japanese territories—all of these have been periodically the direct targets of Russian military threats or diplomatic power plays. As is characteristic of most nation-states, Russia has invariably justified its expansionist moves as dictated by minimum security needs; and, to be sure, its long history of constant suffering from attacks by enemies on all sides gives considerable credence to the posture. From such a perspective the West—particularly Britain, France, and later the United States—in attempting to build a *cordon sanitaire* to hem in Russia, appeared

4. The popular geopolitical view was articulated by Walter Lippmann's assertion in early 1917 that "we are face to face ... with the most serious calamity that could happen to our civilization—the disintegration of sea power." Quoted by Robert E. Osgood, *Ideals and Self-Interest in America's Foreign Relations* (University of Chicago Press, 1953), pp. 117–18.

to be driven by imperial ambitions.[5] Add to this the Soviet Union's deep suspicion since 1917 that, as a socialist nation, its continued existence was intolerable to the capitalists—who were now driven to strangle it through a strategy of encirclement—and the reverse image to the world view of Anglo-American geopolitics is striking.[6]

When the end of World War II left the United States and the Soviet Union—somewhat to their surprise—the rival superpowers Tocqueville had predicted, strategists on both sides tended to dip into preexisting geopolitical lore, which gave their hunches the appearance of historically determined inevitability.[7] As crises piled up on one another there

5. Bernard Pares, *A History of Russia* (Knopf, 1947); Anatole Mazour, *Russia Past and Present* (Van Nostrand, 1951); E. Day Carman, *Soviet Imperialism: Russia's Drive toward World Domination* (Public Affairs Press, 1950).

6. According to the *Survey of Fifty Years of the Soviet Union*, published by the Central Committee in 1967, the socialist industrialization of the USSR "had to be undertaken in conditions of our country's capitalist encirclement, and of constant danger of an armed attack by the aggressive power of imperialism." Quoted by Alexander Werth, *Russia: Hopes and Fears* (Simon and Schuster, 1969), p. 30. For the persistence of this belief see Adam B. Ulam, *Expansion and Coexistence: The History of Soviet Foreign Policy 1917–67* (Praeger, 1968); and Louis J. Halle, *The Cold War as History* (Harper and Row, 1967).

7. Dean Acheson mixed traditional geopolitics and ideology most deftly in attempting to persuade congressmen to help suppress the Greek rebellion: "Only two great powers remain in the world . . . the United States and the Soviet Union. Not since Rome and Carthage had there been such a polarization of power on this earth . . . [It] was clear that the Soviet Union was aggressive and expanding. For the United States to take steps to strengthen countries threatened with Communist subversion was not to pull British chestnuts out of the fire; it was to protect the security of the United States—it was to protect freedom itself. For if the Soviet Union succeeded in extending its control over two-thirds of the world's surface and three-fourths of its population, there could be no security for the United States, and freedom anywhere in the world would have a poor chance of survival." Acheson's remarks of February 27, 1947, at the White House, as paraphrased by one of the State Department officials in attendance; Joseph M. Jones, *The Fifteen Weeks* (Viking, 1955), pp. 138–41. See also Dean Acheson, *Present at the Creation* (Norton, 1969), p. 219. The perceptions of the Russian threat prevailing in Washington at the time are detailed in Seyom Brown, *The Faces of Power: Constancy and Change in United States Foreign Policy from Truman to Johnson* (Columbia University Press, 1969), pp. 31–45.

was little time for anything but improvisation. The conceptual legacies of the past would just have to do.

By the early 1950s the official wisdom in Moscow and Washington reflected a set of remarkably similar geopolitical notions, presumed in both capitals to be self-evident: The outcome of earlier wars, the evolution of technology, and the ideological struggle had combined to leave the world with two opposing poles of attraction—the United States and the Soviet Union. Nations would coalesce around one or the other of the poles on the basis of location and ideology, with bipolar competition centering on the geographical areas in between: Central Europe and the great Eurasian rimland stretching from the Middle East to Southeast Asia.

The New Military Relationships

The military aspects of cold war geopolitics, having been inherited from the prenuclear, premissile, presupersonic age, eventually would have to be altered as the scientific and technological revolution continued to affect the geographic factors of military capability—particularly the functions of distance and natural barriers. It was not until the 1960s, however, that the massive political implications of these new military relationships began to be fully appreciated by the policy-making elite and laymen, and strategies and military commitments based on the older geopolitics began to lose support.

As missiles have become truly intercontinental, neither superpower needs distant allies to extend its lethal reach into the home territory of the other. Such allies are perhaps still strategically desirable for confounding enemy defenses and complicating enemy offensive targeting, but they are no longer essential to the success of the basic mass-destruction mission. Nor does either superpower, with reconnaissance systems in orbit around the earth, need bases near the other's frontiers to gain adequate warning of menacing deployments or impending attack.

For the superpowers the military value of allies for deterring or fighting strategic war has been receding, while the costs and risks of attempting to protect their allies by direct military action have been rising. Any war between the United States and the Soviet Union, it is recognized on both sides, carries the danger of spiraling into total war; and total war in the thermonuclear age would mean virtually total destruction of one's own society. The U.S. secretary of defense on numerous occasions throughout the 1960s publicly estimated up to 100 million fatalities on each side from the immediate blast of a thermonuclear exchange and the resulting fire storms, let alone radiation and other after-effects.[8] Officials of the Soviet Union have made similar calculations, admitting that "the nuclear bomb does not distinguish between the imperialists and the working people, it hits great areas, and therefore millions of workers would be destroyed for one monopolist."[9]

This mutual inhibition by the superpowers at the level of strategic warfare, at least against one another, was formally codified at the United States–USSR summit meeting of May 1972. The treaty limiting antiballistic missile deployments and the interim agreement for putting a numerical ceiling on offensive weapons were acknowledged by the leaders of both countries to have been the product of their "common determination that in the nuclear age there is no alternative to conducting their mutual relations on the basis of peaceful coexistence. . . . The USA and the USSR attach major importance to preventing the development of situations capable of causing a dangerous exacerbation of their relations. Therefore, they will do their utmost to prevent the outbreak of nuclear war. . . ."[10]

The balance of terror was now duly certified. But if this were to become *the* decisive logic defining U.S.-Soviet relations, it would have far-reaching implications for the military alliances on both sides. An unconditional inhibition on war between the two nuclear giants would mean that even if one of them should attack an ally of the other, the attacked party's superpower could not be relied on to enter the fray. Or, as General de Gaulle used to envision the apocalypse: There might come "some awful day" when "Western Europe should be wiped out

8. For a typical set of estimates of American and Soviet fatalities in general war see U.S. Department of Defense, "Statement of Secretary of Defense Robert S. McNamara before a Joint Session of the Senate Armed Services Committee and the Senate Subcommittee on Department of Defense Appropriations on the Fiscal Year 1966–70 Defense Program and 1966 Defense Budget" (1965; processed).

9. Open letter from the Communist Party of the Soviet Union (CPSU) Central Committee to Party Organizations and All Communists of the Soviet Union, July 14, 1963; complete text in William E. Griffith, *The Sino-Soviet Rift* (M.I.T. Press, 1964), pp. 289–325.

10. "Basic Principles of Relations between the United States of America and the Union of Soviet Socialist Republics," full text in *Weekly Compilation of Presidential Documents*, Vol. 8, No. 23 (June 5, 1972), pp. 943–44.

from Moscow and Central Europe from Washington."[11] Such anxieties had already provided strategic justification for the British to stay in the nuclear club, for the French and Chinese to join, and for the Japanese, the Indians, and the Israelis to keep alive their technical options to develop independent nuclear forces.

In an attempt to allay the exacerbation of these fears in the context of the continuing bilateral strategic arms limitation talks, President Nixon and General Secretary Brezhnev in their 1973 summit meeting in Washington pledged to "refrain from the threat or use of force against the other Party, against the allies of the other Party, and against other countries, in circumstances which may endanger international peace and security."[12] The deliberately loose wording was picked up immediately by commentators all around the world as further confirmation that the superpowers were giving their bilateral détente priority over all other relationships.

Indeed, twice during the span of the previous decade the Soviet Union had backed away contritely from rendering military support to an ally when to do so would have involved the Russians in a military encounter with the Americans—in the Cuban missile crisis of 1962, and the mining of Haiphong harbor in 1972. A few months after their 1973 no-war pledge, both superpowers prudently backed off from the direct confrontation into which they found themselves propelled as a result of their escalating support of Middle Eastern clients.

Some sovietologists caution against predicting Soviet crisis behavior in the present strategic context of full parity on the basis of the previous period of asymmetrical deterrence. Given the developing correlation of forces, the Kremlin is rather envisioned as more tempted to engage in preemptive local interventions in the hope that by staking out its claims first it will thrust onto the United States the burden of initiating U.S.-Soviet warfare, with all its dangers of escalation.[13] The strategic standoff between the superpowers, it can be argued, far from nullifying the military reasons for extended alliance systems, has enhanced their importance; for without very firm and unambiguous commitments to come to the defense of one's friends, the enemy would

11. Quoted by Brown, *The Faces of Power*, p. 296.
12. Text of "Agreement on Prevention of Nuclear War," *New York Times*, June 23, 1973.
13. See especially Zbigniew Brzezinski, "Peace and Power: Looking toward the 1970s," *Encounter* (November 1968), pp. 3–13.

in fact discount the risks of staging faits accomplis. This only states the problem without resolving it, however, since it is precisely the disproportion between the terrible physical costs of a major war against the opposing superpower and the less tangible political costs of backing out of an alliance commitment at the moment of truth that has reduced the credibility of alliances.

Washington's desire for firm military alliances was sustained for a time by the notion of flexible response. The strategists who most influenced defense planning in the United States during the 1960s argued that the emerging balance of terror at the strategic level would again bring into prominence limited contests for local position with conventional military forces. It was thought that without special U.S. provisions to maintain local balances of military power, either in the form of standing forces or through rapidly deployable capabilities, the communist countries could frequently compel the anticommunists to choose between local surrender or global holocaust. Thus, even though intercontinental missiles and reconnaissance capabilities might be reducing the value of overseas bases and allies for strategic deterrence, such outposts were even more needed to deter or fight local aggression.

While deprecating the U.S. doctrine that military conflict between the superpowers could under some circumstances remain limited in geography and weapons, the USSR continued to develop and deploy forces oriented toward particular arenas of local combat. In the early 1960s Soviet military strategists usually justified their continued interest in theater warfare capabilities by the need to follow up the results of the nuclear-missile phase of war. By mid-decade the American strategy of flexible response was taken more seriously by Soviet generals, and some of them were pushing the proposition that Soviet forces should be prepared not only for strategic nuclear war but also for local operations restricted to conventional arms or with a limited use of nuclear weapons.[14]

The revival of limited-war doctrines in the 1960s probably postponed for a time a full review and reconstruction by both the United States and the Soviet Union of the geopolitical assumptions contained within their respective alliance policies. But the very fact that nonnuclear war was again to be taken seriously stimulated national secu-

14. The evolution of Soviet military doctrine toward a begrudging acceptance of limited warfare is traced by Thomas W. Wolfe in his *Soviet Power and Europe, 1945–1970* (Johns Hopkins Press, 1970), pp. 211–16, 451–58.

rity planners to apply the fruits of the technological revolution to conventional operations as well as to strategic nuclear ones. This in turn led the military planners to reassess the importance of various locational and topographic factors in determining what foreign objectives are worth fighting for and how to fight for them.

By now it is widely recognized among strategists that communication and transportation technologies have reduced the significance of distance from the front in assessing the material costs of a military campaign. These developments have increased the ease with which military operations in remote theaters can be commenced and sustained. They have also reduced the military significance of some traditional intercontinental access routes as improvements in air freight capabilities and economies in ocean shipping have lowered the comparative costs of substitute routes. Today about six straits are considered geopolitically crucial whereas two decades ago about twenty straits were so considered. Developments in airlift, sealift, and instant communications have also reduced the military requirements for prepositioning troops and weapons in the locale of potential conflict.[15]

15. "It was rather common until recently," observed Albert Wohlstetter, "to talk of the comparative disadvantage to the United States in fighting eight to ten thousand miles from home against an adversary whose home base is near the scene of the conflict. . . . This has been [challenged] . . . by detailed studies of the comparative logistics at present levels of technology in several areas of possible non-nuclear conflict—in Thailand, in the Himalayas, in Iran and in Lebanon—and in the *actual* conflict in Korea.

"The most striking fact displayed by these studies is that the long-distance lift capacity of each side massively exceeds its short-distance lift inside the theatre, especially in the very short ranges in which the battle would be joined." Albert Wohlstetter, "Strength, Interest, and New Technologies," *The Implications of Military Technology in the 1970s*, Adelphi Paper No. 46 (London: Institute for Strategic Studies, 1968), pp. 1–14; quotation from p. 8.

The military effects of these advanced technological developments are not all one-sided, however, as is evident in the increasing vulnerability of surface naval power to attack from submarines—a fact that revives the importance of overseas prepositioning of military manpower and equipment for short limited wars. Eventually the major maritime nations may consider deploying cargo submarines to compensate for the inability to protect surface transport, but in the interim a combination of airlift and dangerous escalation threats to deter submarine warfare are likely to be featured in military contingency plans. See Paul Cohen, "The Erosion of Surface Naval Power," *Foreign Affairs*, Vol. 49, No. 2 (January 1971), pp. 330–41.

Simultaneously, the value of remote military bases as communication links for local wars has been declining. For conventional as well as strategic warfare, reconnaissance methods have been reassessed in the light of technological innovations—particularly the deployment of earth-satellites for surveillance and information relays—which can supplant battlefront or nearby observation posts and command and control headquarters.[16]

The military importance of topographic and political barriers will be further reduced by the major improvements in vertical takeoff and landing capabilities of aerospace vehicles expected during the coming decade. Much military planning still conceives of access and defense primarily in *horizontal* terms, and a new geopolitics reflecting the predominantly *vertical* dimensions of contemporary war is still developing. But even its anticipation, as in the American "Big Lift" exercises of the 1960s, weakens the mutual defense foundation of unity of the coalition.

The Arab oil embargo during their 1973 war with Israel stimulated new interest by Western strategists in the natural-resource components of military power. But for the most part their response to anticipated shortages of raw materials has been to advise a reduction in dependence on particular foreign suppliers by exploring for new sources or by developing synthetic substitutes.[17]

Although industrial country dependence on the Middle East for oil is bound to increase further before it declines, perhaps sometime after 1985, there is little prospect for a renewal of the kind of alliance-building that earlier polarized the region between American and Soviet clients. Saudi Arabia, the biggest oil producer and key to any concerted Arab policy, is the least likely Russian ally. The main regional rival of the Saudis is Iran, traditionally at odds with Iraq, which in turn is a traditional rival of Egypt. Local cross-pressures preclude any of these countries from being a loyal camp follower of any nonregional power—as

16. See Neville Brown, "Reconnaissance from Space," *The World Today* (February 1971), pp. 68–76.

17. Although the steadily rising worldwide demand for petroleum products, especially for fuel and energy purposes, was visibly increasing the dependence of industrial countries on Middle Eastern sources before 1973, it was not until the Arab nations used their oil as a political weapon against pro-Israel countries that the United States and its alliance partners began vigorous efforts to develop other sources of energy.

both the United States and the Soviet Union have learned from bitter experience.

Moreover, energy shortages are as likely to divide ideological coalition partners as to unite them. The Soviet Union's role, both as a source of crude oil and natural gas and as a world petroleum entrepreneur, can be exploited by the Kremlin in commercial and political bargaining with the West. Russia's partners in the Warsaw Pact, however, many of whom are increasingly dependent on Soviet oil, should not be very pleased at this prospect. Concurrently, the competition between the United States, Western Europe, and Japan for preferred access to Middle Eastern or Russian sources promises to become more keen. Such political implications of the world energy problem for the most part cut across the old cold war bipolarity and, if anything, are accelerating the disintegration of the superpower coalitions.

None of these trends presage a full dismantling of the U.S. and Soviet alliance systems. Although advanced technology is making it less critical for the superpowers to become militarily engaged on foreign soil, and easier for them to disengage from previous commitments, it is also making it physically easier to establish a presence in remote areas. The USSR has become a global commercial power, able to provide naval escort to its shipping in all theaters, and is deploying in the Mediterranean, Persian Gulf, and Indian Ocean capabilities that might facilitate future interventions in local conflicts.[18] With the coming of age of huge transport aircraft and naval capabilities for speedy deployment of troops and supplies, the United States can base limited-war forces primarily at home and maintain a low military profile in client states without diminishing its security commitments.[19] This means that while the costs of being denied access to many areas of the globe (previously defined as strategically essential) are easier to bear than the costs of fighting for the territory, the relative costs of getting there are also reduced. Both the United States and the USSR can cast their interest nets more widely, but fewer external interests merit being considered vital in a military sense.

18. Barry M. Blechman, *The Changing Soviet Navy* (Brookings Institution, 1973); David Fairhall, *Russian Sea Power* (Gambit, 1971); Thomas W. Wolfe, "The Soviet Quest for More Globally Mobile Military Power," No. RM-5554-PR (RAND Corp., 1967).

19. See George C. Wilson, "Shaping a 'Heartland Strategy,'" *Washington Post*, Aug. 16, 1970.

In determining how much to invest in the protection of foreign countries more weight must now be given to nonmilitary criteria—ideological or cultural affinity, marginal economic advantage, or simply how one's reputation for fidelity and toughness might be affected by a failure to protect even a marginal interest when challenged. In cases where such criteria still compel the preservation of a mutual defense relationship, there will be attempts by partners to assure one another of continued fidelity through symbolic deployments, joint exercises, and other visible acts that make it politically costly to renege on established commitments. But as no nation can be assumed to have an unswerving commitment to defend the interests of another nation, the major nations can be expected to incline increasingly toward postures of self-reliance when it comes to protection against military attack—self-reliance meaning mass-destruction capabilities under their own control and sufficient diplomatic flexibility to make deals unilaterally with their adversaries.

In sum, the technology-induced erosion of the military rationale for the extended mutual security systems associated with the cold war is an important and probably irreversible source of the serious weakening of coalition unity. In the process, elaborate and relatively permanent alliance infrastructures—such as those found in NATO—are likely to be regarded as diplomatic liabilities; for where the visible physical apparatus of alliances and military assistance agreements is large, publics and parliaments become involved in alliance issues. As statesmen seek more flexibility to make limited security commitments on an ad hoc basis, they will attempt to reduce the domestic costs of realignment and opting in and out of alliances.

The Slackening of Ideological Bonds

The pace and extent of the fragmentation of the cold war coalitions will depend on more than just the weakening of their military foundations. The willingness of the powerful coalition leaders to assume high risks to protect smaller partners will continue to be a compound of military and political, economic and cultural, material and moral, selfish and altruistic, hard and soft calculations. But given the high interdependence of these various considerations, a significant constriction of the military-security elements can itself work to dislodge some of the nonmilitary foundations of the coalitions. The reverse is also true: If there is to be hope for sustaining the military foundations, the other ingredients relied on for cohesion will have to be particularly strong. But as will be argued in the following pages, the nonmilitary foundations too are being directly weakened under the impact of new socio-economic and political forces.

The Legacy of Ideological Polarization

From the outset of their formation each of the cold war coalitions was assumed to be a community of basic common beliefs no less than an alliance to marshall power for the defense of territorial objectives. Although the standard code words such as "free world" and "socialist commonwealth" were inadequate descriptions of the values adhered to by members in each camp, they did reflect a very real difference in general approach to domestic and world order that established two rival ideological centers of gravity around which most nations tended to coalesce. The collective military force of each coalition was presumed to be available to protect a "way of life" or the "rules of the international game" as well as pieces of real estate critical to the balance of power.

The socialist camp, as viewed from Moscow, was a community of communist political parties—in some countries in control of the government, elsewhere still in opposition—which represented the class interests of the proletarians. Differences in tactics and priorities that might exist between national branches of this movement were dwarfed by their common adherence to "proletarian internationalism," which put them in universal opposition to governments and parties representing the capitalist classes. The allocation of tasks for the grand struggle against the capitalists, for the time being, required all parties to support the state interests of the USSR. But specialization of effort also obligated the USSR to protect weaker elements of the community in their confrontations with locally powerful capitalists—subject to the proviso that local communist parties could not expect to be bailed out of suicidal situations that were the product of un-Marxist adventurism (namely, moves in advance of the full ripening of the historical process).[20]

By attaching credibility to the ideological motives in Soviet foreign

20. See Zbigniew Brzezinski, *Ideology and Power in Soviet Politics* (Praeger, 1962), pp. 97–113.

policy and to the international behavior of other communist regimes and parties, the leaders of most of the free-world countries—at least those in the North Atlantic region and Japan—gave a serious ideological content to the noncommunist coalition. The concept "free," however it might be stretched with respect to the character of domestic society, came to mean being anticommunist internationally. It became necessary to resist the assumption of power by communists or regimes willing to align themselves with the international communist movement on important international issues, as well as to resist the overt extension of communist control by military aggression. Who was in whose camp ideologically would largely determine the extent of military commitments by the superpowers and the lineup of military allies in case of general war. From the point of view of the United States, being against the extension of communism was usually sufficient to qualify a nation as a member of the free world coalition; and the ideologies of national self-determination and international pluralism countenanced the presence in the coalition of some rather curious species of free society.

As both sides continued to propound their respective views on the nature of the global struggle, ideology became of even greater moment in defining coalition interests. By the high cold war period (the early 1950s through the early 1960s), leaders in the United States and the Soviet Union appeared to believe that a failure to fight for "freedom" or "socialism" wherever challenged might be regarded as a sign of a reluctance to fight for anything other than one's own survival. The opponent might misconstrue a failure to hold the line at the community's outermost peripheries as a general retraction of the coalition leader's sphere of defense—in Secretary of State Rusk's words, "the crime of tempting thieves." Less powerful members of one's coalition would then wonder when they too might be considered dispensable and would be tempted either to provide for their own self-defense or to explore the possibility of a separate peace with the opposing coalition.

As mutual thermonuclear deterrence called into question the American pledge to use whatever force might be necessary to prevent Western Europe from being overrun, President Kennedy felt it important to proclaim "*Ich bin ein Berliner.*" And when the rising costs of the American involvement in Vietnam stimulated skeptical criticisms of the strategic importance of Indochina, U.S. officials began to talk increasingly of "organizing the peace" as a reason for continuing to expend blood and resources. (Those with a realpolitik orientation justified

U.S. persistence in the war by pointing to the adverse effects upon Japanese confidence in the United States security guarantees if the Americans were to quit when the going got too rough.)

The Russians, however resourceful in putting the ideology of Marxist-Leninism at the service of the state interests of the USSR, were nonetheless prone to allow messianic aspects of their ideology to affect political commitments and military risks at some dramatic junctures in the cold war. Soviet leaders have been aware that a single-minded pursuit of Russian state interests, even if justified by the necessity of first securing "socialism in one country," would degrade the authority of the Kremlin as the Vatican of the world communist movement, especially in the face of the eastern schism of the Chinese.

Premier Khrushchev's insistence that he needed President Kennedy's pledge not to invade Cuba in return for the removal of Soviet missiles was prompted by "soft" consideration of maintaining Kremlin prestige in the socialist fraternity as much as by "hard" requirement for a friendly naval port of call in the Caribbean. Indeed, Castro had by this time become an economic liability for the USSR and, after October 1962, a substantial military risk.

A similar process of amorphous ideological considerations mixing with traditional realpolitik concerns seems to have been at the root of the opportunistic but ambivalent Soviet entanglements in the Middle East. From a strict security point of view, the Soviet Union would do better to attempt to maintain reliable access through the Black Sea straits and a naval presence in the Mediterranean and the Persian Gulf without incurring the high risks of an American confrontation involved in its military support of the Arabs against Israel. Having visibly committed itself to the Arabs' cause, however, the Kremlin would lose face and future influence over Arab policy by not backing them in an Arab-Israeli war, at least to the point of readily supplying armaments. The more the new strategic realities have called into question such extended obligations, the more the Russians, like the Americans, have had to fall back on the fiction of a community of like-minded peoples, in this case the so-called anti-imperialists, to sustain their commitments to reckless clients.

The Process of Depolarization

The greatest binding force in each of the cold war coalitions has been the premises about the malevolent character of the opponents and their motivations rather than the principles around which one's own camp is organized. The need to present a united front against the clearly bad has been a powerful spur to the coalescence of political communities throughout recorded history.[21] Conversely the disappearance of the villain—either by his defeat, his reform, or simply the neutralization of his capabilities for doing harm—has frequently been an important cause of the disintegration of previously united communities.

Subsequent chapters will examine aspects of the ideological erosion that have their sources primarily in intrabloc developments. Here the concern is with general developments in the international system that are casting doubt on assumptions which heretofore have been crucial to cold war bipolarity.

Of cardinal importance to the ideology propounded by the USSR has been the experience, for over five decades now, of a growing acceptance by the noncommunist countries of a relationship of coexistence with the communists. Communist theoreticians have attributed the fact of coexistence to the skillfulness of Soviet diplomacy and, more recently, to the great growth of their military power which has made a world war too costly for the capitalists. Yet, according to orthodox Leninism, the growing power of the socialist forces should have brought the world that much closer to the inevitable cataclysm, since the capitalists were not expected to come to terms peacefully with the new correlation of forces. On the contrary, the Leninists believed it was precisely out of fear of being on the losing side that the capitalists, anticipating a shift in the balance of power, would be most likely to launch an intendedly preventive but ultimately suicidal war. However, once it was admitted by the Kremlin that a world war would be mutually suicidal—the official Soviet doctrine since the mid-Khrushchev period—the prediction of a final bloody struggle to bring about the worldwide victory of socialism needed revision. In a thermonuclear war the workers would lose more than their chains. The final victory would arrive rather, as Marx himself had forecast, as the ultimate result of a succession of transformations of the capitalist states *from within.*

The primary job of socialist diplomacy, therefore, became one of stabilizing relations among states to the degree necessary to prevent global war while the historical revolutionary process works itself out

21. See Crane C. Brinton, *From Many One* (Harvard University Press, 1968).

in the varied domestic societies of the noncommunist world.[22] The military power of the Soviet Union was still a prime concern, but now more as a necessary environmental condition for the policy of peaceful coexistence than as a sword for actively furthering proletarian internationalism. As explained by the American sovietologist, Marshall Shulman, the strategy of peaceful coexistence, originally a tactical response to adverse situations requiring a breathing spell, became "elongated in time" and was "extended into a long-term strategy, implying a continued acceptance of the necessity for an indirect and more political way of advancing Soviet interests than the militant advocacy of revolution and the use of force."[23]

During the 1960s as détente became a grand strategy instead of just an expediential tactic, as the cultivation of normal state-to-state relations with members of the opposing ideological bloc eclipsed postures of militant hostility, and as a sequence of arms limitation agreements underlined the common overarching interest of the Soviet Union and the United States in reducing the likelihood of general war, it became increasingly difficult for the Kremlin to sustain the Marxist myth of two implacably contradictory social systems. If world politics was not simply the anticipation of the impending worldwide class war, the urgency for attaining a completely autarchic economy in the socialist commonwealth faded, as did the need to mobilize the camp in a rigidly hierarchical system. Commerce with the developed noncommunist world, much of it bilateral between individual Eastern European and Western European countries, began to play a more important part in many of the economies of the Soviet-led coalition. The doctrine of "many roads to socialism" was elaborated in principle and in the practice of states such as Czechoslovakia, Hungary, and Yugoslavia (now once again accepted as a member of the socialist community, despite its continuing international posture of nonalignment).

Thus the gradual mellowing of Soviet international ideology interacts with the geopolitical limitations on Soviet revolutionary activism and shows signs of producing a long-term secular moderation of Soviet grand strategy. A third factor interacting with mutual deterrence and

22. My analysis of the evolution of Soviet ideology relies heavily on William Zimmerman's carefully researched study, *Soviet Perspectives on International Relations, 1956–1967* (Princeton University Press, 1969).

23. Marshall D. Shulman, *Beyond the Cold War* (Yale University Press, 1966), pp. 53–54.

the erosion of the two-camps ideology—namely, the increasing nationalism within the Soviet sphere—will be analyzed further in Chapters 3 and 4. The hypothesis advanced here is that these three interacting factors arise from transformations in the overall system of world politics, that they are mutually reinforcing, and that therefore it would be inaccurate to dismiss the observed changes in Soviet international behavior as only ploys to get the anticommunists to let down their guard.

In the West, transformation of the image of the major opponents from a monolithic band of revolutionaries into a feuding group of self-interested states had indeed been gradually eroding an important foundation of the extensive U.S. system of alliances. Once it became generally accepted, as Secretary of State Rusk maintained in 1964, that "the Communist world is no longer a single flock of sheep following blindly one leader,"[24] and that the Soviet Union was unflinchingly putting its state interests ahead of its missionary impulses, then it would appear unnecessary to the security of the whole noncommunist community to oppose each and every expansion of communist influence. Distinctions among communist countries would now seem to be in order, less on the basis of the internal character of their regimes than on the basis of their intentions and capabilities for major international aggression against important Western interests.

With the contest between the communist and noncommunist ways of life removed as the central explanation for the struggle for global influence between the superpowers, some of the mutual defense obligations in the U.S.-led coalition were bound to be devalued. It was now much less credible that the United States should use its own military force wherever such action might be necessary to prevent the spread of communism.

In contrast to the popular American mood in the early 1960s, when President Kennedy could proudly proclaim that "destiny" had made the United States "the watchman on the walls of world freedom," the public temper by the early 1970s had swung decidedly against overseas commitments that could require direct U.S. military involvement. The American Institute of Public Opinion (Gallup) asked a "representative sample" of Americans in 1971 how the United States should

24. "United States Policy and Eastern Europe," address by Secretary of State Rusk, Feb. 25, 1964, in the Council on Foreign Relations, *Documents on American Foreign Relations* (1964), pp. 144–49.

respond in the event of attack by communist-backed forces on certain countries. Among the more revealing results were the following:[25]

Country suffering a communist-backed attack	Response favored by indicated percentage of those polled			Percentage of those polled answering don't know
	Send troops	Send supplies only	Refuse to get involved	
West Germany	28	41	22	9
Japan	17	34	38	11
Thailand	11	36	38	15
Turkey	10	36	37	17

Once the Americans extricated themselves from Vietnam, a more restrictive set of criteria would determine whether and how the United States should intervene to redress a local imbalance of power favoring the communists. The importance of a particular country's alignment for the global balance of power, the degree of direct involvement in the local conflict by either the Soviet Union or China, and the symbolic or emotional importance attached to the preexisting commitment—all of these would become more weighty considerations than any general obligation to support members of the free world against a communist takeover.[26]

25. Adapted from Albert H. Cantril and Charles W. Roll, Jr., *Hopes and Fears of the American People* (Universe Books, for Potomac Associates, 1971), pp. 86–89.

26. This reassessment of the importance and desirability of a global resistance to communism was well under way by the mid-1960s, when the United States government invoked the hyperbolic ideological conceptions of the mid-1950s to justify its military intervention in Vietnam. But, as Leslie Gelb has demonstrated, this reflowering of cold war concepts—especially the notion that U.S. anticommunist alliances were a seamless web of commitments, which if cut at one place would unravel the whole system—was no mere post facto rationalization of inadvertent involvement in the Vietnam war. The Vietnam intervention was rather the *product* of the earlier world view which saw some high global stakes involved in preventing the communists from overrunning Indochina. Commitment was piled upon commitment by successive U.S. administrations to the point where a failure in 1965 to fight to prevent a communist victory would be regarded as a momentous U.S. capitulation under pressure. See Leslie H. Gelb, "The System Worked," *Foreign Policy*, No. 3 (Summer 1971), pp. 140–67.

The Nixon doctrine, first proclaimed by the President at Guam in late 1969 and reiterated in annual State of the World messages, rather strongly suggested that in applying these criteria the United States would consider the use of its own forces warranted only to resist military aggression across established international boundaries; and even in such cases the United States would probably refrain from becoming an active belligerent as long as the Russians or the Chinese communists were not direct military participants.[27]

To be sure, this movement in U.S. policy toward a highly selective set of criteria for determining to whom the United States should be committed, and against what, could be arrested by a turn toward aggressive expansion on the part of either the Soviet Union or China. But short of a rapprochement between the two communist giants that appeared to be part of a conspiracy to establish a global duopoly, a rebuilding of military alliances by the United States on a worldwide basis seems highly unlikely. Because of the larger international developments already outlined and the changes taking place within the communist world that will be elaborated in Chapters 3 and 4, a policy of major expansion by military means by either or both of the great communist powers is not visible on the horizon. If such a reversal of present trends were to occur, however, it is most improbable that it would happen without considerable warning in the form of political and economic pressures and a sequence of crises signaling a repolarization of world politics. There will be more on the constraints against such a repolarization in Chapter 6.

27. Richard Nixon, *U.S. Foreign Policy for the 1970's: A New Strategy for Peace* (Government Printing Office, 1970), p. 55.

CHAPTER TWO

Strains in the Anticommunist Coalition:
The Rise of Nonmilitary Issues

During the high cold war period economic relations among the non-communist industrial nations frequently reinforced and rarely were allowed to undermine the military and ideological foundations of the U.S.-led coalition. But the close intercontinental economic cooperation that characterized the period might not have outlasted the postwar recovery of Europe and Japan were it not for the high priority given to countering the rising power of the communist countries. Today, given the weakening of the political foundations of coalition unity, national and special economic interests are demanding an expansion of opportunities to pursue international transactions on their "merits" (mainly economic) rather than with primary reference to the global balance of military power. Subcoalitions along economic lines have become more prominent, undermining the authority of the coalition leader, giving prominence to intracoalition issues, and stimulating uncoordinated diplomatic interaction with members of the opposing coalition and with Third World countries. Now the disintegrating forces in the larger coalition appear to be mutually reinforcing, and the unifying forces seem to be on the defensive.

Effects of the Decline in Security Concerns

To be sure, the raison d'être of the coalition was never simply the containment of communism. A dominant belief among Western statesmen after World War II was that the important economic interests of the major industrial nations were in the main compatible, and that the

NEW FORCES IN WORLD POLITICS

enlightened pursuit of economic self-interest would advance the well-being of all, provided it was carried on within a structure of mutually acceptable rules designed to reduce barriers to international trade and payments.[1] Yet without the agreement to maintain an advantageous balance of power against the Sino-Soviet bloc, it is doubtful that Western Europe and Japan would have remained as willing as they did to defer to U.S. concepts for organizing the world economy, or that successive United States administrations could have continued to fend off domestic pressures to protect the American economy from growing European and Japanese competition.

The clear dominance of security issues was in evidence up through the early 1960s when Charles de Gaulle tried to form a Bonn-Paris axis of economic, technological, and military collaboration. Important segments of the German economy were anxious to limit the U.S. presence in the European Community (EC), but Bonn was unwilling to support measures that might lead the Americans to reduce their military deployments in Germany.[2] The rising differences between the United States and its Atlantic partners over payments, trade, and monetary matters still were subordinated to the need to resolve the main issues of NATO defense policy: the strategies for holding the ground against Soviet attack in Western Europe and the question of sharing or centralizing control of strategic nuclear weapons.[3]

In the 1970s collective defense continued to be the most important task of the U.S.-led coalition and the primary reason for continuing to regard the United States as coalition leader. But the coalition, with the United States at the helm, appeared to be functioning effectively as a

1. See William Diebold, Jr., *The United States and the Industrial World: American Foreign Economic Policy in the 1970s* (Praeger, 1972), pp. 3–44.
2. Robert L. Gilpin, "The Politics of Transnational Economic Relations," in Robert O. Keohane and Joseph S. Nye, Jr., *Transnational Relations and World Politics* (Harvard University Press, 1972), pp. 64–65.
3. Characteristically, it was the bilateral discussion on nuclear sharing between Kennedy and Macmillan that triggered de Gaulle's veto of British entry into the Common Market. De Gaulle probably would have vetoed British entry into the EC regardless of the Anglo-American tête-à-tête at Nassau; but it was this presumed evidence of a continuing special relationship between Britain and the United States in violation of the *common defense* ideology of NATO that allowed de Gaulle to claim that in the most important matters there would remain an unbridgeable gulf between the Atlantic nations and continental Europe.

group only in NATO military planning exercises and, to a lesser degree, in East-West arms control negotiations. Moreover, collective defense against communist attack was receding as an everyday concern of the top political leadership of the various members of the coalition—a sign that the coalition itself had a reduced overall importance in world politics.

The first reason for the reduced role of the coalition was elaborated in Chapter 1, namely, the decline in the perceived threat of aggressive expansion by the Soviet Union or China. The second reason is the rise of nonmilitary issues as the major subject of political bargaining among members of the coalition. It has been the reduction of external security concerns, however, that has provided the opportunity for the nonmilitary issues to rise, both relatively and absolutely, to a level where they now are frequently challenging the institutions and ethos of the anticommunist security community itself.[4]

Today the differences in membership and purposes of the North Atlantic security community and the Western European economic community are prominently exposed and have substantial effect on the bargaining in both communities. With opposition to the power of the rival ideological bloc less compelling as an overriding common purpose, the principle that everyone should do his part for the good of the whole is more difficult to enforce. Those with the greatest military and economic power do not automatically exercise the greatest authority, and conflicts of interest within the community are harder to resolve than previously. Moreover, where nonmilitary matters are at issue— access to energy supplies, trade barriers, currency exchange rates, the terms of technological cooperation, environmental controls—there is more opportunity for subnational and transnational interest groups to press their demands not only upon their own governments but also upon the deliberative assemblies and bureaucracies of the coalition.

It is still true that an essential feature of the so-called free world

4. See Richard N. Cooper, "Trade Policy is Foreign Policy," *Foreign Policy*, No. 9 (Winter 1972–73), pp. 18–36; Robert E. Hunter, "Troops, Trade and Diplomacy," *Atlantic Community Quarterly*, Vol. 9, No. 3 (Fall 1971), pp. 283–92. For effects of this trend on the academic discipline of international relations see Edward L. Morse, "The Transformation of Foreign Policies: Modernization, Interdependence, and Externalization," *World Politics*, Vol. 22, No. 3 (April 1970), pp. 371–92; and Susan Strange, "International Economics and International Relations: A Case of Mutual Neglect," *International Affairs*, Vol. 46, No. 2 (April 1970), pp. 304–15.

coalition—if restricted to North America, Western Europe, Japan, and Australasia—is that the member nation-states remain armed for potential conflict with the communist nations. Yet it has become increasingly difficult to coordinate coalition action, as evidenced by the reluctance during the 1973 Arab-Israeli war of various NATO countries to allow use of their bases, or even overflight of their territory, to transport U.S. military supplies to the war zone. Partly this results from the growing heterogeneity of military security interests within the alliance. It also reflects the rising importance of other issues which have been exacerbated by the oil crisis.

Debates over the size, composition, and deployment of forces by the various NATO members, it is now widely recognized, are less concerned with how best to deter or defend against military attack than with the distribution of economic burdens of alliance membership. Previously when the United States insisted that economically thriving NATO countries provide more for their own defense and purchase military equipment in the United States to offset the U.S. balance-of-payments costs of American forces in Europe, it was easier to compel agreement on the basis of the overriding imperatives of mutual security. But to the extent that questions of military burden-sharing are linked to monetary and trade issues or projects for cooperation in the energy field, the United States must progressively bargain against a coalition of EC countries within NATO.

Similarly, Japan's hand for bargaining with the United States on both economic and security matters appears to have been strengthened by the devaluation of cold war alignments in Asia, signaled by the American President's visit to China in February 1972. Tokyo's first reaction was one of shock at not having been adequately consulted or informed about this demarche in U.S. policy. But the more lasting effect probably has been to liberate Japan somewhat from the tight Japanese-American security relationship, which Washington was in the habit of hinting could be undermined by Japanese intransigence in the trade and monetary fields.[5] Now free to pursue intensively its own bi-

5. The fact that the U.S.-Japanese negotiations on the reversion of Okinawa to Japan were concluded simultaneously with the loosening up of security alignments in Asia added to Japan's bargaining strength vis-à-vis the United States. On the question of Okinawa reversion Japan had been the demander and therefore vulnerable to U.S. suggestions that Japan's economic policies might be straining the larger web of U.S.-Japanese relations.

lateral relationships with mainland China, the USSR, and the Third World, Japan could begin to play off other options against suggestions from the United States that it had nowhere else to go.[6] By the time of the Middle East conflict of 1973 Japan felt free to make its own deals with Arab oil producers against the wishes of the United States.

Growing Tensions in the Economic Realm: Multipolarity and Interdependence

Underlying the increasingly hard bargaining among the major members of the anticommunist coalition has been the realization in all capitals that the United States has abandoned the posture of economic altruism it adopted as coalition leader during the early postwar period and the heyday of the cold war. Washington's tougher stance toward its coalition partners in the early 1970s, in trade and monetary policies and in rhetoric, conveyed that the United States was no longer inclined to make generous concessions. According to administration spokesmen this more mature relationship was only natural. Instead of there being just two superpowers, observed President Nixon in July 1971, "when we think in economic terms and economic potentialities there are five great power centers in the world today." Western Europe and Japan, the two emergent power centers in the "free world," have become "very potent competitors of the United States—friends, yes; allies, yes, but competing, and competing very hard with us throughout the world for economic leadership."[7]

The prospect of a European economic union becoming powerful enough to compete with the United States was foreseen by the American policy community as far back as the Marshall Plan. It was widely believed that this competition would be a healthy stimulus to modernization on both sides of the Atlantic, and that the United States and Europe, once the latter had completed its postwar recovery, would cooperate in freeing that competition from artificial restraints on trade—

6. Selig S. Harrison, "Nixon Journey Spurs Japan to Recast Policy," *Washington Post*, March 2, 1972; Don Oberdorfer, "Japan-China Pact: Gains for Both, Risks for U.S.," *Washington Post*, Sept. 30, 1972.

7. Richard M. Nixon, address to midwestern newspaper and broadcasting executives in Kansas City, Mo., July 6, 1971, *Department of State Bulletin*, Vol. 65, No. 1674 (July 26, 1971), pp. 93–97.

thus the U.S. Trade Expansion Act of 1962 and the Kennedy Round of tariff-reduction negotiations with Western Europe. Furthermore a strong European partner was the keystone to the containment of Soviet expansion westward, and even if the growing economic competition would involve some readjustment difficulties in the United States, it was thought the temporary sacrifices would be worth the long-term gain in overall power for the anticommunist coalition.[8]

American attitudes toward the postwar recovery of Japan were more ambivalent. Unlike Germany a rebuilt Japan could not be submerged in a regional bloc. Moreover the war with Japan was thought to have been a direct result of the Japanese economic imperialism of the 1930s. Even when the anticommunist containment policy was extended to Asia in 1950 with the consolidation of Mao's rule in China and the outbreak of the Korean war, there was no intention on the part of the United States to help restore the Japanese "co-prosperity sphere." The future economic health of Japan, confined as it was to its home islands, would have to depend primarily on its fitting into the evolving world trading system. Thus successive United States administrations, as a matter of high policy, paved the way for Japan's resurgence as a major competitor—but less through direct aid, as in the Marshall Plan for Europe, than through fighting for fair access by Japan to the American and European markets.[9] The expectation was that once Japan recovered from the war it would reciprocate by reducing its barriers to foreign goods and direct investments and by generally helping the United States to construct a more open world economy.

Thus the resurgence of major competitors in Europe and Asia was anticipated and encouraged by most of the cosmopolitan and liberal economists in the American foreign policy establishment during the cold war. What may not have been sufficiently anticipated was the degree to which economic regionalism in Europe would be accompanied by discrimination against the United States and Japan. Nor was it foreseen how weak elements in the U.S. economy and Japanese parochial sensitivities against foreign penetration would stimulate politicians on both sides to revive the specter of a trade war.[10]

8. Lawrence B. Krause, *European Economic Integration and the United States* (Brookings Institution, 1968), pp. 25–28.

9. Diebold, *The United States and the Industrial World*, pp. 47–52.

10. Harold B. Malmgren, "Coming Trade Wars? (Neo-Mercantilism and Foreign Policy)," *Foreign Policy*, No. 1 (Winter 1970–71), pp. 125–26.

Probably the least anticipated and most significant aspect of the tripolar economic rivalry was the fact of its emergence in the détente-minded world of the early 1970s. With reduced priority accorded to global rivalry with the communists, the subordination of short-term national or special interests to the long-term goal of a stronger and more cooperative free-world community became highly problematical. Everyone's grand design for an orderly world economy began to be looked at suspiciously by everyone else as a cover for some narrow domestic objective. The whole became less than the sum of its parts.

Henry Kissinger's call in April 1973 for "a new Atlantic charter" that would "identify [common] interests and positive values beyond security in order to engage once again the commitment of peoples and parliaments" was received coolly in Western Europe. The Europeans were particularly chagrined at Kissinger's stated premise—"The United States has global interests and responsibilities. Our European allies have regional interests"—and at his strong implication that, if the Europeans were not more cooperative on trade and monetary matters and on the sharing of NATO defense costs, the United States might have to reconsider its own outlays for European security.[11]

In response the European Community proposed two declarations: the first on economic relations between the EC and the United States emphasizing that henceforth in this field there would have to be a two-party dialogue to resolve transatlantic issues; the second on common defense issues among the fifteen members of NATO. In contrast to earlier notions that the treaty organization would expand its functions with the waning of the cold war, the North Atlantic community was to be constricted to the security field and the United States would be treated as a kind of adversary in economic matters. This was hardly what Mr. Kissinger was requesting.

The ground was rapidly crumbling underneath the coalition when the energy crisis was exploited by the Arabs in 1973 to pressure Europe and Japan to support their cause against Israel. Again Europe and Japan

11. The text of Henry Kissinger's "Year of Europe" address to the annual meeting of the Associated Press editors in New York City on April 23, 1973, appears in the *Department of State Bulletin*, Vol. 68, No. 1768 (May 14, 1973), pp. 593–98. For European reactions see Alvin Shuster, "Europe Cool to U.S. Design for New Ties," *New York Times*, May 22, 1973; and Flora Lewis, "Redefining Atlantic Ties: Difficult Hurdles Lie Ahead," *New York Times*, Sept. 13, 1973.

deeply resented Kissinger's suggestions that America's coalition partners were looking out for their narrow self-interests while the United States was left with the job of preserving world order. By early 1974 the disintegration had progressed to such an extent that even Washington's generous offer to pool current and future energy resources in return for a common industrial-country front against the price-gouging of the oil cartel was deprecated in European capitals as a stratagem for reviving U.S. hegemony.[12]

With a decline in community spirit among the nations of the North Atlantic region and Japan, economic interdependence, involving as it does the capacity of societies to harm one another as well as advance one another's welfare, has become less an engine of community-building than a spur to intramural strife. Without substantial joint community efforts to ameliorate the sometimes harsh effects of economic interdependence, the strife is bound to increase, perhaps to a level where the larger pattern of interdependence is perceived as intolerable by politically important groups, who then actively mobilize to discredit and dismember the larger community. In the decade since President Kennedy called for a "Declaration of Interdependence" between Europe and America—a mutual pledge to build a "great Atlantic Community" —the negative effects of economic interdependence seem to have assumed higher political salience than its potential positive effects.[13]

Paradoxically, the growing political prominence in the 1970s of the economic tension between major noncommunist countries is in large part the result of the success of the previous efforts to remove barriers to trade and capital movements.

The freer international flow of goods and investments would presumably lead to the ultimate benefit of all by allowing production to take place where factor costs are lowest and allowing consumers to purchase goods in the cheapest market. But it would be impossible to avoid generating fears and resentments on the part of those whose sources of income might be adversely disturbed by the tougher competition. National political leaders, particularly if they retain office on the

12. "Text of Address by Henry Kissinger in London on Energy and European Problems," *New York Times*, Dec. 13, 1973; "Europeans to Confer on Nixon's Oil Meeting Invitation," *Washington Post*, Jan. 11, 1974.

13. See Richard N. Cooper, "Economic Interdependence and Foreign Policy in the Seventies," *World Politics*, Vol. 24, No. 2 (January 1972), pp. 159–81.

basis of narrow electoral margins, often must be responsive to these fears and resentments. Governments are consequently pressured to become the international agents of weak and uncompetitive elements of the national economy. Fortunately for the goal of a more rational and mutually beneficial order, governments are also pressured by those who expect to thrive in the wider competitive market to negotiate for a general reciprocal lowering of international economic barriers. But a period of general success in the direction of freer trade, such as the Kennedy Round negotiations ending in 1967, may help create a situation in which the stronger competitors are relatively satisfied with the degree of openness achieved, but the weaker elements feel more vulnerable than ever to displacement. Since the late 1960s was also the beginning of a dramatic thaw in the cold war and a loosening of security-community bonds within and between national governments, the coalition of supporters of "free-world" interdependence would be falling apart just at the time that protectionist pressures were increasing.[14]

In the early 1970s the defection of most of organized labor from the ranks of those supporting liberal foreign economic policies undercut the ability of the American government to take the lead in negotiating further reductions of trade barriers. Moreover the Economic Policy Committee of the AFL-CIO was actively lobbying for additional import quotas and for new restrictions on the activities of U.S.-owned multinational corporations.

According to three spokesmen for organized labor, this protectionist shift in labor's historic position derived from the cruel conditions of international economic life:

To integrate world economies is next to impossible. Realistically the natural limit of economic integration should be national. National goals such as economic welfare, security and peace, equitable distribution of wealth and expansion of individual freedom and human dignity are difficult enough to attain in our own country, let alone trying to develop integration between nations. . . .

14. C. Fred Bergsten, "Crisis in U.S. Trade Policy," *Foreign Affairs*, Vol. 49, No. 4 (July 1971), pp. 619–35; National Planning Association Advisory Committee on U.S. Foreign Economic Policy for the 1970s, *U.S. Foreign Economic Policy for the 1970s: A New Approach to the New Realities* (National Planning Association, 1971); Harold B. Malmgren, *Trade Wars or Trade Negotiations: Nontariff Barriers and Economic Peacekeeping* (Atlantic Council of the United States, 1970).

For more than thirty years, the United States has scrupulously followed trade and investment policies designed to implement reciprocity and most favored nation (MFN) principles without interference and with the relatively free flow of goods and dollars. The hope was that adherence to these policies would induce other countries to follow suit and reduce their trade restrictions. Unfortunately, just the opposite has occurred.[15]

As examples of the failure of other countries to adhere reciprocally to liberal trading principles, the labor spokesmen pointed to the Common Market's preferential trading agreements with other European and African countries, its common agricultural policy, its value-added tax which allegedly offers incentives for exports, and its restrictions on imports from Japan and other Asian countries—"all of which occurred while the United States continued to pursue its open-door policy."

Labor's souring on liberal trade doctrines also derived from its having to face the new mobility of capital:

The age-old theory of comparative advantage . . . assumes that the factors of production remain fixed. This assumption no longer holds true today . . . U.S. multinational corporations have been investing overseas at phenomenal rates in recent years. The U.S. labor force, on the other hand, is not mobile. The result—products produced overseas that take advantage of cheap labor using the most modern of the U.S. or world's technology enter the world market and seriously disrupt job opportunities in the United States. Today, the comparative advantage is, in most cases, simply cheap labor.[16]

At the turn of the decade it looked as though the interest group most strategically located to affect U.S. national elections had shifted decisively against a liberal U.S. trade policy. Moreover the cause of liberal trade got little help from the progressive sectors of management, who traditionally might have been expected to exert the most persistent pressure on behalf of export expansion policies. They appeared less concerned about commodity import restrictions by the United States or other countries than about policies that might restrict the international investments of multinational firms, for whom the ability to maintain a variety of production and marketing subsidiaries in a number of coun-

15. Rudolph Faupl (International Association of Machinists), Thomas Hannigan (International Brotherhood of Electrical Workers), and Howard Samuel (Amalgamated Clothing Workers of America), in dissenting comments to the NPA report, U.S. *Foreign Economic Policy for the 1970s*, pp. 44.

16. Ibid., pp. 44–45. See Chapter 8, below, for other reactions of different segments of labor to the multinational corporation.

tries is of greater account than reducing the barriers to trade across national boundaries.[17]

For academic economists, internationally minded journalists and lawyers, and citizen groups who traditionally have championed world order the early 1970s were not particularly congenial to the generation of popular support for further liberalization of U.S. trade. This was partly a result of the intense national preoccupation with a new generation of domestic problems (see below). It was also the result of the intensification of public dispute on international economic issues among the major governments, creating the impression that the spirit of the General Agreement on Tariffs and Trade (GATT) was dying anyway. This being the general international temper, few Americans were willing to have their country make the first economic sacrifices.

Apart from the segments of the U.S. economy which deal in imports, and some consumer interest groups, the trade liberalization lobby appeared to be left pretty much to the farmers interested in removing foreign barriers to the American agricultural exports. Though a dwindling portion of the population, the farmers remain a dominant political force in many states and thus also a nonnegligible national voting bloc capable of swinging presidential elections. But the apparently solid commitment by the European Community to its restrictive Common Agricultural Policy had reduced the farmers' expectations of achieving general international liberalization as opposed to special trading deals (some with communist nations) and continued domestic subsidies.

The dramatic unilateral protectionist move made by the United States in August 1971 would have been unthinkable a decade before. The 10 percent surcharge on imports and other "buy American" devices were set up to compel an international adjustment of currency exchange rates in order to reduce the price of U.S. goods in world markets and increase the price of foreign goods in the United States. However vociferously this protectionist move might be condemned by some American economists, it would not be immediately unpopular with any politically powerful domestic American interest group.

The White House apparently was somewhat taken aback, however, by the intensity of foreign reaction to its unilateral move, and by the reactions of American firms active in the transnational economy along with influential elements of the U.S. foreign policy community, who

17. Bergsten, "Crisis in U.S. Trade Policy," pp. 623, 624.

feared a complete unraveling of the GATT and International Monetary Fund (IMF) system. Although billed as part of a temporary set of measures designed to reverse the domestic inflationary spiral and the associated adverse balance of international payments, the United States' move of August 1971 was viewed abroad as sloughing off the special responsibility of stabilizing the world economy that America had assumed as far back as the Bretton Woods conference of 1944. Americans henceforth would lose some of their credibility in the international arena as the protectors of the rules, their claim to special authority as defenders of the system. And other countries would feel more justified in putting their immediate self-interests ahead of the long-term general interest. If this was the way the game was to be played it would be harder for the United States to object on political or moral grounds to the European Community's "variable taxes" on imports such as grain, beef, poultry, and dairy products—taxes designed to make sure that foreign agricultural goods entering the Common Market would not be less expensive than European farm products. Nor could the United States convincingly claim the political high ground in objecting to the many EC nontariff devices (product standards, border taxes, and other technical restrictions) specially directed against imports from most countries in the Western hemisphere and Asia.

Similarly, while the unilateral approach to the new economic policy of August 1971 may have been conducive to subsequent liberalization of Japan's restrictions on imports and direct investments, the longer run effects of the new American toughness toward Japan were problematical. If the United States henceforth would respond to the growing Japanese competition by threatening to raise retaliatory barriers against imports and investments or by bringing pressure on the yen, Japan was not without alternatives. It could attempt to improve its global competitive position by lessening its dependence on the United States market. This would mean finding other major markets for its industrial products in communist and developing countries and perhaps creating its own preferential trade and investment area, in emulation of the EC's special association and trading arrangements with Mediterranean and black African countries.[18]

18. See Martin Bronfenbrenner, "A Japanese-American Economic War?" *Quarterly Review of Economics and Business*, Vol. 11, No. 3 (Autumn 1971), pp. 7–16.

Perhaps in recognition of such implications of a return to unfettered unilateralism, perhaps in response to the nearly universal negative reactions from international economists and foreign finance ministries, the United States softened the more pugnacious aspects of its new foreign economic policy. It has entered into a series of protracted negotiations with the other industrialized nations to achieve a stable system for adjusting currency exchange rates. And at the September 1972 meeting of the International Monetary Fund and the World Bank, the American secretary of the treasury proposed a comprehensive set of principles for monetary reform to "avoid a breakup of the world into antagonistic blocs."[19] But less than a year would pass before the United States again angered its trading partners by sudden unilateral action —this time slapping export controls on some of its agricultural products and raw materials as a domestic anti-inflation measure.

The post-1972 shift from protection against competitive imports to policies designed to counteract fears of domestic shortages in food, energy, and other raw materials, while superficially conducive to trade "liberalization" negotiations, is more accurately seen as a symptom of the deepening contradictions between international economic interdependence and political nationalism. Indeed, as C. Fred Bergsten notes, the adoption of export controls by the leading industrial nations "raises the specter . . . of nationalistic beggar-thy-neighbor policies at least as vicious as those which occurred in the 1930s."[20]

Given the depth of the socioeconomic and political trends, international and domestic, that underlay the scuttling of the Bretton Woods system in the early 1970s and the recent nationalistic responses to impending raw-material shortages, it seems highly unlikely as of this writing that any major rehabilitation of the free-world economic order is pending. Most sober analysts would agree with Miriam Camps that the required "quantum jump in collective management . . . does not appear to be in the cards."[21]

Nor is there discernible movement toward the frequently expressed

19. Statement of Secretary of the Treasury George P. Shultz, Washington, D.C., Sept. 26, 1972; text in the *New York Times*, Sept. 27, 1972.

20. "Interdependence: Now a Cold Reality," *Washington Post*, Jan. 13, 1974.

21. Miriam Camps, "Sources of Strain in Transatlantic Relations," *International Affairs*, Vol. 48, No. 4 (October 1972), pp. 571–72.

post-cold war objective of a "community of developed nations"[22] to be built outward from a highly integrated core area comprising Western Europe, North America, and Japan. Rather the dominant tendencies now seem to portend increasing rivalry among the three industrialized areas of the noncommunist world. There will probably continue to be greater interdependence, in the sense of heightened sensitivity and domestic vulnerability to one another's actions, but not yet substantial integration, in the sense of adherence to jointly decided and binding distributions of burdens and benefits.

The Pull of Domestic Problems

For most members of the erstwhile anticommunist coalition, the receding of global military concerns and the rising prominence of international economic issues has lessened the claim of alliance solidarity as a consideration in the allocation of national resources. When it could be credibly argued that deterring external enemies and lining up foreign friends were necessary to prevent imminent threats to the survival of the whole society, governments could override popular pressures to give domestic problems first consideration. That this was one of the hallmarks of cold war politics is reflected by the fact that in most of the developed democracies executive agencies responsible for national security affairs were relatively insulated from popular and legislative oversight. Governments fashioned and implemented commitments of mutual security assistance with minimum domestic debate and often only pro forma legislative ratification. Intracoalition bargaining over strategy toward the opposing coalition and distribution of mutual security burdens within the coalition could be conducted among national executive establishments, under the assumption that they had been delegated considerable prerogatives in these matters by their legislatures.

The changing nature of the issues at the top of the international agenda in the 1970s cuts deeply into executive prerogatives associated with national security, which in turn subjects coalition obligations to increased competition from the domestic concerns of each of the members. Moreover this return to neglected domestic issues after a period of preoccupation with external military threats comes at a time when

22. This phrase is from Zbigniew Brzezinski, *Between Two Ages: America's Role in the Technetronic Era* (Viking, 1970).

the strain of postindustrialism in many of the advanced noncommunist societies has itself been forcing an inward reorientation of public attention and resources.

The postindustrial crisis, whose sources and effects will be discussed in greater detail in Chapter 9, has most visibly interacted with foreign policy problems in the United States. A widespread disillusionment with overseas commitments, brought on by the country's failures in the Vietnam war, has shattered the twenty-year bipartisan consensus for a security policy based on an elaborate web of alliances. At the same time, the anomalies of poverty, crime, fuel shortages, and environmental degradation in the midst of general affluence have spawned popular anger at public authorities and a general antipathy toward minding other people's business before America puts its own house in order.

With variations in the intensity of particular causes of domestic discontent, other countries in the coalition—Britain, Japan, France, West Germany, Canada—are all faced with similar ailments of affluence. Urban overcrowding, imprudent energy policies, pollution, unprecedented health and welfare problems, youth alienation, rapidly changing moral standards, and a general erosion of civic order face all these national societies with the need to reassess the fundamental design of their political and economic systems. Consequently new demands by the United States for a more equitable sharing of the burdens of common defense, now that postwar recovery needs have been met, have not been particularly welcome.

Even the most internationalist of Western European statesmen have little patience today for schemes to revive the Atlantic community. In each country the reconciliation of competing domestic interests into a consensus behind participation in the EC has been extraordinarily difficult in itself. Major concessions have been given along the way to parochially minded but politically powerful groups such as the German and French farmers. The enlargement of the EC in 1973 to include Britain and other European Free Trade Association countries only compounded the problem of reconciling domestic interests. For the time being, therefore, all policies advanced in the name of the preexisting cold war coalition—even policies having to do with East-West security issues in Europe—are likely to be assessed first and foremost in terms of their effects upon the still-fragile bonds of the Community.

It is even less likely that external policies designed to further long-term objectives of world order—from reconstructing the world monetary system and facilitating freer trade to rationally allocating world energy supplies and promoting economic development in the Third World—will be able to preempt the political high ground in legislatures and bureaucracies. The constituencies for any of these concerns must do battle with constituencies for domestically oriented programs, and the burden of proof is on the proponents of internationalist policies to show their particular programs will better promote the *domestic* welfare and assure *domestic* tranquility.

In sum, this is not a propitious time for a movement toward the goal of Atlantic partnership or a community of developed nations, let alone a more integrated free-world community. Multinational community building, to be sure, has been proceeding in the Common Market; but the pace and direction of this effort is determined more by narrow intra-European political and economic issues than by grand designs for world order. To the extent that the elaboration of the EC is a movement at the geopolitical level of world affairs, it is now as much an assertion of economic independence from the United States as an effort to rally Western European strength against the power of the Soviet sphere.

It has become evident to statesmen on both sides of the Atlantic and in Japan that the tight alliance pattern of the 1950s is unsustainable, and even the looser relationship of the 1960s is coming apart on many issues. More and more the coalition is being transformed into a vast web of intersecting adversary and cooperative relationships. And it is this latter feature that progressively defines and sets the tone of international politics outside the communist sphere.

CHAPTER THREE

Cracks in the Soviet Sphere

The divisions and special alignments emerging in the Soviet-led coalition pose a more critical threat to its existence than do the self-assertive forces in the U.S.-led coalition to its basic structure. In the West, even in the heyday of the cold war, pluralism has been regarded as one of the essential principles of the coalition, subject only to the need to concert policies against the common opponent. But where strict orthodoxy and rigid hierarchy have been the central structural elements, a little dissent can seem dangerously destabilizing, and any tendencies of subunits to define and pursue their own goals may appear to risk disintegration of the whole coalition.

Washington's and Moscow's fears of the security consequences of coalition disintegration have also been asymmetrical. The major allies of the United States have been a part of its forward defense, located (with the exception of Canada) across the seas, organized to prevent the local expansion of the Soviet Union and China. Even in the unlikely event that the main U.S. allies in Europe and Asia came under hostile control, there would still be a fall-back position to "Fortress America." By contrast, the main Soviet allies since World War II have been in the USSR's immediate security belt in Eastern Europe and, if China is included, on its Siberian frontiers—the staging grounds for invasions of Russian territory for centuries. The perfection of its long-reach retaliatory capabilities has only partially alleviated the Soviet Union's historic fear of invasion, and it continues to be very edgy about subversion of nationality groups in its border areas. Moreover, major defections from the existing socialist commonwealth of nations, particularly in Eastern Europe, would be accompanied by a severe erosion of Moscow's authority in communist parties all around the world; and whichever Soviet leadership group presided over this deauthorization

45

of the Kremlin would be disgraced in the Communist Party of the Soviet Union (CPSU) itself.

The ability of the Soviet leaders to sustain their directive role in the world communist movement has been a compound of physical power and nonphysical elements, the latter including the capacity to command respect on the basis of political skill, ideological vigor, embodiment of the virtues of the movement, and general social creativity —in a word, legitimacy. In the early aftermath of World War II the legitimacy component of Soviet authority was practically immune from serious challenge within the communist movement. The USSR's emergence from the war as a victorious superpower, along with the United States, seemed to vindicate even Stalin's excesses in his prewar consolidation of power. Leaders of communist parties the world over paid obeisance to the Kremlin and the great wartime leader who had helped save the world from fascism. Now, in attempting to consolidate their own power, many of these indigenous communist leaders would not only seek material aid and blessings from Moscow but also often emulate their hero's brutal techniques. In their deference to Moscow and identification with Stalin, the local leaders apparently were acting with the approval of most of their party followers. There were, of course, exceptions to this general pattern by communist leaders (Mao, Ho Chi Minh, and Tito) who took over their countries largely without Soviet help and established themselves as independent authorities with whom the Kremlin had to bargain rather than command. But by and large the imperial relationship between the Kremlin and most national communist parties—in power and vying for power—was accorded broad legitimacy throughout the movement while Stalin lived.

The growing polycentrism in the world communist movement of the 1970s is both a result and a reinforcement of the declining legitimacy of Kremlin hegemony over the movement, which in turn is traceable to destalinization, the Sino-Soviet split, and inherent contradictions in the Marxist-Leninist approach to international order.

Destalinization and Desatellization

Paradoxically, much of the erosion of the authority of the CPSU has its source in the effort by Nikita Khrushchev to enhance the legitimacy of Soviet power through the destalinization program. The Khrushchev faction apparently believed that, as socioeconomic development proceeded within the Soviet Union and its satellites, attempts to induce adherence to Kremlin policy by terror would be perceived as inconsistent with Marxism-Leninism and consequently would negate the moral leadership of the CPSU. The legitimacy of Kremlin authority was seen increasingly as requiring voluntary consensus—internationally among the diverse nation-states of the socialist commonwealth and internally among the domestic elite within each of the states. But when Premier Khrushchev, particularly in his address to the Twentieth Party Congress (1956), destroyed the myth of Stalin's wisdom, he also fatally weakened the Soviet party's role as the authoritative interpreter of Marxism-Leninism. The CPSU, after all, was Stalin's main instrument for assuring ideological conformity, and many of the men now at the pinnacle of the party were functionaries under Stalin. The process of wrong-headed doctrine passing for revealed truth could repeat itself.

The delegitimation of CPSU authority (an inadvertent result of destalinization) combined with Khrushchev's early moves to relax the coercive aspects of USSR-satellite relations (symbolized by a reconciliation with Tito) weakened the hierarchy of the bloc more rapidly than anyone had anticipated. In the fall of 1956 the Poles threw off their Moscow-run regime and installed the nationalist communist, Wladislaw Gomulka. Soviet military intervention was stayed at the last moment by evidence of Gomulka's strong support in the working classes and the army. In Hungary, however, antigovernment and antipolice rioting and a general condition of political confusion gave the USSR the pretext for reinforcing its military garrisons. In the context of the news from Poland, the Kremlin intervention only galvanized anti-Soviet activity as revolutionary committees and workers' councils sprang up all over the country. A new nationalist government, headed by Imre Nagy and containing only three communists in its thirteen-member cabinet, negotiated a cease-fire and a withdrawal of Soviet troops from Budapest, and then announced that Hungary would no longer be a one-party state and would leave the Warsaw Pact. This last was clearly intolerable to the Kremin, which poured military reinforcements into Hungary, set up an alternative government under Janos Kadar, and rolled tanks with heavy guns into Budapest. Massive strikes and underground resistance continued through the winter of 1956–57, and some 200,000 refugees escaped into Austria.[1]

Viewed from the 1970s, the significance of this sequence of events lies not in the Russians' threat of a military response in Poland and their actual intervention with impunity in Hungary. (After all, bipolarity was the order of the day in 1956; this was the Soviet sphere of control; and not surprisingly the United States, despite its liberation rhetoric, made no threat of counterintervention.) The significance lies rather in the signs of the USSR's inability to fashion a legitimate empire even in its own immediate zone of dominance. The Kremlin, of course, could not bring itself to view the lessons of the past decade that starkly. But it was notable and portentous that in the wake of the uprisings of 1956 there was no general reinstitution of Stalinism. On the contrary, the Khrushchevian concept of "many roads to socialism" within a socialist commonwealth of nations was embraced with even greater commitment in Moscow in the hope of refurbishing the legitimacy of the USSR's continued hegemony in the communist world.

That the Kremlin had to use major military force against a member of its own camp to compel conformity was more important to the long-term evolution of world politics than the immediate fact of the successful suppression of dissidence. Twelve years later this was also the deeper significance of the tragic "Prague Spring of 1968." The suppression of the Czechs was all the more momentous for revealing that the cracks in the Soviet sphere were manifestations of inherent contradictions in the Soviet system of organizing life among nations, and not attributable simply to Stalinist rigidity or the sudden thaw of the early Khrushchev period.

The August 1968 invasion of Czechoslovakia was immediately condemned by all the top officials of the Czech government and party, and for a full week Czechs and Slovaks participated in a massive show of nonviolent resistance. Over the next few months Party Secretary Alexander Dubcek, primarily to avoid a blood bath and secure a withdrawal of the invasion forces, gradually bargained away the popular reforms to which his regime had committed itself earlier in the year. His efforts bought mainly time, the lives of millions of his countrymen who were ready to participate in a suicidal insurrection, and perhaps

1. Adam B. Ulam, *Expansion and Coexistence: The History of Soviet Foreign Policy 1917–67* (Praeger, 1968), pp. 589–96.

some restraint on Kremlin factions anxious to stamp out all traces of anti-Soviet nationalism. But the Soviet troops stayed. Meanwhile his domestic backing fragmented as militant nationalists accused him of selling out to the Kremlin. Moscow no doubt was playing a different game, cajoling and coercing Dubcek himself into carrying out normalization measures—namely, the suppression of political pluralism and civil liberties and the reversal of market-oriented economic reforms— thus weakening his domestic support. Then at the opportune moment Dubcek was replaced by a more subservient successor, Gustav Husak.[2]

Thus the Kremlin gained in the short run by preventing what it feared would be a runaway pluralization of Czechoslovakian politics and deposition of a Moscow-oriented ruling party. In the long run, however, these gains may be far outweighed by the further depreciation of the legitimacy of the USSR's hegemony throughout the world communist movement along with the intensification of anti-Soviet nationalism in a satellite that since the late 1940s had been reliably pro-Soviet. Moscow's resort to force in Czechoslovakia and subsequent announcement of the so-called Brezhnev doctrine, justifying a continued interference in the domestic affairs of other communist states, can be seen as refurbishing the Soviet Union's reputation for the unsqueamish use of power when it perceives its vital interests to be at stake. But as Adam Bromke reports,

The fact that, as a last resort, communist unity has been maintained by the paramount Soviet power has aroused a good deal of resentment, if not hatred, of the Russians on the part of the East Europeans. These sentiments are widespread among the masses and are also present among the ruling elites. Moscow's repeated use of force in some ways has strengthened the tendencies of the different Eastern European nations to try to escape from Russian suzerainty. . . .

The Soviet invasion of Czechoslovakia in August 1968 and the enunciation of the Brezhnev doctrine has slowed down, but has not reversed the disintegration of the communist monolith in Eastern Europe. . . . Indeed, in some respects at least, the new demonstration of naked Soviet power has strengthened the resolve of East Europeans to resist it.[3]

In nearly every communist party factional controversy has sharpened since 1968. There is unprecedented public dissent on the part of

2. See H. Gordon Skilling's chapter "Czechoslovakia," in Adam Bromke and Teresa Rakowska-Harmstone (eds.), *The Communist States in Disarray 1965–1971* (University of Minnesota Press, 1972), pp. 43–72.

3. Adam Bromke, "Polycentrism in Eastern Europe," in *The Communist States in Disarray*, pp. 5–6.

nonruling parties to the Kremlin's reiteration of the standard Soviet line that the socialist community's interest in proletarian internationalism takes precedence over national sovereignty.

When the frequently postponed International Conference of Communist and Workers' Parties finally convened in May 1969, China and Albania, as expected, refused to attend. But North Korea, North Vietnam, and Yugoslavia also stayed away, and Cuba sent an observer only. The nonruling parties who boycotted the conference included those from Japan, the Netherlands, New Zealand, Thailand, Indonesia, and Malaysia. There were strenuous objections voiced by quite a number of the participating parties to the CPSU's stress on unity of the camp. The British and the Norwegians refused to sign the final declaration. And the Italians and Australians were the most outspoken defenders of national autonomy.[4]

More than ever before, the issue that dominates debates among the communists has become the role of the Soviet Union—its right to direct the global strategy of and speak authoritatively for a fragmented world movement. This question is now central to doctrinal disputes over different paths to socialism and the means of conducting the struggle against the capitalists.

Ramifications of the Sino-Soviet Split

The cracking in the monolithic communist sphere Russia had hoped to establish in Europe is, as it were, geologically related to the Sino-Soviet split: Shocks along the larger East-West fault line reverberate in the Eastern European fissures and vice versa. The disturbances radiate outward to communist movements in Western Europe, Africa, Latin America, and South and Southeast Asia. Destalinization and the following authority crises in the Kremlin and Eastern Europe might not have produced such severe structural strains in the bloc as a whole were it not for the existence of a rival pole of Marxist-Leninist orthodoxy and world revolutionary strategy in Peking. But without the centrifugal tendencies on Russia's western flank, the opportunities for China to increase its own magnetic pull on other Marxist parties, and in-

4. Alexander Dallin, "The USSR and World Communism," in John W. Strong (ed.), *The Soviet Union under Brezhnev and Kosygin* (Van Nostrand Reinhold, 1971), pp. 193–234.

deed on the noncommunist world, would be considerably less. Thus any assessment of the longer term implications of polycentrism in the Soviet sphere depends heavily on one's assumptions about the sources, depth, and likely future dynamics of the Moscow-Peking rivalry.

The intensity of the animosity between the two communist giants is difficult to fathom for anyone not a national of either country. It is partly the product of historic animosities with racist overtones and of imperial ambitions which overlap, literally and symbolically, at a 4,000-mile common frontier. On one side lies a Eurasian multination striving to be a great Western power in dominating or absorbing the "backward" peoples on its Asian peripheries; on the other side are the bitterly proud descendants of the glorious Middle Kingdom whose wealth, territory, and culture had been cannibalized by Russians among others during the centuries of Caucasian colonial expansion. Overlay these ancient resentments with the antagonism between rival dogmatic claimants to the mantle of revealed Marxist truth, and the only surprise in the Sino-Soviet relationship should have been their decade of limited cooperation after Mao's 1949 defeat of Chiang Kai-shek.[5]

Since the early 1960s, when the deep cracks in the facade of unity in the Eurasian communist coalition were displayed publicly in the epistle war between Moscow and Peking, Western analysts of the Sino-Soviet relationship have become virtually unanimous in assessing the split between the two powers as fundamental and their coalescence as inherently unstable. Most scholarly observers of the communist world now reject as inadequate Chou En-lai's explanation that "the split between Moscow and Peking developed because Nikita Khrushchev took the road of revisionism and peaceful coexistence rather than continuing vigorous revolution after he came to power in the nineteen fifties."[6] They also regard as superficial the standard Soviet polemics against the Mao personality cult.

Chairman Mao himself has traced the conflict back to when "Stalin tried to prevent the Chinese revolution by saying there should not be any civil war and that we must collaborate with Chiang Kai-shek."[7]

5. O. Edmund Clubb, *Twentieth Century China* (Columbia University Press, 1964).

6. See John W. Strong, "The Sino-Soviet Dispute," in *The Communist States in Disarray*, pp. 21–42; quotation from pp. 22–23.

7. Mao Tse-tung, "Speech to the 10th Plenary Session of the Eighth Central Committee, Sept. 24, 1962," *New York Times*, March 1, 1970. For

The actions of the USSR toward the Peoples Republic of China since 1949 provide ample evidence that, from the Kremlin's point of view, the conflict lay not in the deficiencies of Maoism for China's internal development but rather in China's unwillingness to be a subordinate of the Soviet Union. China's growing power, not her weakness, has been the primary threat. Thus the USSR at critical junctures has found all manner of excuses for not providing capital for China's industrialization and not helping China develop an independent nuclear capability. The Chinese party's real heresy is not in the substance of its doctrinal disputes with the CPSU but rather in its attempts to be an alternative pole of attraction within the world communist movement.

When Khrushchev proposed "many roads to socialism" in the 1950s, the Chinese party argued for unity in the camp. In the late 1960s Brezhnev insisted on only limited sovereignty for smaller communist nations in the coalition, but China was now the champion of absolute sovereignty. While the Kremlin was still cool to neutralism in the Third World, Chou En-lai was warmly courting Nehru, Nasser, and Sukarno at Bandung. During the next decade Mao was to bitterly attack Russia for becoming a status quo power and engaging in diplomatic minuets with the capitalist countries; but in the early 1970s the toasts to coexistence in Peking's glittering dining halls set the tone for East-West diplomacy.

Probably the most galling aspect of the rift, from the point of view of the Kremlin, has been China's use of the centrifugal tendencies in the Eastern European segments of the Soviet sphere to prosecute its rivalry with the Soviet Union.[8] Recent examples are China's criticisms of Russia for invading Czechoslovakia in 1968, its public interpretation of the Polish crisis of 1970 as a reaction against "Soviet social imperialism," its joint statements with Rumania against big power hegemony, and its encouragement of separatist movements among the Ukrainians and other nationalities of the USSR.

Since the late 1950s, when the Chinese began to express openly

---

a detailed examination of the early tensions between Mao and Stalin, see Robert North, *Moscow and the Chinese Communists* (Stanford University Press, 1953).

8. See Hemen Ray, "China's Initiative in Eastern Europe," *Current Scene*, Vol. 7, No. 23 (Dec. 1, 1969), pp. 1–17.

their long string of grievances against the USSR, Russia has periodically attempted to call a truce to this feature of their rivalry. As early as 1960 the USSR formally renounced its leading role in the world communist movement and offered to stop public criticism of Mao's policies in China if Mao would stop his propagandistic interference in the affairs of Russia and Eastern Europe. But the Chinese have consistently refused to grant the legitimacy of a sphere of Soviet influence even in Eastern Europe as the minimum basis for a modus vivendi.[9]

Opposition to superpowerism and social imperialism has become the essence of the Chinese worldwide rivalry with Russia for influence over other communist parties, both ruling and nonruling, and also for influence among Third World countries (see Chapter 5, pages 105–06). Even if China's post-Cultural Revolution diplomacy leads to a more tempered line toward national liberation struggles and to sustained cordial relations with capitalist countries, China is unlikely to relent in its efforts to stimulate greater autonomy within the Soviet sphere. If anything, given the continuation of the trends in Europe, the opportunities for such meddling will increase, especially as China participates in more international forums and institutions and becomes more active in world commerce.

Partly by way of retaliation, the USSR has been attempting to establish itself as friend and potential protector of the countries around China. But here it is dealing mostly with regimes whose political survival depends upon their ability to demonstrate a fierce independence from foreign domination. It is doubtful that Russia can be successful where others have failed, or that the Chinese are very worried.

The USSR's ultimate trump card—the threat of nuclear war with China—becomes less and less usable as China develops its own punitive strike-back capability, while simultaneously cultivating an image of international respectability. (A Soviet attempt to conquer China by invasion and occupation has never been militarily credible.) Moreover the degree of escalation of the border conflict is largely in China's hands. It is the irredentist and can pretty well manipulate the dispute to suit its external and internal political requirements. Finally, the Chinese know—and are aware that Russia knows—that the USSR's mili-

9. Richard Lowenthal, "Russia and China: Controlled Conflict," *Foreign Affairs*, Vol. 49, No. 3 (April 1971), pp. 507–18.

tary, economic, and political capabilities for controlling events in Eastern Europe would be depleted by a major embroilment in a protracted Asian war, whether over the Sino-Soviet border or growing out of some third-party conflict.

The Future of the Socialist Commonwealth in Europe

Despite the growing challenges to Soviet authority in the world communist movement, the likelihood of major defections from the Soviet-led coalition in Eastern Europe has been considered low by most prominent analysts and statesmen in the West. This prognosis usually has rested on three assumptions: (1) The USSR will continue to find it a threat to its military and political security to have other than loyal subordinate allies in Eastern Europe. (2) The economic and political weakness of the Eastern European nations, accompanied by the continued fear of a revived German imperialism, will allow the Kremlin to maintain control at relatively low cost to the USSR. (3) Wherever and whenever the Kremlin decides it is necessary to apply overwhelming force to maintain its Eastern European security belt, it will not shirk from doing so. Among the most dramatic aspects of the emerging pattern of world politics are indications that even these cardinal "permanently operating" factors may be subject to erosion.

With respect to the first factor, it was pointed out in Chapter 1 that the military value of contiguous allies as buffers against attack is being rapidly devalued by the technology of contemporary warfare, particularly for a superpower with long-range weapons of mass destruction. Given the buildup of its strategic capabilities, the Soviet Union should be able to deter attack from any quarter without having to deploy its troops beyond its borders or to depend on help from its neighbors. Bordering nations actively hostile to the USSR, though perhaps not a vital security threat, can be expected to remain intolerable long into the future for a country with Russia's historical memories. But there need be no objective security reason why the USSR must continue to fear a belt of neutrals in Eastern Europe, especially if they were substantially demilitarized. This is not to say that Russia will no longer *prefer* to maintain a belt of military allies around its western frontiers, but only that from a military planning perspective it should be able to find alternative means of guaranteeing its own security. These alternatives may become more attractive, especially with a rise in the political costs of attempting to maintain military allies.

A central reason put forward by the USSR for maintaining a militarized buffer area on its western flank was German *revanchism* for World War II. This argument became less salient in the early 1970s with the negotiation of the Bonn-Moscow, Bonn-Warsaw, and Bonn-Prague treaties renouncing the use of force and pledging to respect the existing territorial status quo, the Berlin agreement, and the normalization of relations between the East and West German states. To the degree that détente and increased East-West intercourse supplant deterrence as the basis for security in Europe, the geopolitical rationale is further weakened for maintaining major deployments of Soviet troops in Eastern Europe and a tight, Kremlin-controlled military alliance system. Other, more embarrassing reasons for the Soviet military presence come into focus: (1) Moscow's desire to maintain its newly acquired empire; (2) the CPSU's fear of a revival in Eastern Europe of nationalism, economic liberalism, and pluralistic democracy, and of the spread of such tendencies into the Soviet Union; and (3) the advantages perceived by a number of the communist leaders in Eastern Europe, for purposes of keeping themselves in power against domestic opposition, of being able to request or invoke the specter of Soviet military intervention.[10]

But as the underlying political reasons for the continuation of a heavy Soviet presence come into focus, they also become a clearer target for nationalists and reformists. In most of the Eastern European countries the growing unpopularity of the Soviet presence confronts the domestic regime with a most delicate balancing task: If it becomes openly the spokesman of anti-Soviet nationalism and reformism, as did the Dubcek government in early 1968, it risks being forced out of power by the Kremlin; yet if it fails to be adequately responsive to the growing popular pressures, it risks becoming the target of progressive agitation and even determined subversion. Clever politicians—and there are many in power today in Eastern Europe—can turn this delicate situation into a major bargaining asset vis-à-vis the USSR. They

10. For an up-to-date and well-documented analysis of the rise of the political security concerns in Eastern Europe concurrent with the decline in the military-geopolitical concerns, see Peter Bender, *East Europe in Search of Security* (Johns Hopkins University Press for the International Institute of Strategic Studies, London, 1972).

must be able to bring home the bacon, so to speak, especially on intrabloc economic matters, to demonstrate to their countrymen that constructive participation in the socialist commonwealth has its rewards.

Political leverage by the satellite leaders has been increasing concurrently with intrabloc economic issues, which result from the rather impressive though uneven progress in economic development throughout Eastern Europe during the past two decades. Apparently it is within the Council for Mutual Economic Assistance (COMECON) that the toughest international bargaining takes place, and Russia by no means always gets its way.

Observers of economic relations among the COMECON countries report that the primary issues concern the pricing of goods exchanged among the members; the design and management of multilateral projects, such as the development of nuclear energy or cooperation on the Danube; and economic intercourse with the noncommunist countries.

Coalitions within COMECON for bargaining on these issues tend to follow the natural economic cleavages within the region. The most pervasive, natural coalition derives simply from the overweening size and diversity of the Soviet economy which establishes a colonial type of tension between the USSR and each of the other COMECON members. Attempts by the Soviet Union to institutionalize a "socialist division of labor" within the camp exacerbate this cleavage between superpower and small power. As economic modernization proceeds throughout the region the concept of the socialist division of labor also tends to open up other crosscutting cleavages: between the developed and less-developed countries of the alliance, essentially the northern and southern tiers; and between the traditional international traders (Hungary, Czechoslovakia, and Poland), which are more interested in moving toward a greater dependence on market forces, and the others who are inclined to insulate their national economies from outside disturbances.[11]

The USSR cannot simply command conformity with its preferences on these issues; nor can the Kremlin apply gross economic or military coercion when its preferences are resisted, without drastically undermining the already weakened legitimacy of its claim to supreme authority in the international communist movement. As economic growth,

11. Philip E. Uren, "Patterns of Economic Relations," in *The Communist States in Disarray*, pp. 307–22.

nationalism, and the declining external military threat reinforce each other in Eastern Europe, the big question is whether the Soviet Union will gradually raise its threshold of tolerance for pluralism. Additional perspective on this still unpredictable scene may be gained by a closer look at the three Warsaw Pact countries—Rumania, Hungary, and Poland—that have continued to expand their narrow range of autonomous action in the post-Czechoslovakia period.

The Rumanian Deviation

The Kremlin's major noncoercive adaptation to the decline in direct political control over its satellites through the international communist party apparatus has been its sponsorship of top-heavy supranational procedures in both the Warsaw Pact organization and COMECON. This is why Rumania's defiance of the USSR in recent years, while not the immediate critical threat to Soviet geopolitical interests that Czechoslovakia posed in 1968, constitutes in some respects the most frustrating challenge to Soviet leadership.

Rumania has been able to hit at the basic organizing principles of the Soviet bloc without inviting coercive discipline. Unlike Czechoslovakia, whose internal reforms were branded as counterrevolutionary, Rumania has been one of the slowest in the bloc to loosen its authoritarian and highly centralized structure. Moreover, whereas a defection by Czechoslovakia could be seen as opening up a traditional invasion corridor from Germany, Rumania's disloyalty would not in itself constitute a security threat to the USSR. The most menacing recent hints of Soviet military intervention in Rumania were in connection with the Czechoslovakian crisis and apparently were to deter Rumanian attempts to mobilize international sentiment against the Soviet occupation of Prague.

Rumania's dissidence has been expressed in a number of arenas: international communist party congresses, the military planning committees of the Warsaw Pact, COMECON, various all-European forums, where, as in the nonproliferation treaty negotiations, Rumanian delegates have openly attacked Soviet-sponsored proposals as "profoundly discriminatory" against nonnuclear countries.[12] The USSR would like to dismiss Bucharest's dissent as a hangover of prewar

12. Thomas W. Wolfe, *Soviet Power and Europe, 1945–1970* (Johns Hopkins Press, 1970), pp. 303–08, 348–59.

romantic nationalism and the traditions of fickle Balkan diplomacy, "soft" factors which communist internationalism will in good time eradicate. But the strongest Rumanian grievances at being fully integrated into the socialist bloc emanate from the modernizers, most of them pragmatic tough-minded materialists.

Bucharest early saw the contemplated socialist division of labor as unpalatable. If Rumania were to restrict its commerce with its COMECON partners according to the principle of comparative advantage within the bloc, it would remain the supplier of petroleum products, hard minerals, and grains in exchange for machinery and finished consumer goods provided by the more industrialized East Germans, Czechs, Poles, or the Russians themselves. As put by Premier Ion Gheorghe Maurer, "Why should we send our corn to Poland? So Poland can fatten its pigs and buy machinery from the West? We can sell the corn directly and buy the machinery we need ourselves."[13]

Not only has Rumania prevented COMECON integration from proceeding according to the USSR's preferred designs, but it has also been

13. Quoted by Anatole Shub, *An Empire Loses Hope: The Return of Stalin's Ghost* (Norton, 1970), p. 204. Rumania's basic "declaration of independence," published in 1964 in the form of a statement of the Central Committee of the Rumanian Workers' party, provides a glimpse of the deep conflict of interests existing within COMECON: "Our party . . . declare[s] that . . . shifting some functions of economic management from the competence of the respective state to that of superstate bodies or organisms . . . [is] not in keeping with the principles that underlie the relations among the socialist countries . . . The sovereignty of the socialist state requires that it hold . . . in its hands all the levers of managing economic and social life. Transmitting such levers to the competence of superstate or extrastate bodies would turn sovereignty into a meaningless notion. . . . Bearing in mind the diversity of the conditions of socialist construction, there are not nor can there be any unique patterns and recipes; no one can decide what is and what is not correct for other countries or parties. It is up to every Marxist-Leninist party, it is a sovereign right of each socialist state, to elaborate, choose, or change the forms and methods of socialist construction . . . There does not and cannot exist a 'parent' party and a 'son' party, or 'superior' parties and 'subordinate' parties, but there exists the great family of Communist and workers' parties, which have equal rights." From "Statement on the Rumanian Workers' Party Concerning the Problems of the International Communist and Working Class Movement," April 1964. Text in William E. Griffith, *Sino-Soviet Relations 1964–1965* (M.I.T. Press, 1967) pp. 269–96.

instrumental in stimulating opposition within the Warsaw Pact against Soviet proposals for greater military specialization, sharing of financial burdens, and complete unity of policy toward the West.[14] Rumania's leverage within the Warsaw Pact and COMECON has been due in no small degree to an ability to cultivate ties with countries outside the region, not only China but also noncommunist countries, particularly France, various Third World countries, and the United States.[15] Throughout the 1960s it expanded and intensified its participation in international organizations, notably the Danube Commission, where it sponsored West Germany's candidacy for full membership, and the United Nations Conference on Trade and Development (UNCTAD).[16] Not surprisingly, Rumania has been one of the most vigorous champions of the East-West Conference on European Security and Cooperation and of negotiations on mutual force reductions in Europe, and has doggedly agitated for procedures in these forums that would reduce the role of the superpowers and enhance the weight of the smaller powers.

Why has the great Soviet Union put up with such frustrations and public embarrassments from its small neighbor? To be sure, they do not threaten Soviet security, but they do constitute nonnegligible obstacles to the USSR's designs for the socialist commonwealth and to its reputation as an effective coalition leader. The answer, clearly, is that for the Soviet Union to harshly suppress Rumania's independence would be in itself a profound admission of Kremlin impotence in the noncoercive elements of authority. And evidently the USSR has decided to try to strengthen this noncoercive authority not only internationally but at home.

14. Fritz Ermath, "Internationalism, Security, and Legitimacy: The Challenge to Soviet Interests in Europe," No. RM-5099-PR (RAND Corp., March 1969), pp. 33–52. One practical result of Rumania's procedural maneuvering has been the inability of the Soviet Union to get Warsaw Pact agreement to any military operation that would bring Russian troops on Rumanian soil.

15. Robert Farlow, "Romanian Foreign Policy: A Case of Partial Alignment," Problems of Communism, Vol. 20, No. 6 (November–December 1971), pp. 54–63.

16. See William Zimmerman, "Hierarchical Regional Systems and the Politics of System Boundaries," International Organization, Vol. 26, No. 1 (Winter 1972), pp. 18–36.

Hungary's Experimentation

The Rumanians have been reflecting and augmenting the contradictions in the organizational principles of the socialist commonwealth and thereby undermining the authority of the USSR over the alliance. In contrast the Hungarians' economic innovations have been exposing the contradictions in the Soviet model for a domestic society and in so doing are undermining the ideological authority of the CPSU. On the one hand the Rumanians thus far have protected themselves against Soviet punishment for their international deviance by remaining internally orthodox. The Hungarians, on the other hand, have been loyal to all Soviet political stances internationally since 1956, which seems to have allowed them some elbow room for internal experimentation and substantial economic intercourse with the West. Cumulatively there exists in Eastern Europe considerable international and internal liberal deviation from Soviet preferences, which the Soviet Union has now set a precedent of tolerating. But as yet it has not tolerated both internal and international deviation from the same country, except for Yugoslavia, which has long been sui generis.

Apart from Yugoslavia, Hungary is the only country in Eastern Europe that has been experimenting with major economic reforms. Significantly, the greatest momentum in Hungary's reforms has come since 1968, which underlines the argument above that the Czech crisis did not turn back the basic secular trends in Eastern Europe eroding Soviet control. The Hungarians, to be sure, are engaged primarily in *domestic* experiments, and since the tragedy of 1956 they have been impeccable in their deference to Soviet views on intrabloc political relations. But the reforms contained in Budapest's New Economic Mechanism (NEM) have only increased Hungarian needs of Western machinery and technological know-how and have made Hungary progressively more anxious to become a full participant in the world economy, as reflected in its application for membership in GATT—all of which must, to some degree, reduce the USSR's influence over Hungary's political economy.[17] The fact that the Hungarians have surpassed the USSR in economic innovation is in itself of potential political significance. To the degree that they are successful, the claim of the Kremlin to be the Vatican of the socialist world will be further eroded. The larger question, however, and the one that the Kremlin is un-

17. Zimmerman, "Hierarchical Regional Systems," pp. 34–35.

doubtedly most concerned about, is to what extent liberalism in the economic field will spill over into liberalism in the political field so as to threaten the dominance of the Moscow-oriented communist party.

The Hungarian NEM varies from the Soviet model for organizing a socialist economy, particularly with respect to the locus of decisions on production schedules, investments, and price-setting. In Hungary these functions have been transferred in large measure to enterprise managers who draw up their own plans in response to local productive potential and set prices in response to market demands, both domestic and foreign, including noncommunist markets.[18] In these matters the NEM already goes considerably further than similar Czechoslovakian experiments in 1968.

At the time of this writing the enthusiasm for economic experimentation appears not to have expanded into political reformism, which is what brought the Czechs into a confrontation with the Soviet Union. But the potential for such spillover is inherent in the economic modernization now under way and may not be contained for more than a few years.

Continuing economic modernization is producing new middle classes skeptical of the elitist basis of one-party dictatorship and the ideological orthodoxy which sustains it. About 15 percent of the population is now composed of professionals, managers, and intellectuals who, according to contemporary studies by Hungarian sociologists, embody values that are primarily nonideological and individualistic.[19] To avoid isolating the communist establishment from the most dynamic elements of Hungarian society and to prevent the latter from being so alienated that they refuse to lend their best energies to further national development, the Kadar regime has been gradually expanding civil liberties and cautiously increasing the opportunities for special interest groups to participate in the political process.

Such pragmatic accommodation to the values of the expanding middle class may not be enough to stave off the nationalistic revival which always lurks around the corner in Hungary. The country's traditional fierce nationalism has strong anti-Russian overtones. It was suppressed

18. George F. Ray, "Reforms in Eastern Europe," *The World Today* (December 1971), pp. 530–40.

19. Bennet Korvig, "Decompression in Hungary—Phase Two," in Peter A. Toma (ed.), *The Changing Face of Communism* (University of Arizona Press, 1970), pp. 193–213, at pp. 207–08.

and intensified by the Soviet invasion of 1956 and the continued presence of 80,000 Soviet troops on Hungarian soil. The Kadar government, and any likely successors that Russia would prefer, must therefore preside as a basically unpopular regime unless there is a substantial loosening of Soviet control over the Warsaw Pact countries generally.

To open up the governing ranks to extensive popular participation would be to encourage anti-Soviet nationalism. In Eastern Europe popular politics means nationalism. The Russians know it and the current rulers in the area know it. So up to a point the interest of a regime in power coincides with that of the Communist Party of the Soviet Union in supporting proletarian internationalism. *Destalinization* and *desatellization* need not proceed simultaneously. But in Hungary to keep these processes apart may be only a temporary condition. The economic reforms already in motion require degrees of freedom of individual choice and decentralization of control that imply considerable political liberalization somewhere down the road. And greater liberalization may well bring to the fore greater national self-assertion. Periodically ideological pressure is applied to Budapest, as in the spring and summer of 1972 when Soviet and Czechoslovakian newspapers ran editorials against the threat of "bourgeois nationalism" in Hungary, urging certain adjustments in the NEM. At a summit meeting between Brezhnev and Hungarian party leader Janos Kadar, the Hungarians agreed to modify some details in their five-year plan and the Soviet leader indicated that he might even recommend that the USSR adopt some of Hungary's innovations. By the end of the year relations apparently returned to their normal amicability.[20]

Clearly, Hungary's experimentation poses profound dilemmas for both the USSR and the Moscow-oriented loyalists in Budapest. Either the Kremlin must progressively loosen its control over its satellite and allow it greater self-determination, or else the authority of the CPSU increasingly will be regarded as illegitimate by the classes whose support is most crucial to the survival of a modernist regime. The maintenance of authority in the face of such opposition would require Stalinist terror. But terror would further undermine the legitimacy of authority and thereby further alienate the modernist elements from their own government and the Soviet Union.

20. Tad Szulc, "Soviet, Hungary in Serious Split," *New York Times,* April 4, 1972; James Feron, "Brezhnev Backs Kadar's Reforms," *New York Times,* Dec. 3, 1972.

The Nationalist Potential in Poland

In Poland the Eastern European dilemmas faced by the Kremlin could appear in their starkest form. Lagging behind Rumania in foreign policy independence and behind Hungary in domestic economic experimentation, Poland is still only a potential threat to Soviet leadership. But the USSR probably fears an outburst of Polish self-determination more than any other development in Eastern Europe save a revolution by the East Germans tempting Western intervention.

The communist lid over Polish nationalism has been threatening to blow off in Russia's face ever since World War II. As indicated above, this nearly happened in 1956 at the time of the Hungarian revolution when Gomulka triumphantly faced down the threat of Soviet military intervention. In 1956 Khrushchev made his peace with Polish nationalism by granting Gomulka more autonomous control over his internal affairs than was allowed any other member of the Warsaw Pact. In return Gomulka was willing to defer to Soviet leadership on international questions, since the support of the USSR was considered a necessary balance against expected demands from Germany to recover its former territories east of the Oder-Neisse.

But in the 1960s Gomulka's sluggish response to the pace of social and economic change inside Poland discredited him with his countrymen as a nationalist hero. Simultaneously, in the warming climate of East-West détente as reflected in West Germany's growing cordiality toward Poland, there was a reduced need for total reliance on the Kremlin to protect Polish security interests. The deposition of Gomulka in December 1970 was dramatic less for its suddenness than for what it indicated about the deep currents of change in Poland and Eastern Europe as a whole.

The pressures for change in the Polish status quo have been building up simultaneously against three fronts: restrictions on civil liberties, economic planning on the Soviet model, and overdependence on the Soviet Union on economic matters. All of these pressures carry the banner of Polish nationalism, and any regime that ignores them now risks being overturned as insufficiently patriotic. Rapid industrialization and the increased demand for educated subelites has created an ambitious younger generation (almost half of all Poles were born since the war), angry at restrictions on freedom and impatient with the sluggishness of the older managerial and party cadres. Consumerism pervades the working classes and is reversible only at the cost of considerable unpopularity. "Indeed," observes Adam Bromke, "had the new trends in Europe not been abruptly reversed by the Soviet intervention in Czechoslovakia, Gomulka probably would have been removed from power earlier. The suppression of Czechoslovakia, however, only postponed, but did not eliminate, pressure for change in Poland."[21]

Today, with charismatic leadership out of the picture and competing elites at the top of party and bureaucracy, popularity becomes an essential requirement of rule even in a nondemocratic country. This means that responsiveness to the diverse demands of this increasingly pluralistic society can no longer be put off. Since the demands from different segments are not always compatible—for example, labor's desire for higher wages is opposed to management's wish to remain competitive in the international market—leadership must hold aloft the banner of the national good, the national interest, to sustain sufficient popular support in the face of tough allocative decisions.

Polish society currently needs to participate fully in the modern world with a sense of self-respect. A lack of Soviet responsiveness to these needs could push Polish nationalism beyond the point of no return. The USSR would of course eventually overpower the Poles in any physical conflict, but it would involve a blood bath that would grimly overshadow the Hungarian and Czech episodes. More likely, however, is a continuation of the uneasy but pragmatic accommodation between Polish nationalist sensitivities and the Russian compulsion to be assured of a reliable satellite to buffer Germany.

The Poles not only hate the Russians probably more than do any of the other Eastern European nations but also need them more. The first axiom of Polish foreign policy is that an alliance with Russia is essential as a balance against Germany, even a friendly Germany.[22] Thus even in the context of growing East-West détente Poland has been more consistently supportive of Soviet international positions under the regime of Edward Gierek than it was during the Gomulka period. No doubt there has been the usual necessary quid pro quo between Gierek and Brezhnev, the latter having come through with badly needed credits and other indications of support while Gierek was consolidating his power. But the recent directions in Soviet foreign policy,

21. Adam Bromke, "Beyond the Gomulka Era," *Foreign Affairs*, Vol. 49, No. 3 (April 1971), pp. 480–92; quotation from p. 484.
22. Peter Bender, *East Europe in Search of Security*, pp. 48–81.

on their merits, fit well with Poland's own international inclinations. Rapprochement with Germany and a general East-West détente have been important for facilitating Polish access to Western technology and markets and for reviving traditional cultural ties with Western Europe. Moreover the Poles all along have been strong champions of an all-European security system, perceiving that in the long run this would enhance their international bargaining position, including their influence vis-à-vis Moscow in COMECON and the Warsaw Pact.[23]

In sum, it appears that important cultural and economic currents running through Eastern Europe are undermining the hierarchical basis of the Soviet coalition and in so doing are increasing the costs to the Kremlin of maintaining tight control. In the main, these costs take the form of the demoralization of the most creative and productive elements within the communist world, which in the long run could affect the balance of power on which the physical security of the Soviet Union itself finally depends. Increasingly the Soviet leadership is therefore faced with the profound dilemma of balancing immediate control against real power over the long term.

Meanwhile the costs of protecting the Asian border areas from Chinese irredentism have also risen. And Russia is investing heavily in military and nonmilitary capabilities for projecting Soviet commercial and political power on a global basis. In this context Soviet proposals for arms limitation and collaborative ventures in Europe should not be interpreted simply as a ploy to achieve a one-sided disengagement of U.S. power from the European balance. The Kremlin may well be probing for means of maintaining influence in all-European affairs at reduced costs.

The cracking of the Soviet sphere, though part and parcel of the depolarization and demilitarization of world politics, also has its dangerous side. Ideological opponents of the Soviet Union could revive their efforts to accelerate the disintegration in ways that could provoke irrational violent responses on the part of the Kremlin. A prudent Western statesmanship in the coming years would avoid interventionist temptations and sustain an environment in which the USSR will not mistake the increasing pluralism in the communist camp, which is mainly generated by internal developments, for externally sponsored subversion.

23. Adam Bromke, "Poland Under Gierek: A New Political Style," *Problems of Communism*, Vol. 21, No. 5 (September–October 1972), pp. 14–17.

CHAPTER FOUR

Spans across the Ideological Divide

Until recently the most severe strains in the U.S.-led and Soviet-led coalitions were largely intramural. The Atlantic alliance was nearly torn apart in 1956 by the differing responses of its members to Egypt's nationalization of the Suez Canal. And France almost walked out of NATO over nuclear command and control issues. The Sino-Soviet split antedated détente. The altercations between Moscow and Havana have been mostly over Castro's militancy. The turbulence in Eastern Europe, as shown in the previous chapter, has emerged primarily from internal pressures—economic stagnation on top of the rapid growth of developmental needs, intellectual ferment, and nationalism. But today many of the intracoalition pressures, whether for autonomy or modernization, are stimulated by the enlarged openings for East-West contact, which in turn affect and are affected by the centrifugal process in each coalition.

There is no doubt that increasing contact with the West can, like applying fresh oxygen to boiling liquid, strongly increase the chances of major eruptions in the communist countries. Thus as incentives and opportunities for cross-alliance interactions rise, the risks—particularly to the Soviet Union's control over Eastern Europe and over its own restive national groups—also rise considerably. The Kremlin is well aware of these dangers, as vividly demonstrated by its interventions in Hungary and Czechoslovakia and by its recent tightening of controls on internal dissidence; but the dangers are inherent in an atmosphere of détente, which the Soviet Union has powerful reasons to sustain. Moreover the process of East-West interaction, particularly with China a full participant in the arena, is not something that the Russians themselves can turn off. It takes two to tango, but now there are other partners willing to dance.

The increasing salience of East-West cooperation is also affecting politics within the anticommunist coalition. Previously the subject produced only marginal disagreements in the West. Some members of the coalition recognized the Peoples Republic of China; some did not. The Federal Republic of Germany used to be more adamant than most of its allies in isolating East Germany. The United States unsuccessfully tried to prevent others from trading with Castro's Cuba and with North Vietnam. But in recent years, with the rapid maturing of détente with the Eastern Europeans and the Russians and the full welcoming of China into the international system, the question of how to pursue relations across the ideological divide has become a central political issue in the coalition.

Economic Ties between Russia and America

In the early 1970s most Western statesmen were convinced that the USSR was furthering the idea of peaceful coexistence as more than a stratagem for sowing dissension in the anticommunist coalition. Not only did Russia appear to be especially anxious to stabilize its western front in order to concentrate on its conflict with China, but also, as the U.S. secretary of commerce explained, "the Soviets had reason to feel that a new Soviet foreign policy was in order if the new direction of Soviet economic strategy were to bear fruit. In short, their domestic economic strategy, which was once tied to sustained high levels of political tensions, now may be tied to its minimization."[1]

There were signs that the Kremlin's view of the global "correlation of forces" now included the following appraisal: A technological gap between the two halves of the industrialized world (communist and noncommunist) was threatening to negate much of the international influence the Russians gained as a result of their rapid modernization, industrialization, and strategic buildup.[2] Continuing modernization now required the Soviet Union to make a substantial shift of resources into many of the high technology, largely civilian areas which, until recently,

1. Peter G. Peterson, *U.S.-Soviet Commercial Relations in a New Era* (Department of Commerce, August 1972), p. 8.
2. See Richard V. Burks, "Technological Innovation and Political Change in Communist Eastern Europe," No. RM-6051-PR (RAND Corp., August 1969).

had been given low priority in comparison with military and space needs. But taking off into the kind of advanced industrialization that would allow the Warsaw Pact countries to maintain military parity *and* satisfy rising consumer demands would require substantial inputs from the West, especially in the fields of information technology and electronics.[3] These expensive inputs could not be had for nothing. They would have to be purchased in the world economy, and this in turn would require flexible economic decision-making capable of responding to demand changes in the world market. Only a fully credible Soviet policy of peaceful coexistence, however, would stimulate the noncommunist developed countries to extend credits, to liberalize their strategic lists, and otherwise let down their political barriers to East-West commerce.

An early indication that a major change in the Kremlin's foreign economic policy was in the works was the public revision of the doctrine that the socialist commonwealth ought to produce all its own economic requirements. The feasibility and desirability of autarchy was officially negated by the directives of the Twenty-third Party Congress in 1966. "It is becoming more and more evident," explained Premier Kosygin, "that the scientific and cultural revolution under way in the modern world calls for freer international contacts and creates conditions for broad economic exchanges between socialist and capitalist countries."[4]

Henceforth decisions about whether to produce a commodity or purchase it in the world market would be based heavily on considerations of the cost of production relative to the cost of importation. In a complementary move, producers in the Soviet Union were to have their quotas and product specifications formulated with greater sensitivity to the world market than previously. "At last," according to Samuel Pisar, "the communist economies were to be reoriented toward a more

3. See Richard W. Judy, "The Case of Computer Technology," in Stanislaw Wasowski, *East-West Trade and the Technology Gap: A Political and Economic Appraisal* (Praeger, 1970), pp. 43–72; Ivan Berenyi, "Computers in Eastern Europe," *Scientific American*, Vol. 233, No. 4 (October 1970), pp. 102–08; Henry R. Lieberman, "Broad Soviet Drive to Automate Economy," *New York Times*, Dec. 12, 1973.

4. Quoted by Samuel J. Pisar, *Coexistence and Commerce: Guidelines for Transactions between East and West* (McGraw-Hill, 1970), pp. 33–34.

active recognition of the principle of a world-wide international division of labor."[5]

The Soviet leadership sought and found ample scriptural justification for the abandonment of autarchy. Thus in a major 1970 speech on trade expansion with the West, N. Patolichev, the minister of foreign trade, defended the growing Soviet worldwide commercial activity by invoking

Lenin's idea that the improvement of political relations facilitates the fuller utilization of opportunities for trade and economic cooperation between countries of different social systems [and], at the same time, the development of mutually advantageous economic relations is an important means of normalizing the international political situation.

Patolichev went on to catalog in considerable detail how "trade, economic, scientific, and technical ties between the U.S.S.R. and the capitalist countries have become broader and more diversified," outlining the long-term agreement with France to expand bilateral trade and scientific cooperation during the 1970–74 period, and a similar agreement with Italy, as well as special contacts with British and West German firms. "The facts of contemporary reality," concluded the Soviet trade minister, "confirm anew Lenin's thesis to the effect that objective economic interest is stronger than the policies of those imperialist powers who seek to hold back the development of business cooperation with the Socialist world."[6]

At the Twenty-fourth Party Congress Brezhnev called special attention to the "economic, scientific, and technical ties, in some instances resting on a long-term basis," being developed "with the countries of the capitalist world." And he labeled as *"basic* concrete tasks" cooperative projects for "conservation of the environment, development of power and other natural resources, development of transport and com-

5. Ibid., p. 34.
6. N. Patolichev, "Economic Cooperation Is the Path to Strengthening Peace in Europe," *Pravda*, June 18, 1970; translation in *Current Digest of the Soviet Press*, Vol. 22, No. 24 (July 14, 1970), pp. 6–7. In the context of official American interest in exploring opportunities for expanding U.S.-Soviet commerce aroused by the President's 1972 visit to Moscow, an elaborate reconstruction of Lenin's attitudes toward economic cooperation was published in *Foreign Affairs* by a senior Soviet official of the UN Secretariat: Evgeny Chossudovsky, "Genoa Revisited: Russia and Coexistence," Vol. 50, No. 3 (April 1972), pp. 554–77.

munications, prevention and eradication of the most dangerous wide-spread diseases, and the exploration and development of outer space and the world oceans."[7]

Heretofore general expressions of Soviet interest in a major expansion of trade with the United States were usually dismissed as not containing sufficiently credible and precise indications of where additional opportunities for American sales could be found in the Russian market, and what the Russians could provide in return to earn the necessary foreign exchange. Nor did the U.S. government give much attention to arguments by American entrepreneurs that they should be allowed to compete more effectively against the Europeans and Japanese for Soviet purchases. But in 1971 the increasing deficit in the U.S. balance of payments and the heightened economic tensions with the EC and Japan, coming simultaneously with serious Soviet anxiety over the new U.S. approach to China, apparently gave the White House fresh economic and political interests in the Soviet overtures to trade.

Rather suddenly, it seemed, firms anxious to cultivate new commercial relationships with the USSR began to experience success in getting the U.S. government to reduce long-standing political and national security barriers to East-West trade. A dramatic example came in advance of the highly publicized November 1971 visit to the Soviet Union of the American secretary of commerce, when the government approved a billion dollars' worth of export licenses to American firms attempting to obtain orders from the huge Soviet truck and diesel engine factory being constructed on the Kama River near Moscow. The previous year the Defense Department got the Ford Motor Company to back out of negotiations for participation in the Kama River project, arguing that some of the trucks might find their way to North Vietnam for use in the war.[8]

Collateral moves on both sides during the fall of 1971 indicated that the logjam in their commercial relations was loosening. The Russians, having suffered a very poor harvest, arranged a $1 billion purchase of American surplus food grains; the State Department said it was ready

7. *Report of the Central Committee of the Communist Party of the Soviet Union*, delivered by Leonid Brezhnev, March 30, 1971 (Moscow: Novosti Press), pp. 33, 37.

8. J. V. Reistrup, "Truck Deal in Russia Approved," *Washington Post*, Nov. 19, 1971.

to reduce the advance notification required from Soviet ships entering U.S. ports, bringing them into line with regulations for other Eastern European countries; and bilateral talks were scheduled to effect additional mutual easing of shipping restrictions. Other prospective agreements and obstacles to them were revealed in numerous background stories from government ministries in both countries. The most lucrative deals were foreseen in cooperative efforts to develop and market the copper deposits and other raw material sources in Siberia, including natural gas. Preceding these ambitious joint undertakings, however, there would be an expansion of the more usual types of trade and technological exchanges, which would require a normalization of commercial relationships. From the American point of view normalization should be accompanied by Russian settlement of their still outstanding Lend-Lease war debts to the United States; the USSR, as a quid pro quo, would want the same trading privileges in the American market that are enjoyed by other countries—namely, government credits from the U.S. Export-Import Bank and "most favored nation" status for tariffs.

By the time of the preparations for the May 1972 visit of President Nixon to Moscow, there was enough momentum on all these fronts for the subject of a U.S.-Soviet commercial rapprochement to be made a major item on the agenda. Indeed, it was probably the Russians' enthusiasm about normalizing economic relations that, more than anything else, convinced the White House it could proceed with highly coercive actions against North Vietnam (including the mining of Haiphong harbor) without thereby provoking the Kremlin into canceling the summit.

Not surprisingly, a central plank in the declaration signed on May 29, 1972, by President Nixon and General Secretary Brezhnev affirmed:

The U.S.A. and the U.S.S.R. regard commercial and economic ties as an important and necessary element in the strengthening of their bilateral relations and thus will actively promote the growth of such ties. They will facilitate cooperation between the relevant organizations and enterprises of the two countries and the conclusion of appropriate agreements and contracts, including long-term ones.[9]

9. "Basic Principles of Mutual Relations between the United States of America and the Union of Soviet Socialist Republics," May 29, 1972. Full text in *New York Times*, May 30, 1972.

The accompanying joint communiqué marking the end of the President's state visit cleared the way for accelerated negotiations to remove political barriers to their economic intercourse. "Both sides . . . agree that realistic conditions exist for increasing economic ties," said the communiqué. "These ties should develop on the basis of mutual benefit *in accordance with generally accepted international practice.*" (Emphasis added.) It was further agreed that new credit arrangements should be facilitated and that a Lend-Lease settlement should be negotiated concurrently with a trade agreement. Detailed negotiations were to be responsive to guidelines developed by a Joint U.S.-Soviet Commercial Commission, which was also charged with the responsibility of working out a comprehensive bilateral trade agreement.[10]

By the end of 1972 the tally of successful negotiations was long enough to convince even the most skeptical that an extraordinary shift in U.S.-Soviet relations was under way. Among the breakthroughs: (1) agreement by the Russians to pay back $722 million, by the year 2001, on their wartime Lend-Lease debt, in return for which President Nixon would now authorize the Export-Import Bank to extend credits and guarantees for the sale of goods to the Soviet Union; (2) a commitment by the Nixon administration to seek congressional extension of most favored nation tariff rates to the Soviet Union; (3) provision for the United States to set up government-sponsored and commercial offices in Moscow to facilitate the work of U.S. businessmen seeking contracts, and similar provisions for the Russians in Washington; (4) the delivery of 440 million bushels of wheat to the Soviet Union; (5) a maritime accord opening forty ports in each nation to the other's shipping, with only a four-day advance notice of entry; (6) an agreement between the navies of the two countries to take steps to prevent high-risk incidents at sea; (7) the start of joint work on the U.S. Apollo–Soviet Soyuz combined space flight planned for 1975; (8) a series of projects to solve environmental problems in which Soviet and American experts are to work together in both countries; (9) an agreement to set up the International Institute of Applied Systems Analysis, a multinational think tank involving social scientists and others from both countries as well as from Britain, France, Japan, West Germany, East Germany, Czechoslovakia, Poland, Italy, Canada, Rumania, and Bulgaria, to study problems of industrialized society; and (10) joint U.S.-

10. Ibid.

Soviet projects in medical research, oceanography, and environmental problems.[11]

Clearly the Russians were most anxious for the détente to bear economic fruit. Following the Moscow summit of 1972 Kremlin officials, playing on the growing American fears of an energy shortage, gave major emphasis to various negotiations that were still only in progress between American companies, the Soviet Union, and Japan for shared financing and construction of two huge trans-Siberian pipelines, associated liquification plants, and tankers to carry natural gas from the Soviet Union to Japan and the United States. The Russians had already negotiated large-scale and long-term agreements with West German, Italian, and Austrian firms for the construction of pipelines to deliver natural gas to Western Europe from the Soviet Union.[12]

Soviet interest in the trinational Siberian project seemed to have been spurred by the Russian desire to counter China's courtship of both the United States and Japan, but it also apparently reflected serious Soviet economic needs as well as geopolitical considerations. It would cost an estimated $10 billion and probably take seven years to build. Gas would start flowing out of the Soviet Union by 1980, after which the three countries were to maintain a special supplier-consumer relationship for twenty-five years, with United States companies expected to purchase more than $40 billion worth over the life of the contract.[13] The Russians and Japanese meanwhile were involved in collateral negotiations con-

11. For background, see *US-USSR Cooperative Agreements*, Hearings before the Subcommittee on International Cooperation in Science and Space, House Committee on Science and Astronautics, 92 Cong. 2 sess. (1972).

See also Bernard Gwertzman, "U.S. and Russians Sign Agreements to Widen Trade," *New York Times*, Oct. 19, 1972.

Reporting on the 1972 agreements, *U.S. News and World Report*, usually hard-line on East-West issues, recognized: "Far more than a spectacular expansion of trade is resulting from the changed relationship between the United States and the Soviet Union. After decades of cold war and confrontation, the world's two mightiest powers suddenly are building not one but many bridges across the gap that separates capitalism and communism." ("Bridging the U.S.-Soviet Gap—Trade Is Just the Start," Nov. 27, 1972, pp. 39–42; quotation from p. 39.)

12. See John P. Hardt, "West Siberia: The Quest for Energy," *Problems of Communism*, Vol. 22 (May–June 1973), pp. 25–36; "Oil Flows in New Pipeline from Siberia to Europe," *New York Times*, April 23, 1973.

13. Nick Kotz and Thomas O'Toole, "Soviets, U.S. Near Gas Deal," *Washington Post*, Nov. 3, 1972.

templating Japanese technological help in exploiting other Siberian resources needed by Japan—especially coking coal, copper, and lumber —plus the construction of harbors and transportation systems necessary to move them to Japan.[14]

Perhaps the most significant sign of confident expectations for a long-term commercial rapprochement is the interest of major U.S. banks in financing Soviet-American trade. In 1973 the Chase Manhattan Bank opened an office in Moscow (1922 was the last time an American bank had an office in Russia), and the Bank of America and the First National City Bank were preparing to follow suit.[15]

In quantitative terms—say, as a proportion of the gross national product (GNP) of either country—the volume of trade between the United States and the Soviet Union is unlikely to become very large over the next decade. Even if it rises to a level of some $5 billion annually by the 1980s (the most optimistic predictions), it still will lag well behind the other major trading relationships of both countries. In the early 1970s, for example, Canadian-American trade was running at more than $14 billion a year, and Japanese-American trade at $9 billion. During the same period the Russians were trading with their COMECON partners in Eastern Europe at about $7 billion annually.

The gross trade statistics do not, however, indicate the greatest significance of the transideological demarche in commerce and technological cooperation. More important for world politics is the extent to which the widening bands of interaction are essential to the modernizing process in the communist countries, and the fact that many of the burgeoning arrangements are not just one-shot, buy-and-sell transactions but involve plans to institutionalize and expand relationships in specific sectors over the long term.

Once again, as during its first two five-year plans (1928–37), the Soviet Union is importing turnkey plants from the West—full production units with all the technical accessories installed by Western technicians, who in turn train Soviet personnel for continuing operational tasks. British, West German, Italian, French, Swedish, and Japanese industries have been leaders in this activity during the past few years,

14. Selig S. Harrison, "Japanese to Help Siberia Develop," *Washington Post*, Feb. 28, 1971; Morton H. Halperin, "The Superpower and the Quiet Power Disagree," *New York Times*, Oct. 14, 1973.

15. Interview with David Rockefeller, *U.S. News & World Report*, Aug. 13, 1973, pp. 35–40.

setting up factories within the USSR to produce a range of goods from industrial fibers to automobiles. But whereas in the earlier period the Russians assumed such modular transplants from the capitalist world would rapidly *reduce* the need for imports, specialized imports are currently viewed as a continuing and growing necessity to keep the new industries operating.

There also are indications of a willingness on the part of the Russians and the Americans to consider long-term joint projects involving shared responsibilities at operational levels—production and marketing, particularly—the kind of arrangements that are increasingly evident in joint projects among the Eastern and Western Europeans. As seen by Secretary of Commerce Peterson, there now ought to be substantial incentives for both Americans and Russians to move into this deeper level of industrial cooperation:

The Soviets may realize that . . . they are going to need substantial implants of foreign technology directly into their economy through a variety of devices—not only through one-time, know-how arrangements and one-time, turn-key factories and projects. . . .
From our point of view, U.S. corporations are not always eager to embark on projects which have one-shot impacts and raise problems of maintaining the incentive of continuing growth. From the Soviet point of view, they must understand that the know-how and technology which firms are most eager to sell them may turn out to be know-how and technology which the seller knows he can make obsolete. For both sides to derive the full benefits of joint efforts, I would suspect that there will have to be the promise of a long term relationship which, in turn, will require a comprehensive commercial structure in which both we and they can have long term confidence.[16]

Similarly, some Soviet trade experts have begun to make this case in their public writings. They argue that the Russians are unlikely to earn enough hard currency, simply from their exports to the United States and other countries, to purchase the needed high-technology hardware and software on the open market. Probably only through various forms of joint ventures, therefore, can the USSR hope to finance the desired technological inputs from the West.[17]

While the lines of U.S.-Soviet contact continue to proliferate, there remains a large residue of suspicion on both sides—some of it war-

16. Peterson, *U.S.-Soviet Commercial Relations in a New Era*, p. 10.
17. Hedrick Smith, "U.S. Widens Trade Role, Triples Exports to Soviet," *New York Times*, Jan. 17, 1973.

ranted—that the other's motives in all of this commercial and technological activity are not innocent of hopes of cold war political advantage. But it is also apparent that the negotiations on practical cooperation are part and parcel of a larger attempt by at least some statesmen in each country to make a transition to a post–cold war era in U.S.-Soviet relations. As Secretary of Commerce Peterson put it:

Closer economic ties bear both cause and effect relationships to relaxation of political tension. Improvement in political relationships is a prerequisite for improved economic relationships, but, once in place, economic ties create a community of interest which in turn improves the environment for further progress on the political side.

Once set in motion, the cause-and-effect process can portend a downward spiral in political tension, a mutually beneficial economic foundation for the new relationship and tangible increases in the welfare and safety of the peoples of both countries.

It is toward these goals . . . that President Nixon authorized the Joint U.S. Soviet Commercial Commission. . . .

It is most emphatically not our purpose to bargain away the nation's security simply to see our trade statistics rise. Our security is not negotiable. Products and technology in sensitive and proprietary areas will continue to be protected.

Our purpose is rather to build in both countries a vested economic interest in the maintenance of an harmonious and enduring relationship. A nation's security is affected not only by its adversary's military capabilities but by the price which attends the use of those capabilities. If we can create a situation in which the use of military force would jeopardize a mutually profitable relationship, I think it can be argued that our security will have been enhanced.[18]

The U.S. secretary of commerce was in these remarks being faithful to concepts worked out in the political side of the house by Henry Kissinger. "For two years we have been engaged in negotiations on a broad range of issues with the Soviet Union," explained the President's adviser on national security affairs in a presummit news conference. "We are on the verge not just of success in this or that negotiation, but of what could be a new relationship of benefit to all mankind, a new relationship in which, on both sides, whenever there is a danger of crisis, there will be enough people who have a commitment to constructive programs so that they could exercise a restraining influence."[19]

18. Peterson, *U.S.-Soviet Commercial Relations in a New Era*, pp. 3–4.
19. Henry Kissinger, news conference of May 9, 1972; excerpts from the official transcript, *New York Times*, May 10, 1972.

The linking of détente and Soviet-American trade, however, has also provided a handle—on the American side at least—for those who are dissatisfied with the behavior of the other party to bring pressures to bear. The need for congressional authorization to extend most favored nation status and credits to the Soviet Union was seized as an opportunity by American Jews, angered at Russian emigration restrictions, to demand changes in Kremlin policy. The Soviet Union did in fact lift some of its restrictions in early 1973 in order to head off congressional obstacles to the expansion of trade; but this concession has only strengthened the conviction of groups wishing to effect reform in the Soviet system that the Russian hunger for commerce with the West provides substantial leverage.

The administration, while willing to exploit such leverage to obtain Russian cooperation in ending the war in Vietnam and achieving a cease-fire and peace settlement in the Middle East, has opposed loading it with demands for changes in Soviet society. A moderate Soviet policy in international affairs has been and continues to be the necessary condition for détente, both political and commercial, argues Dr. Kissinger. But, he insists, "the demand that Moscow modify its domestic policy as a precondition of MFN or détente was never made while we were negotiating [at the summit in 1972]; now it is inserted after both sides have carefully shaped an overall mosaic. Thus it raises questions about our entire bilateral relationship.... We shall urge humane principles and use our influence to promote justice. But the issue comes down to the limits of such efforts. How hard can we press without provoking the Soviet leadership into returning to practices in its foreign policy that increase international tensions? ... And will this encourage ... the well-being or nourish the hope for liberty of the peoples of Eastern Europe and the Soviet Union?"[20]

The American secretary of state's request to the American people to tread delicately on the spans across the ideological divide and to leave détente diplomacy to the professional diplomats came at a time of increasing congressional and popular reaction against executive prerogatives in the foreign field policy. Détente had been generally popular, but the attempt to insulate it from other popular causes could undermine its support in the United States just as loading it with Western de-

20. Henry Kissinger, speech given at the Pacem In Terris Conference, Washington, D.C., Oct. 8, 1973; Department of State Press Release No. 362.

mands to liberalize the Soviet system could undermine its support in the Politburo.

Openings in the Great Wall of China

In contrast to the Soviet moves toward a full-blown détente, which have been the result of weighty economic as well as political considerations, Communist China's motivations in its post-Cultural Revolution efforts to normalize relations with the rest of the world appear to have been overwhelmingly political. On the American side, too, the shifts toward rapprochement with China, appearing much later than détente policies toward the USSR, have been primarily part of the larger political strategy of the Nixon administration in adapting to a "multipolar" world.

Peking still conveyed an impression of being very wary of economic dependence on foreigners and did not seem to have made a decision (as Moscow apparently did in 1966) to abandon its policy of essential autarchy. According to most Western analysts the Peoples Republic of China, in currently sloughing off the isolationism and xenophobia that characterized her foreign policy throughout most of the 1960s, primarily recognizes that this is the best way to counteract Soviet influence.[21] From many reports such an assumption about Chinese motivation was a central aspect of the U.S. policy demarche toward Peking in the early 1970s. It can also be surmised, but not documented, that the U.S. government saw in improved relations with China new opportunities for inducing the USSR to be more accommodating toward the West.[22]

The Nixon administration assumed office coincident with China's post–Cultural Revolution campaign to reinstitute diplomatic ties with Third World countries and to expand its scope of relations with non-

21. See A. Doak Barnett, *A New U.S. Policy toward China* (Brookings Institution, 1971).

22. United States officials of course would not admit to any calculated objective of playing off the two communist giants against one another. "We see no advantage to us in the hostility between the Soviet Union and Communist China," said President Nixon in his 1971 State of the World Report. "We do not seek any. We will do nothing to sharpen that conflict—nor to encourage it." *U.S. Foreign Policy for the 1970's: Building for Peace* (Government Printing Office, 1971), p. 106.

communist industrialized countries.[23] China's new diplomatic priorities were displayed in its 1970 negotiations to establish diplomatic relations with Canada and Italy, especially in its flexibility on the Taiwan issue. Previously Peking had demanded from any country with whom it was to have diplomatic relations an unequivocal endorsement of its claim to rule over Taiwan. But now it was willing that Canada and Italy "take note" of its claim without requiring their explicit endorsement.[24]

President Nixon made it known within his administration early in 1969 that he wanted to reopen the whole question of U.S. policy toward China. While this internal review was proceeding, the United States government continued the cautious "toe in the water" feelers toward the mainland regime (and not incidentally toward the American public) that had characterized U.S. behavior since the early 1960s.[25] That an important policy shift had taken place was communicated in the President's first Foreign Policy Message to the Congress in February 1970, where he indicated the United States was now prepared to enter into a "more normal and constructive relationship" with Communist China and to "promote understanding which can establish a new pattern of mutually beneficial actions."[26]

The subsequent events, including the Chinese invitation for an American ping-pong team to visit China and the lifting of the U.S. embargo on trade in nonstrategic goods in the spring of 1971, need not be recounted here. It is, however, important to note the fact of a fast-moving but nonetheless considered cluster of interactions between the

23. In 1969 France was the only Western country represented in China by an ambassador. The United Kingdom, which had officially recognized the communist government in 1950, was represented only by chargés d'affaires.

24. Jay Waltz, "Canadians Set up Tie to Red China and Drop Taiwan," *New York Times*, Oct. 14, 1970; Anatole Shub, "Italy, China to Establish Ties Today," *Washington Post*, Nov. 6, 1970.

25. For background on the early moves of the Nixon administration see Barnett, *A New U.S. Policy toward China*, pp. 15–24; and Don Oberdorfer, "Nixon's Swing on China," *Washington Post*, April 23, 1971. These accounts are corroborated by the President himself in Richard Nixon, *U.S. Foreign Policy for the 1970's: Shaping a Durable Peace* (Government Printing Office, 1973), pp. 16–21.

26. Richard Nixon, *U.S. Foreign Policy for the 1970's: A New Strategy for Peace* (Government Printing Office, 1970), pp. 140–41.

two countries preceding the President's announcement in July 1971 that he would visit China in 1972 at the invitation of Premier Chou En-lai. This was no simple spontaneous improvisation on either side. Nor were the considerations as simple as the President's stated rationale for the visit: that "there can be no stable and enduring peace without the participation of the People's Republic of China and its 750 million peoples."[27] In explaining to the Chinese people what, given the legacy of intense anti-American propaganda, must have seemed a 180-degree turnabout, the Peking government probably came closer to revealing the realpolitik involved: Reprinting a 1940 article by Mao defending the wartime policy of collaboration with the imperialists in order to resist the Japanese invasion, the official Peking journal *Hungchi* defended the wisdom of "uniting with forces that can be united while isolating and hitting at the most obdurate enemies."[28]

In Peking other considerations were now evidently secondary to the objective of building a world-spanning structure of diplomatic counterweights against the Soviet Union. Even though the United States was still an opponent on matters of major importance to the Mao regime—the war in Southeast Asia and relations with Taiwan (in the October 1971 UN vote admitting Communist China, the United States fought very hard to keep Taiwan in the organization under a "two Chinas" formula)—the door was kept open for the American President's visit.

At the conclusion of his visit, President Nixon and Premier Chou En-lai issued a communiqué affirming that "progress toward the normalization of relations between China and the United States is in the interests of all countries." While explicitly forswearing "agreements or understandings with the other directed at other states," the Shanghai communiqué nonetheless echoed some of the concepts the Chinese had been advancing in their conflict with the Soviet Union. Of specific interest to the Chinese was the joint reiteration of *their* version of the principles of peaceful coexistence:

that countries, regardless of their social systems, should conduct their relations on the principles of respect for the sovereignty and territorial integrity of all states, nonaggression against other states, noninterference in the in-

27. Text of President Nixon's announcement of his planned trip to China, *New York Times*, July 16, 1971.

28. Tillman Durdin, "Peking Explains Warmer U.S. Ties," *New York Times*, Aug. 22, 1971.

ternal affairs of other states, equality and mutual benefit, and peaceful coexistence. International disputes should be settled on this basis, without resorting to the use or threat of force.[29]

And, with the Brezhnev doctrine obviously a target, the communiqué held that "it would be against the interests of the peoples of the world . . . for major countries to divide up the world into spheres of interest."[30]

There was agreement to further interaction between the United States and China in the fields of science, technology, culture, sports, and journalism and to facilitate the progressive development of trade between the two countries. On the sensitive issue of Taiwan the Americans and the Chinese agreed to disagree—a concession on the part of Peking—but the United States did promise that it would "progressively reduce its forces and military installations on Taiwan as the tension in the area diminishes."[31] On both sides, clearly, there was an effort to subordinate the issue of Taiwan, up to now central to considerations of national security, in favor of their newly found interest in a normalization of relations.

It was also evident, however, that the immediate opportunities were still sparse for building commercial and technological interdependence with China analogous to that between the noncommunist industrialized countries and Russia. Following the intensification of China's conflict with the Soviet Union in the early 1960s, nearly 80 percent of China's foreign trade was oriented toward the noncommunist countries, its most important trading partners being Japan, Hong Kong, the Federal Republic of Germany, Singapore, and Canada. The Maoist doctrine of self-reliance, coupled with a relatively low level of industrial development, however, kept its total foreign trade around $4 billion annually.[32] Experts on the Chinese economy expect not only a gradual expansion of capacity to engage in foreign trade over the coming decade but also a continuing political determination to keep the level with any one trading partner low enough to be quickly dispensed with.[33]

29. Text of the U.S.-Chinese Communiqué of Feb. 27, 1972, *New York Times*, Feb. 28, 1972.
30. Ibid.
31. Ibid.
32. Bernhard Grossman, "International Economic Relations of the Peoples Republic of China," *Asian Survey*, Vol. 10, No. 9 (September 1970), pp. 789–802.
33. See Alexander Eckstein, *China Trade Prospects and U.S. Policy* (Praeger, 1971); Stanley Karnow, "U.S. Warns China Trade Isn't Likely to Boom

Major material links between China and the United States and other industrialized countries might eventually insure against a revival of intense xenophobia. For the time being, however, the most critical variable determining China's relations with the noncommunist world would seem to be its rivalry with the Soviet Union. Yet even with high uncertainty about the future, if the United States is to pursue a rational foreign policy it has reason to seize the day and engage China in expanded intercourse insofar as the latter might be willing.

The 1972 demarche in Sino-Japanese relations also can be seen as a sensible adaptive response by both countries to basic trends within and between the cold war coalitions. Historically Japan has been more fearful of Russia than of China; and in the contemporary period, having obtained a return of Okinawa from the United States, Japan's most emotional international demand is for a return of four northern islands seized by the Soviet Union at the close of World War II. In addition, over the next few decades Japan and the Soviet Union are likely to be engaged in numerous protracted negotiations over schemes to develop Siberia. The growing cordiality between Japan and China may make the USSR uncomfortable, but for this very reason it becomes an important bargaining lever for Tokyo. China, for its part, is very wary of Russo-Japanese collaboration in Asia without having itself some leverage over Japan. Since Russian development of Siberia, with or without Japan, is inevitable, Peking's self-interest would seem to lie in some degree of participation by Japan—but a Japan friendly to China. Moreover, both Japan and China can use their thickening band of bilateral interaction to good advantage in the bargaining each is engaged in vis-à-vis the United States. In this larger strategic context Sino-Japanese rapprochement can be viewed as more consistent with emergent power realities than was their antagonistic relationship of recent decades. Although Tokyo's immediate reaction to Washington's unilateral moves in 1971 to normalize relations with Peking was one of pique, it was more at not being consulted in advance than at the substance of the policy.

The 1972 Sino-Japanese negotiations, like those just concluded between President Nixon and Chou En-lai, enabled (indeed compelled) both countries to sort out their central and long-term interests from

Soon," *Washington Post*, Oct. 10, 1972; Stanley B. Lubman, "China Seen Developing New Trade Patterns," *Washington Post*, Dec. 5, 1972.

their peripheral and short-term interests. The communiqué from Peking ending the historic Tanaka visit revealed (as much by what it did not say as by what it said) important concessions by both sides. The Chinese renounced their long-standing demand for Japanese reparations for damage inflicted during the invasion and occupation of China, accepting instead Japan's mild statement of self-reproach. The Chinese also refrained from insisting, as they had done in the past, that Japan end its security treaty with the United States and refuse to harbor American bases. Japan's major concession was to recognize the government of the Peoples Republic of China as the "sole legal Government of China," in return for which Peking abandoned its previous insistence that Japan must stop trading with and investing in Taiwan. Looking toward the future, the communiqué included pledges to hold negotiations aimed at a "treaty of peace and friendship" and intensified negotiations to conclude agreements on trade, navigation, aviation, and fisheries.[34]

Washington might have to make some adjustments in its foreign policy concepts and diplomatic style to accommodate the new bridge-building between Tokyo and Peking. But a successful rapprochement between the two Oriental powers, as long as it was not directed primarily at the United States, would seem to be in the long-term security interests of this country. In a time of continuing disintegration of the cold war coalitions, hostility between China and Japan could stimulate a major program of Japanese rearmament, possibly including nuclear weapons, which could only lead to a protracted arms race between the two and compensating arms increases by the Soviet Union. For the present, the American-Japanese security partnership still seems sufficiently solid to forestall such an eventuality. Given a continuation of the current trends in the Sino-Japanese relationship, with China willing tacitly to accept the U.S.-Japanese tie, Japan might be content with the status of nonnuclear superpower for the rest of the 1970s. Over the long run, however, Japan's willingness to maintain its unique status might come to depend on its ability to develop substantial nonmilitary leverage in its relations with both China and the Soviet Union. If Japan's remaining a nonmilitary superpower is in the American interest, then so are conditions in Asia that would encourage a proliferation

34. "Text of the Chinese-Japanese Accord Signed by Chou and Tanaka," *New York Times*, Sept. 30, 1972.

of technological and economic intercourse—Japan's strong suit—between Japan and China and between Japan and the USSR.[35]

Dangers and Opportunities in Europe

During the 1960s the greatest interbloc economic activity was between the Eastern and Western Europeans, with the Russians standing by ambivalently, sometimes discouraging it, while reportedly debating in the Politburo whether or not to participate on a substantial scale. The USSR attempted to counter this movement through various COMECON devices to achieve a supranationally controlled division of labor and production. But today, having legitimized their own dependence on key technological inputs from outside the socialist commonwealth, the USSR can no longer convincingly object to similar behavior on the part of its COMECON partners. Initial wariness, followed by fascination, and finally by imitation has been particularly characteristic of Soviet attitudes toward efforts by Eastern and Western Europeans to establish multinational ventures—in defiance of the conventional assumption that workable partnerships are not feasible between enterprises in market economies and those in command economies.[36]

A standard arrangement is the agreement of Rheinstahl of West Germany to provide most of the hardware and software required by the Hungarian Danube Iron Works to build a new radiator factory, in exchange for which Rheinstahl gets a fixed percentage on returns from the production over a five-year period or industrial goods of equivalent value. A bit more complicated are agreements for the Western side to provide the designs and specifications, the Eastern partner to do the manufacturing, but *both* to handle the marketing. Progressively popular forms of cooperation involve joint manufacturing operations as, for example, the tractor manufacturing arrangements between Hungary and the Steyr-Daimler-Puch firm of Austria, and between the

35. For the evolving Japanese perspective, see Masoyoshi Ohira, "A New Foreign Policy for Japan," *Pacific Community*, Vol. 3, No. 3 (April 1972), pp. 405–18; and Kei Wakaizumi, "Japan's Role in a New World Order," *Foreign Affairs*, Vol. 51, No. 2 (January 1973), pp. 310–26.

36. *A Foreign Economic Policy for the 1970's*, Hearings before the Joint Economic Committee, Subcommittee on Foreign Economic Policy, 91 Cong. 2 sess., Dec. 8, 1970, p. 1180, and Dec. 9, 1970, pp. 1208, 1215.

Rumanians and Fiat of Italy.[37] Today the Americans and the Russians too, in addition to experimenting with various joint ventures between themselves, are heavily courting partners in Europe across the ideological divide.

Although such transideological economic arrangements are still marginal to national economies in both the East and West, they depart dramatically from expectations of just a few years ago about what kinds of East-West relationships were possible. They also portend internal reforms in the command economies in the direction of decentralization and greater reliance on market mechanisms.[38] Effective participation by the communists in the world market requires that the participating sectors keep well attuned to changing consumer demands abroad and provide their capitalist partners with greater information and access to their own economies. Educational exchanges, internships in one another's industries, freer channels of communication, facilities abroad for sales representatives, hospitality to Western banking institutions, and active participation in international financial and trade institutions become the order of the day.[39]

Whether such burgeoning transideological relationships are allowed to expand to become an essential part of a new all-European system, however, will be largely determined by the future evolution of basic political and security relationships. The legacies of twenty-five years of the cold war still hang menacingly over European politics, and statesmen ignore them at their peril.

Cold War Legacies

The severest effects of cold war bipolarity were felt in Europe. Here the traditional East-West circulation of people, goods, and ideas that was expected to revive with the defeat of Hitler was blocked all along a north-south line from the Baltic to the Adriatic. That the line

37. James A. Ramsey, "East-West Business Cooperation: The Twain Meets," *Columbia Journal of World Business*, Vol. 5, No. 4 (July–August 1970), pp. 17–20. Every issue of *East-West*, a fortnightly published in Brussels, has numerous examples of such transideological arrangements.

38. See Pisar, *Coexistence and Commerce*; and Philip E. Uren, "Patterns of Economic Relations," in *The Communist States in Disarray*, pp. 307–22.

39. Robert G. Kaiser and Dan Morgan provide many revealing examples of these East-West contacts in a twelve-part series of articles in the *Washington Post*, Dec. 17–29, 1972.

of demarcation was unnatural was played up by both sides in the early postwar period, but each offered designs for reunification of Germany and the continent that were totally unacceptable to the other. Each side also suspected the other of strong inclinations to impose coercively its own design on all of Europe and believed that this could only be averted by massive military deployments and tight controls against political subversion. Neither side would grant the legitimacy of many of the regimes in the other's sphere of control. Propaganda battles and shows of force were the essence of East-West politics. During this period of confrontation, which extended into the early 1960s, suggestions from either camp to lower somewhat the barriers to East-West intercourse were suspected of being nothing more than efforts to undermine the cohesion of one's own camp.

In each camp the realization spread that it would be insane to attempt seriously to institute its all-European designs against the will of the other, given the massive military capabilities available. Gradually an uneasy equilibrium evolved which some statesmen on each side felt should be stabilized. An unequivocal stabilization policy, that is, a solid détente premised on the mutual acceptance of two Europes, has remained highly controversial in both coalitions, however, but for different reasons in each.

In the West ambivalence toward détente reflects a number of interrelated concerns. First, policies endorsing the peaceful coexistence of two spheres might seem to convey acceptance of Soviet domination of Eastern Europe and thus completely dash the hopes of liberal and/or nationalist elements. Second, a détente might seem to legitimize a permanent division of Germany, which could revive virulent German nationalism. Third, any suggestion to publics in the Western democracies that the cold war was over could heighten popular impatience with protracted arms control negotiations and generate pressures for premature reductions of the defense budget, unilateral disengagement of U.S. forces from Germany, and dismantling of alliance structures— all of which could reduce Western military power and vigilance below the levels needed to keep the USSR back of the existing line of demarcation.

For the Soviet camp a firm détente would also pose troubles. The implication that both sides now accepted the legality of existing borders and jurisdictions would remove the weightiest excuse for the USSR's heavy troop concentrations in Eastern Europe, namely, the need to defend the area against attack from the West, particularly West Germany. Additionally, Eastern European nationalist pressures to reduce the Soviet military presence in their countries might have to be accommodated if détente were accompanied by serious East-West negotiations for mutual disengagement of superpower military forces from Central Europe and a general thinning down of NATO and Warsaw Pact troops. If peaceful coexistence were accepted as the order of the day in Europe, moreover, the Soviet Union would have less convincing reasons for stage-managing most of the contacts between its allies and noncommunist nations. Finally, even if détente were limited to the recognition of existing frontiers, the side effects might be difficult for the Soviet Union and its satellites to control; for mutual acceptance of the borders as politically legitimate removes much of the rationale for barriers against the normal circulation of goods, people, and ideas.

Yet, despite the carry-over of these fears from the period of confrontation, the late 1960s and early 1970s saw considerable experimentation with normalization and détente strategies by both sides, in which the concept of two different systems in Europe was hesitantly accepted for the time being.

From Détente to Pan-European Interdependence?

The leading catalyst of the movement toward East-West détente, Chancellor Brandt's Ostpolitik, was highly sensitive to concerns in Moscow and the United States that the European equilibrium not be destabilized. Brandt's first normalization agreements were with the Russians; only then did he negotiate directly with Poland and Czechoslovakia, thus deferring to the Soviet Union's strong desire to retain authority over the détente policies of its allies. Brandt was also careful to point out that his program of increasing contacts with the communist countries was fully consistent with his support for greater economic integration and political unity in Western Europe within the larger framework of the NATO alliance. Typical was his April 1972 article in *Foreign Affairs* reassuring the Americans, and not incidentally reminding the Russians, that "in the Federal Republic of Germany there is not a single question of any importance that could be treated outside the context of American-European relations." His Ostpolitik was premised on the expectation that, "as far as security is concerned, the United States and Western Europe will retain their close connection and remain dependent on each other." It would be "foolish," Brandt warned, to contemplate a one-sided reduction in the overall strength of NATO during the complicated negotiations with the East. Most important, any substantial reduction of the American armed presence in Europe "must be a part as well as a result of decreasing tension between East and West."[40]

By the turn of the decade the Russians had accepted Western insistence that any East-West conference on European security should include the United States, despite the fact that Warsaw Pact nations had earlier called for a European security conference designed to extract the weight of the United States from the bargaining balance. The Russians also began to treat the European Community as a legitimate entity for handling economic matters, insisting, however, that "our relations with the participants in this grouping, naturally, will depend on the extent to which they, on their part, recognize the realities existing in the socialist part of Europe, specifically the interests of the member-countries of the Council for Economic Mutual Assistance."[41]

Both sides seemed to be signaling that in the event of détente the opportunities for increased contact would not be exploited for the purpose of subverting institutions already built up on the other side. But would the relaxation of tensions accompanying a full-blown détente allow for sufficient control of cross-coalition interactions to assure the preservation of existing structures? And even if these structures were not consciously subverted by the rival superpowers, could they contain some of the deeper pan-European impulses that have been submerged by the cold war? General de Gaulle used to tap these veins of pan-Europeanism with his call for the renaissance of a web of interacting nations "from the Atlantic to the Urals," belonging to neither of the superpower blocs.

For insight into latent pan-Europeanism it is useful to recall a 1967 study conducted under the auspices of the Council of Europe by the eminent Norwegian social scientist, Johan Galtung. Close to a hundred high-level foreign ministry officials of eighteen European countries (Western, Eastern, and nonaligned) and secretariat officials of

40. Willy Brandt, "Germany's 'Westpolitik,' " *Foreign Affairs*, Vol. 50, No. 3 (April 1972), pp. 416–26; quotations from pp. 418–20.

41. Leonid I. Brezhnev, Speech at the Fifteenth Congress of the Trade Unions of the Soviet Union, March 20, 1972, *Current Digest of the Soviet Press*, Vol. 24, No. 12 (April 19, 1972).

nine intergovernmental organizations were interviewed to determine their impressions of and attitudes toward major trends in Europe. Galtung found tremendous disagreement when it came to interpreting the past (who was responsible for the cold war, etc.); important disagreement about the present, but with the issues more limited and specific; divergence about what will and should happen in the near future; but some very significant patterns of consensus across bloc lines on what Europe would and should be in the more distant future, meaning about ten years hence. The East-West consensus on the more distant future, though vague and abstract, nonetheless revealed more of a convergence on the possibilities for all-European cooperation than could have been elicited ten years previously.

Most of Galtung's respondents foresaw: (1) no major war in Europe, and a continuing decrease in its likelihood; (2) increased economic interdependence, encompassing the whole area; (3) increasingly dense networks of multilateral and bilateral institutions; (4) continued "de-ideologization" of issues; (5) a considerably freer flow of persons, goods, capital, services, and culture across borders between all countries; (6) a general decrease in the significance of international borders in the area (mainly as a consequence of the preceding developments); and (7) some federate or confederate solutions to disputes over contested border areas and territorial jurisdictions.

Galtung's interviews further revealed that, as he put it:

there seems to be substantial agreement that these processes in fact are taking place and will continue to do so, and that also they are by and large desirable. There may be disagreement as to the speed and the concrete details, but not about the idea that this general pattern is "in the cards." And this is of enormous significance since it means that he who reads the cards, and, so to speak, rides on the wave of the future, will also benefit from the trend, whereas he who tries to stem the tide and work against the trend will fight an up-hill fight.[42]

Notably, Galtung's findings were elicited before the Kremlin's 1968 suppression of reforms in Czechoslovakia. When the findings were discussed at an unofficial East-West conference convened under Council of Europe auspices in the aftermath of the Czech crisis, an East-West split was evident on almost all points except the prognosis for no

42. Johan Galtung, "On the Future of European Cooperation," in Galtung (ed.), *Cooperation in Europe* (Oslo: Universitetsforlaget, 1970), pp. 35–62.

major war in Europe. The lack of an interbloc confrontation during the summer and fall of 1968 had confirmed the stability of mutual military deterrence; on matters such as the decrease in the significance of international borders and the end of ideological conflict, most of the Eastern spokesmen now were adamantly opposed to Galtung's formulation of the consensus.[43] But the very adamancy of their objections was in itself an indication of how important indeed was the nerve of deep aspirations that Galtung had revealed.

However attractive the vision of pan-European interdependence, it is obviously impractical so long as either of the blocs is thought to have strong geopolitical or ideological appetites for absorbing the area. But with a fuller flowering of détente, the elaboration of cooperative projects spanning the line of demarcation could well stimulate a revival of the pan-Europeanism that has lain dormant under the surface of the cold war.

Both camps are well aware that the more successful the détente, the more likely it is to become a transitory halfway house to a highly uncertain future. This realization has been reflected in the diplomatic maneuvering surrounding the various East-West negotiations on European security issues.

Before 1970, communist proposals for a multination conference on European security, as well as the Western responses, were more in the nature of a propaganda war than serious efforts to lay the groundwork for an actual conference. The early communist invitations which excluded the United States and Canada were patent attempts to split NATO apart and on this ground alone were unacceptable to the West. Moreover the suggested agenda items were mostly variations on the theme of legitimizing existing boundaries, including the border between East and West Germany. If accepted by the West as a basis for a conference, these items would have conveyed a greater accommodation to the status quo in Eastern Europe than the NATO countries were ready to make. NATO's counterproposals stressed the necessity of dealing with outstanding East-West issues—the division of Germany, the status of Berlin, arms control—as the precondition for any full-dress East-West security conference. If there were to be such a conference, NATO wanted it devoted primarily to specific measures of enhancing security

43. "Protocol from the Vienna Conference on European Cooperation and Security," *Cooperation in Europe*, pp. 345–65.

against military attack, including mutual and balanced force reductions.[44]

By the early 1970s, however, the momentum toward détente began
to engender shifts in the positions of the Soviet Union and the United
States on the purposes of and agenda for East-West negotiations on
the future of Europe. American officials now appeared to see virtues
in the Brandt Ostpolitik of current accommodation to the Soviet
desire to stabilize the territorial status quo as a basis for lowering the
communist barriers against the East-West flow of commerce, people,
and ideas. "We would view a conference on European security and
cooperation in dynamic terms rather than static terms," explained Secretary of State Rogers in December 1971. While opposing any attempt
to perpetuate the political and social divisions of Europe, "We would
see a conference . . . as a step on the long road to a new situation—a
situation in which the causes of tension are fewer, contacts are greater,
and the continent could once more be thought of as Europe rather
than as two parts."[45]

The Russians now appeared to be developing a serious interest in
troop reductions in Central Europe as a means of orienting more of
their combat capabilities toward the Sino-Soviet border. Undoubtedly
the Kremlin recognized the timeliness of entering into troop reduction
negotiations with the United States, in view of growing congressional
pressure, stimulated by the adverse balance of payments, to reduce
American deployments in Europe.

Meanwhile the stakes for the Kremlin in the general conference
had changed. By the time the thirty-five-nation conference convened
in Helsinki in 1973, Bonn had already negotiated treaties with Moscow, Warsaw, East Berlin, and Prague renouncing the use of force and
guaranteeing the stability of existing borders. Consequently, as a device
for legitimizing the territorial status quo in Europe the conference
would be largely redundant. It could endorse the East-West treaties,
but most of its work would be on the other agenda items: (1) "confi-
dence-building" measures in the security field such as exchanging
military observers and advance notices of major troop movements; (2)

---

44. Michael Palmer, *The Prospects for a European Security Conference*
(London: Chatham House: Political and Economic Planning, 1971).

45. Secretary of State William Rogers, address before the Overseas Writ-
ers Club, Washington, D.C., Dec. 1, 1971; Department of State Release No.
279.

cooperation in economic affairs, science, and technology; and (3) widening the opportunities for "human contacts" across political boundaries. The last two items on the security conference agenda were now rivaling, if not surpassing, force-balance issues as the essential substance of East-West political bargaining in Europe. The Russians and their COMECON partners were, overall, more anxious than their Western counterparts to increase opportunities for economic, scientific, and technological intercourse. The Westerners were insisting that for meaningful advances to be achieved in these material fields the East must show some movement in the direction of Western preferences in the politically charged fields of human rights, national self-determination, and a freer East-West flow of people and ideas.

Perhaps of more lasting importance than the immediate outcome of the multiple negotiations now under way is the fact that for the first time in over thirty years the many nations of Europe, with varying social systems and ideologies, have begun discussing with one another in multilateral forums the legitimate design of the international system for all of Europe. This process can only reflect and further stimulate the multiple bases of conflict and cooperation emerging in world politics.

CHAPTER FIVE

North-South Tensions

The opportunities for political, military, and economic intervention that accompanied the postwar decolonization process encouraged both superpowers to export the East-West polarization southward, signing up cold war friends wherever they could be found—in governments or in the bush.

Most Third World countries—poor, nonwhite, located largely south of the Tropic of Cancer—were unable to resist participating in the cold war in one form or another: as a formal ally of one of the super-powers, as a client state not formally aligned, or as a potential ally of either power and therefore an object to be courted by both. A power-ful incentive for such participation was the economic and military assistance thought to be available from either or both superpowers. Thus alliances against communism, alliances against imperialism, and alliances for progress became fashionable. However, with the declining salience of the East-West confrontation many of the Third World countries have found themselves transformed from valued forward sentinels to dispensable pawns. The result has been a search by the poor "South" for non–cold war levers with which to extract concessions from the affluent "North."

Only a few Third World countries have been blessed by nature with raw materials, such as oil, that can be used as a weapon in bargaining with industrial-country customers or used indirectly to accumulate financial assets which can enhance their bargaining position. Some are able to gain leverage from their attractiveness as sites for manufacturing subsidiaries of multinational corporations. But the majority have little influence except that obtained by participating in voting coalitions in international organizations.

Legacies of Cold War Neocolonialism

Comprising most of the rimland countries of classical geopolitics and most of the former colonies of the European nations, the Third World was viewed through thick doctrinal lenses by both superpowers during the height of the cold war. The Third World was considered a huge power vacuum, toward which each superpower suspected the other of imperial designs. The majority of the nations, particularly the newly independent ones, were thought to be politically and economically "underdeveloped," having been exploited as mere economic appendages by the European powers. To avoid sinking into complete misery and chaos, most of the Third World countries were assumed to need substantial economic and technical help (including help in how to structure their societies politically) from the "developed" world. Since only the Soviet Union and the United States emerged from the Second World War with sufficient global interests and capabilities to provide major development assistance, virtually every poor country was expected to choose either one or the other superpower as its primary benefactor, and in so doing become at least a client state if not an explicit ally.

From the middle 1950s to the early 1960s it appeared that the competition for client relationships in the Third World might become the essence of the cold war. New states were being baptized every year. The East-West confrontation over Central Europe was a standoff. Japan was securely in the U.S. camp, China in the Soviet camp. If either side were to pick up weight in the overall global balance of power, it would be in the powerless but nevertheless geopolitically valuable Third World. Both sides suspected this was the way the other viewed the world. The Kennedy administration took Khrushchev's 1961 speech on "Wars of National Liberation" as a serious exposition of Soviet strategy toward the ex-colonial world. The activist-interventionist aspects of the Alliance for Progress and state papers of the First Development Decade were read in Moscow as the real animus behind U.S. development assistance programs. And both were partly correct in their suspicions.

But since none of the underdeveloped countries was individually critical to the maintenance of the global balance of power, neither superpower was really prepared to engage in major sacrifices to gain an additional Third World client. There were plenty of cheaper strategies to ensure that a ruling political faction was favorably disposed: assistance to a friendly regime to expand its power base and suppress opposition; clandestine assistance to friendly opposition groups when the regime was already in the other superpower's camp; and, in the case of an unaligned regime, various combinations of direct government-to-government assistance and assistance to popular groups to bring pressure from below.

The Third World strategies pursued by the United States and the Soviet Union in the 1950s and the early 1960s, however, turned out to be costlier than expected—for the superpowers *and* their clients—and the gains very few. The small were not as tractable in the hands of the big as the latter assumed. Nor were the big as susceptible to political blackmail as the small had hoped.

Throughout the Third World only those capable of mobilizing intense nationalist loyalty were able to rule effectively over the multicultural nation-states carved up out of the old colonial empires. The indigenous leaders with any degree of political longevity (Nehru, Nasser, Sukarno, Nkrumah, Sékou Touré) governed with hybrid ideologies and constitutional structures more suited to the traditions of their particular nations than the ideologies and forms championed by would-be tutors from the United States and the Soviet Union. Moreover, a visible amount of xenophobia was a necessary ingredient of their domestic political appeal, especially as popular aspirations for development remained unsatisfied and frustrations mounted. None of these leaders could hope to be seen as a puppet of an external power and still survive. Indeed it has been the strategy of opposition factions to attach such a stigma to their incumbent rivals.[1] Sukarno, for example, bit the dust at the hands of the nationalistic Indonesian army because he was considered to be too much of a collaborator with the Chinese-oriented communist party of Indonesia.

Regimes that survived primarily as wards of one of the superpowers, however successful they might look in terms of gains in gross na-

---

1. For analysis of the domestic sources of xenophobic foreign policies in Third World countries, see W. Howard Wriggins, *The Ruler's Imperative: Strategies for Survival in Asia and Africa* (Columbia University Press, 1969), especially pp. 221–38. See also Robert C. Good, "State Building as a Determinant of Foreign Policy in the New States," in Lawrence E. Martin (ed.), *Neutralism and Nonalignment* (Praeger, 1962), pp. 3–12.

tional income, sometimes turned out to be political and security liabilities. The imperatives of domestic politics might provoke a beneficiary into dramatic poses of independence, such as rash military moves against local opponents from which it would have to be rescued. U.S. problems with the South Koreans, the Nationalist Chinese, and—most painfully—with a succession of South Vietnamese regimes are cases in point. The Russians too have experienced such embarrassments, disassociating from Castro's attempts to export his revolution to other Latin American countries and pulling the reins on reckless Arab clients. But restraining actions by the superpower often carry their own high price, since the client's acquiescence to more cautious strategies usually requires the superpower to increase the tangible signs of fidelity —meaning more economic and military assistance. To make matters worse, if the ward is frustrated or defeated by its external enemies, it is likely to blame its benefactor for being overly timid (the Russians have had their problems compounded in these situations by the readiness of Communist China to lead the jeers against Soviet caution).

Having confronted the stubborn forces and sophisticated politicians of the Third World, both superpowers in the late 1960s began to tone down their interventionist doctrines.

When the price of the Vietnam commitment became too bloody for the American people to bear, the American government devised a new national security rationale—the Nixon doctrine—for turning over the immediate defense tasks to indigenous anticommunists while the United States gradually withdrew to an offshore blue-water military posture for the Pacific area. During his first year in office President Nixon in a major address also criticized his predecessor's Latin American policies, implying that the Alliance for Progress was based on the illusion that we knew what was best for everyone else and pledging a "new approach" that would "deal realistically with governments in the inter-American system as they are."[2] These new approaches to the developing countries, explained the President in his 1970 State of the World message, were required by "the new era of international relations" in which "the 'isms' have lost their vitality."

Today, these [new] nations have a new spirit and a growing strength of independence. Once, many feared that they would become simply a battle-

2. "Action for Progress for the Americas," an address by President Nixon before the Inter American Press Association, Washington, D.C., Oct. 31, 1969, Department of State *Bulletin*, Vol. 61 (Nov. 17, 1969), pp. 409–14.

ground of cold-war rivalry and fertile ground for Communist penetration. But this fear misjudged their pride in their national identities and their determination to preserve their newly won sovereignty.[3]

Soviet adaptation to Third World realities in the last half of the 1960s was reflected in trade and aid programs which increasingly featured tough commercial criteria—profitable material returns to the USSR.[4] This did not mean that the Russians were withdrawing from the pursuit of political influence with economic weapons. They were still attempting to pick up whatever political benefit they could, be it some show of independence by a firm Western ally (such as Turkey), a greater degree of nonalignment from a westward-leaning neutral (such as Iran), or more consistent support in UN bodies from a friendly African country (such as Tanzania). But political subordination appeared to be regarded more and more as an ultimate by-product of a sustained economic relationship rather than its necessary short-term payoff.

The long-term Soviet goal of becoming the dominant global power was not inconsistent with a nonideological economic strategy toward the Third World. In some respects such a strategy could be more formidable than a policy of sponsoring revolutions, since it puts the onus of ideological politics on those who object to an increased Soviet presence—even in traditional U.S. spheres of influence such as Latin America.[5]

By the late 1960s each superpower seemed to be begging off from designing whole social systems in the Third World and resorting to a more classical mode of state-to-state intercourse based mostly on commercial arrangements. It therefore became increasingly difficult to define conflicts within and among the developing nations as part of the global contest between two incompatible ways of life. As a result it also

3. Richard Nixon, *U.S. Foreign Policy for the 1970's: A New Strategy for Peace* (Government Printing Office, 1970), p. 2.

4. Elizabeth Kridl Valkenier, "New Trends in Soviet Economic Relations with the Third World," *World Politics*, Vol. 22, No. 3 (April 1970), pp. 415–32.

5. For an early analysis of the problems as well as the successes the USSR has encountered with nonthreatening modes of penetration into the Third World, see Herbert Dinerstein, "Moscow and the Third World: Power Politics or Revolution," *Problems of Communism* (January–February 1968), pp. 52–56; for the more recent period, see Morton Schwartz, *The Failed Symbiosis: The USSR and Leftist Regimes in Less Developed Countries* (California Arms Control and Foreign Policy Seminar, 1973).

became more difficult to mobilize popular support in the developed world for sacrifices to aid the poorer countries.

The inherently poor match between new nationhood and membership in either of the cold war coalitions was anticipated by a few far-sighted Third World leaders like Jawaharlal Nehru of India and Julius Nyerere of Tanganyika. It was Nehru's philosophy of nonalignment that animated the first effort toward a broad-based Third World coalition at the Afro-Asian conference held in Bandung in April 1955. The conference produced resolutions on economic and cultural cooperation, human rights and self-determination, problems of dependent peoples, and the promotion of world peace and cooperation. But with many of the participants already implicitly, if not explicitly, members of one or the other of the cold war coalitions and therefore potential enemies of other Third World countries, there was little prospect for translating their shared concerns into concerted international pressure.[6]

Efforts by Egypt and other Middle Eastern countries to assume the leadership of the nonaligned in the early 1960s failed as it became apparent that their main objective was to gain support for their conflict with Israel, rather than to do away with military blocs. After 1967, with Egypt's growing dependence on the USSR making a fiction of its nonalignment posture, symbolic Third World leadership devolved for a time on the few African leaders who had been able to maintain themselves in power without excessive dependence on either their former colonial overlords or the neoimperialists of either cold war coalition. Not surprisingly the 1970 nonalignment conference was held in Lusaka, Zambia, and the most charismatic figures present were Tanzania's Julius Nyerere and Zambia's Kenneth Kauanda. Nor was it uncharacteristic of the trend that the issue most capable of serving as a common denominator of the Third World was the persistence of Portuguese and white regimes in South Africa.[7] Just as the posture of nonalignment seemed to be gaining most adherents in the Third World, however, it lost most of its effectiveness as a means of pressuring the superpowers for special concessions, since the super-

6. Carlos P. Romulo, *The Meaning of Bandung* (University of North Carolina Press, 1956).

7. See the *Lusaka Declaration on Peace, Independence, Development, Co-operation, and Democratization of International Relations* (Lusaka, Zambia: Government Printer, 1970).

powers themselves had begun to consider political and military alliances with Third World regimes as often accruing more liabilities than assets.

The Russians, to be sure, with their steadily lengthening maritime reach, continued to expand their activities in the Third World; but their strategy more and more seemed to be to maintain a diversity of friendships with capitalists and bourgeois nationalists as well as "progressives" so as not to become overly dependent upon the good will or stability of particular regimes. This new Kremlin attitude toward the ideological factor could only lessen the bargaining effectiveness of any given Third World country's coyness regarding its international alignment.

The Soviet Union's increasing embroilment in the Middle East on the side of the Arabs in their conflict with Israel and their recent heavy courtship of India might seem to contradict this general tendency. But the Kremlin's Middle Eastern role in the 1970s is more accurately viewed as a hangover of traditional Soviet strategies and an effort to take advantage of the new political significance of oil rather than as another reversal of policy. The Indian courtship and Brezhnev's vague and still unrealized 1969 proposal for an Asian security pact can only be fully understood in a post–cold war context as directed against China.

For Moscow the Middle East remains a central geopolitical pivot, from which Russia can be either attacked or bottled up in wartime; and its newly acquired status as a maritime power probably does require an assured access southward to the oceans of the world. These objectives could be served just as well, and perhaps better, by a Middle East *not* polarized along cold war lines, and the Russians appear increasingly to realize this. Their habit of exploiting the Arab-Israeli conflict by signing up military clients in the area has, however, been very difficult to reverse, the consequence being a continued counter-engagement in the region by the United States.

The recent record demonstrates the great ambivalence of Soviet policy toward the Arabs: By the early 1970s the Arab-Israeli arms race had drawn the USSR into such deep military collaboration with Egypt that in future hostilities the risk of Soviet personnel becoming involved in battle was quite high. As a price for such deep involvement the Russians apparently wanted to exercise greater control over Egyptian decision making than any Middle Eastern nationalist regime could tolerate. The immediate result was the Soviet-Egyptian altercation of the summer of 1972 in which President Sadat ordered the bulk of Soviet military personnel out of Egypt. This was followed by the Treaty of Peace, Friendship, and Cooperation between the Soviet Union and Iraq—seemingly more a reaction to Soviet-Egyptian friction than an indication of a renaissance of cold war alliance-building. The Russians kept open the pipeline of military equipment to Egypt, Iraq, and Syria, but at the same time intensified their commercial courtship of the major non-Arab powers of the Middle East, Turkey and Iran, and even appeared to be seeking a limited rapprochement with Israel.[8] But the renewal of open warfare between the Arabs and Israel in 1973 once again entrapped the Kremlin into a closer identification with Egyptian and Syrian fortunes than was consistent with the longer-term trends in Soviet Third World policy.

The 1971 Soviet agreement with India—also titled a Treaty of Peace, Friendship, and Cooperation—was not designed as a military alliance, although it was linked to Soviet support for India's position against Pakistan in the Bangladesh war for independence. The obligations to consult in case either party were attacked are very loose and not incompatible with Indian treaties of friendship and cooperation with others. Again the accord was hardly an example of cold war alliance-building. The Russians were primarily at work containing China, and the Indians were attempting to deter concrete collusion between Pakistan and China as happened in the Sino-Indian border conflicts of the previous decade. While economic cooperation between the USSR and India has increased in recent years, the Kremlin has been notably unsuccessful in gaining New Delhi's endorsement of its proposed Asian security pact.

In both the Middle East and Asia, Russia is increasingly viewed by Washington as playing a more traditional balance-of-power game involving many states. The notion of the Third World as the grand arena for confrontation between the two superpowers is fading, though in fits and starts. The Third World had complained of bipolarity, but what was to follow might be even worse. The emerging reality was described some years ago by the internationally respected Indian commentator Sisir Gupta: "With the loosening of the two blocs and the beginning of a cer-

8. See Oles M. Smolansky, "The Soviet Setback in the Middle East," *Current History*, Vol. 64, No. 377 (January 1973), pp. 17–20. For the pattern of Soviet involvement up to the 1970s see A. S. Becker and A. L. Horelick, "Soviet Policy in the Middle East," No. R-504 (RAND Corp., 1970).

tain measure of multipolarity, the nations of Asia and Africa suddenly found themselves reduced to the position of the 'Fifth (or Sixth) World,' in terms of their importance in world politics."[9]

Along with the increasing alienation between the superpowers and many of their former military clients in the Third World, there has been a growing realization all around that the sociocultural sources of economic underdevelopment in many countries are much less tractable than had been supposed by either the Marxist or non-Marxist development economists. To compound the difficulties, just when the magnitude of the problem finally was beginning to be appreciated the industrially developed powers seemed less inclined to allocate resources to the problem.

To be sure, even apart from the major petroleum producers, there have been a few success stories. Taiwan, Singapore, South Korea, Brazil, and Mexico have made rapid progress in industrialization, attaining GNP growth rates of as much as 10 percent. The developing countries averaged a 5.5 percent increase in GNP during the 1960s, and export of manufactured goods from the developing world as a whole accounted for 23 percent of total world exports by 1972. But the success stories and the averages do not adequately reflect the varying capacities and needs of the countries in the Third World. Whereas some appear to be nearing the point of needing little outside help, particularly if they can look forward to enlarging markets for products they can produce efficiently, others lack the experience in modern production and administration to transform their natural resources into new wealth. Still others are vastly overpopulated in relation to their natural resources.[10]

The president of the World Bank has pointed out that during the First Development Decade income grew the least where it was needed the most: in the poorer countries with the largest aggregate population. For those countries with a per capita GNP of less than $200 a year—60 percent of the world's population—"the per capita income growth was so small as to be barely perceptible: a minuscule 1.7%."

9. "The Third World and the Great Powers," *Annals of the American Academy of Political and Social Science,* Vol. 386 (November 1969), p. 56.

10. See *Reassessing North-South Economic Relations: A Tripartite Report by Thirteen Experts from the European Community, Japan, and North America* (Brookings Institution, 1972). See also James P. Grant, "Where Next With Development Assistance?" in Robert E. Hunter (ed.), *The United States and the Developing World: Agenda for Action* (Washington, D.C.: Overseas Development Council, 1973), pp. 56–68.

Moreover, when the severely skewed income distribution in the developing countries is taken into account, "the poverty of the low-income strata—roughly the poorest 40%—is far worse than the national averages suggest."[11] According to the World Bank studies, in twenty of the very poor countries 40 percent of the population has an average yearly income of $80 or less.

It was to raise these per capita figures that the United Nations adopted an overall annual GNP growth target of 6 percent for the 1970s—the Second Development Decade—which was to be made possible by an increase in aid from the industrialized countries. By 1975 the industrialized countries were supposed to be devoting 0.7 percent of their GNP to Official Development Assistance. IBRD President McNamara took a look at the record in the fall of 1972 and concluded sadly,

The truth is that the objective of .7% will not be reached. There seems little likelihood that in 1975 Official Development Assistance will exceed .37% of GNP: only half the Second Development Decade target.

This is a most unwelcome conclusion. But we must face the facts. Not only is there no evidence that ODA as a percentage of GNP will rise above half the target rate, but unless there are prompt and marked changes in attitudes, it is difficult to foresee any great improvement in the second half of the decade. . . .

Given the deficit in ODA, and the consequent increase in the debt burden—all of this compounded by the delay in dismantling discriminatory barriers to trade from the developing countries—many of the poorer nations will fail to reach the Second Development Decade's 6% growth target altogether, and many others will reach it only with very severe difficulties.[12]

Even if there were a more open global economy with all markets more accessible to both the less developed and the developed countries, many poor countries, given their current deficiencies, would stand little chance of competing effectively. Their chances for substantial economic progress would depend on the *political will* of the rich to redress the inherited competitive disadvantages of the poor, whether through direct technical and development assistance or through preferential trading arrangements. But this would now have to be activated by forces other than East-West rivalry.

11. Robert S. McNamara, address to the UN Economic and Social Council, Oct. 18, 1972 (International Bank for Reconstruction and Development; processed).

12. Ibid.

The Group of Seventy-seven

With the declining political leverage of nonalignment, the Third World countries have been attempting to concert their economic demands upon the industrialized countries. The emergence of this cross-pressure on the cold war groupings can be dated from 1964, when seventy-seven countries at the first United Nations Conference on Trade and Development (UNCTAD), over the objections of the Western countries in attendance, turned the conference into a continuing institution for confronting the North on economic issues. (The UNCTAD southern coalition has now expanded to over ninety countries, but the designation "Group of Seventy-seven" has been retained in commemoration of their dominance of the 1964 conference.)

Through a series of general UNCTAD sessions (1964, 1968, and 1972), special ministerial meetings of the Group of Seventy-seven, and catalytic activities of the UNCTAD secretariat (whose first secretary general was the charismatic Raúl Prebisch), the southern coalition has compelled the industrialized countries at least to hear the demands of less developed countries. These demands have included:

• stabilization of world prices at remunerative levels for primary product exports;

• preferential access to the markets of industrial countries for goods from the poor countries, without reciprocal privileged access to poor-country markets;

• better loan terms, including lower interest rates, longer amortization and grace periods, and less tying of purchases to the exports of the lending country;

• supplementary or compensatory financing to protect a developing country's plans against unanticipated export shortages;

• a larger share of Special Drawing Rights (the international reserve assets controlled by the International Monetary Fund), with development needs as well as liquidity needs the basis for allocations;

• the breakup of shipping monopolies, with their artificially high transportation costs.[13]

13. See *Proceedings of the United Nations Conference on Trade and Development, Geneva, 23 March–16 June 1964*, UN Doc. E/Conf. 46/141; and *Proceedings of the United Nations Conference on Trade and Develop-*

The Group of Seventy-seven has also been attempting to act as a bargaining coalition in other international forums, including the GATT, the International Monetary Fund, the various specialized agencies, UN environmental conferences, and law of the sea negotiations. It has been caucusing before and during important international meetings in order to present a common front to both the industrial North and the East.[14] But as it gets down to the details of negotiation on specific issues the southern coalition finds it difficult to sustain its hoped-for unity. Many developing countries have conflicts of interests over how the general Third World demands should be implemented in one's own case. The former French and British colonies in Africa, for example, wish to retain their special access to the European Community in opposition to the Latin Americans' insistence that the EC should treat all developing countries alike. Most of the Third World countries are energy consumers and thus suffer from the concerted rise in prices by the energy producers. In the law of the sea negotiations, the poor countries that are landlocked find themselves in opposition to the coastal states of the Third World on the central issue of how far out coastal-state ownership of seabed resources should extend. Moreover, the efforts of the Group of Seventy-seven to build a broad-based Third World coalition may have *weakened* their bargaining power by stimulating industrial countries to concert their own policies when dealing with the less developed countries.

New Opportunities for Selective Leverage

Third World countries are finding that whatever weight they might have in bargaining over political or economic issues with the industrialized countries is the product of the special relationship a particular Third World country or set of countries has with particular

---

ment, *Second Session, New Delhi, 1 February–29 March 1968*, UN Doc. TD/97; "The Undoing of UNCTAD," *The Economist* (May 27, 1972), pp. 18, 23.

14. Branislav Gosovic, "UNCTAD: North-South Encounter," *International Conciliation*, No. 568 (May 1968); Robert S. Walters, "International Organization and Political Communication: The Use of UNCTAD by Less Developed Countries," *International Organization*, Vol. 25, No. 4 (Autumn 1971), pp. 818–35; Vanya Walker-Leigh, "Was UNCTAD III a Failure?" *The World Today*, Vol. 28, No. 9 (September 1972).

industrialized countries or corporations rather than the result of any generalized confrontation between poor and rich.

The most impressive example is the way the Organization of Petroleum Exporting Countries (OPEC), especially its Arab members, has put the industrialized world on the defensive by its demands for higher prices, better concessionary terms from the multinational oil companies, increased participation in management decisions, and even political concessions from consumer-country governments during the Arab-Israeli war of 1973. To be sure, the ability of the Arab petroleum producers to threaten and then actually go through with production cutbacks if their demands are not met is very difficult to replicate in other commodity fields.

Developed-country consumers of most raw materials have the ability to locate or develop substitute commodities; and incentives to act in concert on the part of the supplier countries may be lacking. But as C. Fred Bergsten has pointed out:

Subtle pricing and marketing strategies could boost consumer costs and producer gains significantly without pushing consuming countries to the development of substitutes, which requires heavy initial investments and start-up costs. Concerted action by copper, tin, and bauxite producers would sharply reduce the risk to each that cheaper aluminum or tin would substitute for higher priced copper, or vice versa.[15]

These strategies could be applied in a discriminatory fashion so as not to harm other Third World countries and industrialized countries willing to be more cooperative on trade and investment issues.

Selective leverage could also be exercised over corporate investments through a number of techniques available to Third World governments, which include confiscation, expropriation with compensation, local export quotas, and reinvestment requirements. Some of these governments may be tempted to repudiate their debts to particular industrialized countries and private lenders with whom relations have deteriorated. Indeed, repudiation of their U.S. debts has already been threatened by a number of countries in the course of debt rescheduling negotiations, and has been avoided only by their obtaining liberal rescheduling terms.[16]

Opportunities for Third World countries to insert levers into the cracks in the Soviet sphere have been very few up to now, India's

15. "The Threat from the Third World," *Foreign Policy*, No. 11 (Summer 1973), pp. 102–24; quotation from p. 113.
16. Ibid., p. 114.

playing off the Soviet Union against China being the outstanding exception. The Sino-Soviet split was of little benefit to most of the developing countries when China demonstrated its revolutionary purity by sponsoring antiregime parties or when, as during its Cultural Revolution (1965–69), it withdrew from most foreign activities to concentrate on building Maoism.

Now as China increases participation in international forums and expands commercial activity among the Arab nations, Africans, and even the Latin Americans, as well as the South and Southeast Asians, the opportunities should widen for countries in these areas to toughen their bargaining with Russia and Eastern European countries.[17] The USSR is clearly on the defensive as the Peoples Republic of China reenters the world diplomatic arena. For centuries a victim of Western exploitation and racial discrimination, an industrially backward country becoming a nuclear power mainly by its own efforts, for the past decade the pugnacious enemy of both the United States and the USSR simultaneously, China appears as the defiant underdog.

The Soviet Union is not at all happy with China's attempts to pick up the anti-imperialist mantle in the Third World, particularly at UNCTAD, the Stockholm environmental conference, law of the sea negotiations, and increasingly in the UN General Assembly and the specialized agencies. Though China's resources for tangible external assistance remain limited, rivalry for influence in the Third World again prompts the USSR to offer developing countries economic and technical assistance and transfers of technology on concessionary terms, especially in the weapons field where its comparative advantage over China is most visible.

Long-Term Prospects

In the context of industrial-country competition for raw materials and new investment and market opportunities, pressures from relatively well-endowed Third World countries—say, Saudi Arabia or Nigeria—for economic concessions or participation in decisions affecting the world economy can be expected to grow. As suggested in the

17. Isham A. Hijazi, "Peking Widening Ties with Arabs," *New York Times*, Feb. 10, 1971; G. Comte, "Peking Shows Its New African Look," *Africa Report* (March 1971), pp. 19–21; Tad Szulc, "China Increasing Her Foreign Aid," *New York Times*, Mar. 5, 1972.

following chapter, the need for the major world powers to build coalitions across a wide range of international issues may revive some of the political influence the diplomatically active southern countries such as Egypt, Brazil, India, and Indonesia had at the height of the cold war.

But any such problematical gains in leverage would still amount to far less than required to coerce the affluent countries into global redistributive policies. Apart from the petroleum producers, few Third World countries can withhold anything of strategic significance. No developing country is of critical importance as a market for the goods of any industrialized country, and the major investor nations and the large multinational corporations are probably able to overcome any economic shocks they might suffer, even from expropriation of their foreign holdings.

Is the only realistic long-term prospect then a despairing acceptance by the rich and poor alike of the grim disparities outlined by World Bank President McNamara? Will the poorer two-thirds of the world's people who live at or below minimum subsistence adjust to the fact that less than one-third of all human beings consume over 85 percent of the world's production? Given the psychological compression of the planet due to contemporary means of transportation and communication, will the affluent minority be able to close their eyes to this situation? Or will the buildup of jealousies on one side and moral guilt on the other produce such tensions along the North-South axis that more drastic reactions are to be anticipated?

It is doubtful that the nightmare of an international class war of the colored poor against the white rich could materialize in the form of organized or highly coordinated and sustained violent action. The animosities and deep suspicions many Third World countries have for one another would impede the integration of strategies and organization. It is not such a fantasy, however, to forecast widespread unofficial support for commando-type violence as a desperate reaction to the frustrations. Demonstrative acts against vulnerable points in the highly industrialized societies may be most tempting precisely because they seem to equalize the relationship in terms of the ability to cause pain. Where popular desperation is combined with xenophobia, the fact that terroristic acts are ultimately self-destructive may be insufficient to deter them. And many Third World governments may find it politically risky to apprehend and punish the radical leaders.

Fears of a radicalization of North-South tensions could conceivably lead affluent societies to reduce all types of interaction with the poor societies, discouraging even tourism in a kind of de facto apartheid of the globe. Both strategies of North-South dissociation, however neat in logic, fail to take into account the persistence and growth of complicating factors: (1) Many important countries will be part of *both* worlds (where will one locate Turkey, Brazil, the energy-producing countries of the Middle East, or even China?). (2) The northern and southern countries alike are simultaneously the perpetrators and victims of mankind's shared predicament—the press of the population explosion and the industrial revolution on the earth's natural resources. (3) Important social sectors within the less developed countries are gaining greater mobility and becoming part of transnational commercial, professional, or cultural networks whose lines run to and from many major industrial centers. (4) Given the globalization of communications, many ethnic groups within the industrialized North are reviving emotional identifications with their ancestral societies in the Third World. (5) Most prominent systems of social ethics in the developed societies (whether Judeo-Christian, liberal-secular, or Marxist) contain strong universalistic imperatives; in some segments of the population (probably the best educated strata), wholesale and consistent violation of these universal obligations would produce strong political counterreactions. Thus the apartheid response to the prospect of an embitterment of North-South relations must be dismissed as highly implausible.

In sum, North-South tensions are likely to increase in the years to come. Various poor countries, out of their frustration, are likely to attempt to bring pressure on the affluent countries by seizing whatever levers come their way—an energy crisis, industrial material shortages, the desire of industrial countries to gain international agreement on coastal jurisdictional boundaries, fears of general environmental degradation. Strategies of avoidance by the wealthy countries can only exacerbate the tensions. What to do about growing international welfare disparities in the midst of a continued growth in gross world product is likely to become a more important issue around which political coalitions form internationally, transnationally, and domestically. But the likelihood of a global North-South polarization is virtually nonexistent. Possible U.S. policy responses to this situation will be discussed in the final chapter.

CHAPTER SIX

The Emerging System of Multiple Coalitions

The cross-pressures on the cold war coalitions highlighted in the previous chapters result from and simultaneously produce new lines of interdependence among societies—new, that is, with respect to those that dominated world politics since the late 1940s. The new lines of interdependence by no means obliterate the cold war coalitions; rather they intersect or supplement the established patterns, sometimes contradicting, sometimes reinforcing them.

What is taking place, however, is not simply a complication of the bipolar system of rival coalitions constructed in the aftermath of the Second World War. A central thesis of this book is that as new lines are elaborated a qualitatively different system of world politics will begin to emerge. The particular characteristics of the emerging system cannot be forecast with confidence, just as the adult behavior patterns of a child cannot be predicted. Tendencies can be observed from which potential courses of development can be inferred; but which main course will be taken, and then which subsequent paths, is highly contingent upon unpredictable environmental and internal events. Yet for a complex social system no less than for an individual certain tendencies are sometimes sufficiently dominant and mutually reinforcing to allow for a gross forecast—though what is being left behind is often more apparent than what lies ahead.

The Dominant Tendencies

The discussion in the previous chapters indicates three interacting tendencies in international relations today, which together constitute a potential for systemic change.

The Waning of Geopolitical and Ideological Bipolarity

The United States and the Soviet Union are today less anxious than in the 1950s and 1960s that shifts by smaller countries toward non-alignment, neutralism, or even the other's coalition will fundamentally affect either of their vital security interests. Changes in military technology have reduced the value of forward bases not only for strategic missions but also for supply and reconnaissance in large-scale conventional war. An exception is Eastern Europe, where the Russians still insist upon a security belt made up of completely loyal allies. Elsewhere superpower protection, having become less credible, loses some of its value, while at the same time the price of securing that protection rises. This generates high incentives for the smaller countries to strike postures of independence in the hope of creating more opportunity for diplomatic maneuver against both superpowers. In turn, the superpowers find the fidelity of their allies less reliable. New geopolitical doctrines that assert a reduced security requirement for allies are given greater play in military planning and foreign policy generally. Ideologies which make it imperative to defend on a global basis the "good" people against the "bad" are pushed aside in favor of more pragmatic considerations.

The Rise of Nonmilitary Issues

The loosening of the hierarchical relationship between both of the superpowers and their smaller allies gives freer play to conflicts over nonmilitary issues, primarily economic ones, while the emergence of these issues in turn reinforces the fragmentation of the coalitions. When protection against a threatening enemy coalition was the most pressing concern, the subordination of political, economic, and cultural interests to the requirements of the common defense was more readily accepted, as was the hegemony of the country with the most powerful military capabilities. Still prominent today are questions concerning the best military strategies for common defense against the opposing coalition and the allocation of military roles and burdens among the members. But the ability of both the United States and the Soviet Union to prevail over their respective allies on security issues has been decreasing. In considerable measure this is because the lesser members, when nonmilitary matters are at issue, are increasingly able to form coalitions with one another or with nonaligned countries, and even with members of the other cold war coalition. Thus the dynamics of bargaining with the superpower give many countries high incentives to push nonmilitary issues to the top of international agendas. To the extent that the rise in nonmilitary issues and the construction of multiple coalitions are the results of East-West détente, these countries develop a vested interest in the further evaporation of cold war issues. In this way the disintegration of the cold war coalitions, once begun, sets in motion other forces that tend to accelerate the pace and force of the erosion.

The Diversification of Friendships

The waning of global bipolarity and the rise of nonmilitary issues open new opportunities and provide greater incentives for countries to cultivate a wider and more diverse range of international friends than was possible previously. In the heyday of the cold war coalitions each superpower, while competing for allies all around the globe, made firm distinctions between its coalition partners and members of the enemy camp. Rarely would lesser members of either alliance deal bilaterally with members of the opposing camp unless the exchanges were stage-managed by the alliance leader. Even for transactions within the camp, when important political or economic issues were being negotiated the superpower was usually heavily involved; and bilateral or multilateral dealings among a subset of members were discouraged, unless of course the superpower was one of the parties. Nonaligned countries, notably India, Egypt, and Indonesia, played the field, but many statesmen and analysts assumed this international stance was untenable over the long run. Now it is precisely such a flexible posture, in many respects resembling nonalignment, that seems to be serving as the model for realistic diplomacy.

More and more, divergences in world view or social systems are insufficient causes to bar cordial relations among countries. The strongest lines of cooperation continue to be those established during the cold war, such as between the North Atlantic countries and Japan, and within COMECON. But economic intercourse, multilateral technological projects, and scientific and cultural exchanges are now considered legitimate among virtually all possible combinations of countries. Organizations and forums for these purposes are increasingly using functional or geographic rather that ideological criteria for participation. Multilateral groupings established for cooperation in various fields have crosscutting memberships: For example, some members of a given security group cooperate on regional environmental control with countries from the adversary security group, and a different subset of each group participates in a space-communications system. This means that rival international coalitions vary in membership according to the issues in dispute.

The Emerging International System

If the dominant tendencies continue to mature as indicated above, an international system whose essential characteristics differed greatly from both the bipolar cold war system and previous balance-of-power systems could probably emerge by the 1980s. These essential characteristics can only be conjectured, and then only in broadest outline. There is admittedly much guesswork inherent in such an exercise, and unpredictable contingencies—such as a rapprochement between the USSR and the Peoples Republic of China plus a renewal of belligerent expansionism by either or both—could halt or reverse the disintegration of the cold war coalitions. But it is not too early to try a sketch of the emerging system, especially its behavioral and structural characteristics: the nature of power; the relationships of the most powerful actors with each other and with lesser actors; the less dominant though important patterns of behavior; and the conditions under which this postulated system is likely to break down or evolve into something fundamentally different.

The Changed Properties of Power

If the international power of a country is defined as its capacity to influence others to accede to its objectives,[1] then in a system characterized by multiple and crosscutting coalitions formed around a variety of issues the properties of power would be significantly different than in the predominantly bipolar system. In the new system the most influential countries are likely to be those that are major constructive participants in the widest variety of coalitions and joint or multilateral ventures, since they would have the largest supply of usable political

1. Seyom Brown, "Power Wielded and Power Perceived," in *The Faces of Power: Constancy and Change in United States Foreign Policy from Truman to Johnson* (Columbia University Press, 1968), pp. 1–4.

currency—in effect, promissory notes for support on one issue in return for support on another. Conversely, threats to withdraw support would serve as negative sanctions.

The power-maximizing country would want its own pledges of support universally and highly valued; this support could be in the form of access to natural or industrial resources, the provision of financial assets, or technical cooperation. Countries would want to be able to convert pledges they have collected from others into currency for their own use; pledges from poorer countries that lack surplus material assets could be in the form of votes in the various multinational forums whose endorsement is important to projects desired by the richer country.

As during the cold war, power in the form of promises to apply or withhold military capabilities would still be of decisive importance in conflicts over vital security interests; but compared with other forms of power it would have little or even negative utility in bargaining over the nonsecurity issues around which coalitions will be forming and re-forming in the post–cold war system. The threat to apply military power carries a high risk of devaluing the other bargaining chips in one's possession, since it is almost certain to alienate the involved societies from one another so that they dismantle their cooperative projects and withdraw from mutual coalition partnerships in virtually all fields. Similar disincentives should also work against policies of economic strangulation, such as those attempted by the Arab oil producers against Israel's supporters in 1973 or by the United States against Castro's Cuba.

Pairs of countries with few interlocking associations (formerly characteristic of relations across East-West lines in the cold war and still characteristic of Arab-Israeli, Sino-Soviet, and Indo-Pakistani relations) can perhaps afford to be indifferent to an increasing alienation between them. But in an international system with elaborate overlapping of interests and coalitions, the most successful participants are likely to be sensitive to the fact that their opponents on one issue are often their supporters on another. If coercive bargaining strategies must be resorted to, the prudent statesman will conserve his overall store of influence by proffering, withholding, and withdrawing assets well below levels that will lead to total nation-to-nation or coalition-to-coalition hostility. Rarely should a specific dispute warrant the loss of influence which would accompany war threats, mobilization of military alliances, and polarization of international politics.

The Powerful Actors

The two countries that dominated international relations in the cold war system could continue to be the most influential in the emerging system by virtue of their command over economic resources, technological skills, and military capabilities. But if they rely primarily on the coercive leverage of their material positions instead of exploiting the new opportunities for participation in multiple coalitions, they may find themselves lagging in usable power. Moreover, in competing for global influence the United States and the USSR will find that constructive cooperation with smaller countries gains more votes in global and regional forums than coercive or denial strategies.

The cumulative power of the members of the European Community and associated countries to the south could begin to rival the power of the United States and the Soviet Union—especially if the two military superpowers continue to act as if the obsolete bipolar confrontation of security communities was still the essence of international relations. The usable power of the Western European group in any case would not derive from its military strength but from industrial capabilities, cultural ties, geography, and diplomatic skill. The EC countries are well situated for building coalitions with the countries in Eastern Europe, for they are partners or competitors in the larger all-European market and in the use of common resources—river basins, seas, energy supplies, air space, and the atmosphere. The Western Europeans also can be expected to maintain and construct North-South interdependencies, building particularly upon France's connections with most of its former colonies in Africa and upon ties of the British Commonwealth.

Japan, though envisaged as equal to or surpassing the Soviet Union in gross national product by the end of the century, is nevertheless likely to contine to rank somewhat lower in overall power as defined here. Although Japan's high technological and financial assets are desired by other countries, its high reliance on others for raw materials (even after nonpetroleum sources of energy are developed) will continue to keep it vitally dependent on the goodwill of others and on the absence of regional or global conflicts that could interrupt its supply lines. With neither the potential for self-sufficiency of the United States or the Soviet Union nor the historic community ties of EC countries to Third World partners, Japan is vulnerably dependent. As such it must please as well as be pleased. A hefty military capability will be of little use in day-to-day bargaining relationships, and in the light of recent history even the slightest attempt to escalate a dispute over economic matters to the military level would surely alienate a large set of its suppliers and revive a broad international coalition against it.

The fifth potential superpower, China, must rely almost entirely upon skillful diplomacy rather than material assets to exert any great influence beyond its borders. The only wide swath it can hope to cut in international coalition politics is as champion of the Third World countries, among which it may continue to be the only one with nuclear arms for some time. But China's nuclear capability, even if useful to deter military attacks upon itself, is unlikely to be pertinent as a bargaining counter on behalf of other members of any Third World coalition. China's opportunities for diplomatic leadership in the Third World will depend rather on the degree and quality of the policies of the United States, the Soviet Union, the EC countries, and Japan. If preoccupation with their own rivalries or a moral indifference to Third World concerns should cause the industrialized superpowers to treat the less developed countries as pawns, the way will be open for China to strike heroic poses in international forums as an aggressive spokesman for the world's poor. China also can be expected to exploit any opportunities for driving wedges between the Soviet Union and the Eastern European countries as a part of its continuing effort to be an alternative pole of attraction in the world communist movement. As either a major market or a source of specialized products, China will be of growing significance, but its economic weight will not be decisively greater than that of important countries or regional groupings in the Middle East, Africa, Latin America, South Asia, or Southeast Asia.

As long as oil remains the world's major source of energy, the petroleum-producing countries of the Middle East possess the capacity, when acting in concert, to disturb the whole international system and directly influence the policies of Japan and the Western European countries. Saudi Arabia, with the largest supply of marketable oil and huge accumulations of foreign exchange, can by itself cause considerable international disruption, though perhaps this leverage could be applied for positive ends.

Balances of Power, Real and Illusory

It would be misleading to characterize the relationships among the most powerful actors in the emerging system as a five- or six-sided balance of power, since this conveys rough equality of weight among them. Most of the various kinds of power at the disposal of each are incommensurate, and in specific categories some of the countries are clearly more powerful than others.

The United States and the Soviet Union may be able to balance one another's military power, but neither is likely to be equaled in this category by any of the other countries or groupings. It is not improbable that a Western European community armed with nuclear weapons could deter direct military attack upon it by the Soviet Union. But it is improbable that the Western Europeans could themselves prevent the USSR from winning a European war or a war for control over some third area, say, the Persian Gulf, if the United States stayed out. China and Japan might be able to balance each other's military power, especially if the latter developed nuclear weapons. If such were the case each of them could probably also deter the Soviet Union although they might lose an actual war against it. Without nuclear weapons Japan would not be able to balance the military power of China, though this asymmetry would not necessarily negate Japan's ability to deter a direct Chinese attack. China should be able to deter the United States from invading or bombing the mainland, but the United States would clearly win any naval encounter.

War between Europe and the United States or Japan or China, or between the United States and Japan, is so implausible that the military balance of each pair would have little effect on any disputes likely to arise between them. Even between the United States and the Soviet Union, the United States and China, or Western Europe and the Soviet Union, the escalation of any particular dispute to the war-threat level would be rarely warranted in the system postulated, given the costs and risks of this pattern of interaction and the availability of nonmilitary means of exerting pressure. The only pair for which the military equation may yet dominate the relationship would be China and Russia, if their border dispute continues.

In the nonmilitary categories of power the relationships often lack any measurable common denominator, and to the extent that there are comparable categories they tend to exhibit imbalance rather than symmetry. Thus the Soviet Union and members of COMECON probably would be more in need of commerce with the West than vice versa. On the other hand the state-controlled economies of the socialist countries could more easily subject their commercial negotiations to the requirements of their international political maneuvers. Japan and the countries of Western Europe would be more vulnerable than the United States, the USSR, or China to economic pressures such as a cutoff or increase in price in essential raw materials, particularly petroleum products.

Of increasing importance are the terms of access to and privileges in the space and ocean environments and the setting of international ecological standards and controls. Who gets what, when, and how depends largely upon the international decision structures set up to allocate benefits and costs and to resolve disputes, and upon the configuration of coalitions in each of these fields. These institutional structures and coalitions are unlikely to be congruent with the hierarchy of power based upon standard military or economic indicators. The relevant balances of power in these new areas will constitute a much wider set of critical actors and interdependent relationships than is contemplated in most visions of a five- or six-power world.

Multipolarity as an Unstable Condition

The emerging international system would not be congenial with multipolarity, a concept frequently invoked in the late 1960s and early 1970s to describe the successor pattern to cold war bipolarity. The concept connotes a magnetic pull by certain powerful countries, presumably over the other nations in their respective regions. In effect it contemplates spheres of hegemonial influence—jurisdictions of domination marked out for themselves by each powerful country and respected by the others.

But such a carving up of the globe, even if ostensibly agreed to by the major actors, could not be sustained under conditions of multiple interdependence and crosscutting coalitions. Smaller countries within a region would actively seek extraregional partners for commerce or other functions in order to retain bargaining leverage against the dominant regional country. Rather than being a pole of attraction, the country with pretensions to hegemony is likely to reinforce the centrifugal tendencies already present in the system.

Attempts by a powerful country to assert local hegemony over others in its region may appear to succeed in the short run; but over time, given the other characteristics of the emerging system, such attempts would tend to produce a subregional coalition against the dominating power. The existence of this coalition would tempt other big powers or coalitions outside the region to subvert the sphere of influence of the dominating power by establishing special ties with the aggrieved nations and publicly championing their causes. In consequence, the would-be hegemonial power would have either to loosen its overbearing influence or apply larger and larger quantums of coercion to keep its would-be satellites in line and keep out extraregional influences. The latter strategy would revive the weight of military factors of power and, if practiced consistently and widely by a number of the big powers, eventually would destroy the underlying preconditions of the postulated system.

Paranoid World as a Perversion of the System

The fragmentation of the cold war alliances and the lack of stable spheres of influence will throw most countries back on their own material resources and diplomatic skill for protecting their interests and could equally well lead to the development of either malign or benign results. If countries with nuclear weapons and other powerful military capabilities invoke their military superiority for purposes of facing down opponents in conflict situations, then military force and militarized diplomacy—bad currency in a kind of Gresham's law of international politics—will tend to drive out the good currency of cooperative and limited coalition-building; and many prestige-seeking countries will want their own weapons of mass destruction. A similar outcome could also result from a pattern of economic coercion.

Although in the emerging international system the nuclear powers have strong incentives not to resort to nuclear diplomacy against one another or against smaller powers, there are no guarantees that irrational behavior will not occur. A few instances of escalation to high-level military or economic coercion by one or some of the most powerful actors could engender a retrogressive chain reaction of coercive diplomacy. Since a return to the classical mode of attempting to balance power by military means would now, for any adversary of a nuclear-armed country, require some sort of devastating second-strike capability, the system of multiple coalitions would soon contain multiple arms races and multiple paranoia.

Prognosis

At the time of this writing the disintegration of geopolitical and ideological bipolarity, the rise of nonmilitary issues, and the diversification of coalition and adversary relationships seem to be the dominant tendencies in international politics. It cannot be forecast with confidence whether a persistence of these tendencies will give rise to a full-blown system of cooperative interdependence, with power exercised largely in the form of constructive exchanges of valued resources, or whether it will lead instead to an unstable world of coercive threats and multiple arms races.

In Washington and Moscow the habits of calculating power primarily in terms of coercive capabilities are still strong, and these capabilities are displayed in conflict situations. The United States has only recently liquidated its direct participation in the Southeast Asian war after applying major military force against a smaller adversary in that region for most of the previous decade. The Soviet Union, having just a few years ago enforced with tanks and bullets a change in the Czechoslovakian regime, is not about to abandon the role of brute force as a control mechanism in Eastern Europe. The NATO countries in Western Europe still view the U.S. troops deployed on the continent as a critical bargaining chip in East-West negotiations. The Sino-Soviet border issues continue to be prosecuted in the classic mode of exhibiting menacing deployments of force on each side. The balance of military power between the Arab nations and Israel is buttressed on each side by equipment from the USSR and the United States, and this together with anticipation that the superpowers would become directly involved in extremis continues to dwarf the nonmilitary factors important to the outcome of the Arab-Israeli conflict. The Arab countries, having reaped considerable short-term gains from their use of oil as a coercive political weapon, do not yet show adequate appreciation of its more consequential long-term disadvantages. In many areas of the globe more removed from great power rivalries, smaller powers often seem even further behind in adapting to the new disutilities of physical coercion as a means of gaining and maintaining international influence.

Over the coming decades the emerging system of multiple interdependence might take the form of its paranoid variant, with each country surviving fearfully at the mercy of its rivals. It may yet evolve into a system featuring benign interdependencies. Which pattern does in fact emerge will be determined mainly by how statesmen in the contemporary period of flux respond to the confused situation facing them. In part their response will depend on their ability to read accurately the changing objectives and strategies of other nations in the system. How world politics as a whole adapts to the changes in international relationships will also be determined in large measure by the response of statesmen to underlying social forces—many of them domestic, some of them transnational—affecting the structural base of the nation-state system itself.

PART TWO

Challenges to the Nation-State System

CHAPTER SEVEN

The Impact of Technology on Community

The disintegration of the cold war coalitions described in Part 1 raises some basic questions of world order. Given recent and prospective increases in the ability of physically separated societies to help or harm one another, should there be a system of institutions politically superior to the separate nation-states? If so, on what basis should this supranational system be organized—global or regional? Since the Second World War, international integration responsive to the twentieth-century scientific and technological revolutions has been hung primarily on the frameworks of the rival cold war alliances. Even non–cold war institutions such as the European Community (EC) and the Organisation for Economic Co-operation and Development (OECD) have been generally responsive to the political imperatives of the bipolar rivalry. At a time of ever greater mobility of men, materials, and ideas, the slackening of cold war tensions thus reopens in a new context the old issue of the adequacy of the nation-state system for performing basic tasks of world order.

The most fundamental imperative of world order—assuring that some humans do not destroy the conditions of healthy survival for the species as a whole—may no longer be able to be adequately implemented by the existing fragmented world political system. Another world war fought with the weapons currently in the inventories of the major nations would be tantamount to species suicide. Or the survival of humanity may be jeopardized, incrementally and inadvertently, by alterations of the natural environment which, though disruptive in the short term only to particular ecological systems, may ultimately create critical imbalances in the earth's biosphere.

At a less apocalyptic level of concern, many of the new technologies, through their transnational operations or effects, call into question the sovereignty of the nation-state as the sustaining principle for orderly international relations. In addition, a system of world politics operating on the premise that existing states must remain the highest secular authorities may be inconsistent with the need to minimize the chances of violent conflict; for many of the earth's resources essential to the health and well-being of some or all nations are progressively capable of being exploited by some in ways that limit their availability to others.

Inescapably, the pace and magnitude of technological change stimulates a need to reexamine the basis of political community. Who is to be responsible for whom? Who is to be accountable to whom? And if there are multiple and contradictory lines of responsibility and accountability, which obligations are to have primacy?

Primacy of the Nation-State System

For some three hundred years now world politics has been characterized by a system of nation-state primacy. Beyond loyalties to their immediate families, individuals have been expected to respond, at least when called upon, to service the needs of the larger nation-state community in which they live. Subnational or transnational community identifications have been maintained in between those of family and nation-state, but they have been expected to give way when required by the demands of national security or national welfare. Whether in democratic or in autocratic societies, when the survival of the nation itself has been thought to be at stake, even loyalty to one's family has been subordinated to the needs of the state.

Communities frequently have fought one another to determine which populations are to be contained within which nation-state; but each geographically defined population and each individual has been assumed to be part of one of these political units and subject to its laws above all others. Normally each nation-state has recognized the authority of other national governments over the populations within their respective territorial confines and has expected to have its sovereignty over its population recognized in turn. Failure to respect a country's exclusive jurisdiction within its territory, particularly if accompanied by tangible acts of intervention, has been grounds for war.

This nation-state system has dominated politics on a global basis, partly by coercion and partly by voluntary consent. The extent of a given country's jurisdiction has been established in many cases by force of arms—military expansion and subjugation of populations, finally checked by countervailing military action of another expanding country or aroused local populace. But the persistence over generations of a particular nation-state usually must be explained by the existence of strong bonds of mutual voluntary obligation among the peoples of the realm. A country would not be able to maintain its prevailing jurisdiction without a conviction on the part of substantial segments of the society that the best way to protect what they value—property, status, or their general well-being—is to cooperate with the established authorities and to support the existing nation-state against its enemies. Failure to maintain the legitimacy of extended jurisdictions in the face of intensified loyalty to local community is of course the main reason for the breakup of colonial empires in the period after World War II. Discontent with the protection and benefits of prevailing jurisdictional demarcations can also result in the voluntary amalgamation of neighboring states into a new and larger sovereign unit. This happened with the thirteen American colonies in the late eighteenth century and may be in the process of happening today in Western Europe.

Despite the breakup of multinational empires or the federation of existing political communities into larger states, the population of the world has remained divided into territorially defined sovereign units. These are accepted by most people living within them as jurisdictions that can legitimately tax them, require their conformity to general behavior norms of the larger community, and if need be command their military service in defense of the homeland. But, as will be argued below, the existing territorial bases of political community are becoming increasingly incongruent with the physical and ecological interdependencies brought about by contemporary technological developments.

Incapacities of the Existing System

Politically, the existing system is still for the most part one of laissez-faire. The more than 150 states are limited in their international behavior essentially by what the market will bear, affected only in the most marginal sense by universal rules and decision processes. External constraints upon national action are imposed by other nation-states; it is they who basically affect the international price of one's contemplated action, not the institutions of the world community nor— with the possible exception of the European Community and the Council for Mutual Economic Assistance (COMECON)—multinational regional institutions. A country's foreign policy decision makers usually ascertain the international price of a contemplated action from the rhetoric, posturing, or concrete deployment of resources by other countries on a case-by-case basis. There are many treaties, to be sure, indicating the intentions of groups of states who expect to interact over an extended period in some field; but most such treaties are riddled with escape clauses allowing each party to interpret its own obligations and to slough off the obligations if conditions change. The United Nations is one of the places where such treaties are made and where resolutions are passed expressing the sentiments of the majority of countries. In some of the specialized agencies and the World Bank group there is a certain amount of communitywide rule-making and enforcement and some allocation of international resources. On occasion UN peacekeeping forces are established on an ad hoc basis to supervise truce lines or disputed borders. But the compliance of countries to these decisions is voluntary. Most of the significant international action, whether cooperative or antagonistic, is still decided and implemented between governments—unilaterally, bilaterally, and multilaterally in only the loosest sense.

Outside of Europe the system still lacks a meaningful capacity to make binding rules for or administer to communities transcending the existing nation-states. Yet very real communities exist at these transnational levels and are being knit together inexorably by the cumulative effects of industrialization and technological change. Within these emergent transnational communities there is an increasing need for stable patterns of positive coordination where economies of scale suggest joint projects or for patterns of mutual restraint where the new interdependencies give different segments of a community the capability of substantially harming one another. But many of these needs must remain unsatisfied in the absence of institutions and procedures for allocating resources and resolving disputes, which are congruent with the emergent communities of interdependence.

Preventing Armageddon

The increasing incongruity between the physical interdependence of societies and the political fragmentation of the world was viewed as a momentous danger at the close of the Second World War by many of the scientists associated with the development of the atomic bomb. It was feared that someday the whole earth would be turned into a ball of fire if nuclear explosives could be used by the separate nations as they saw fit. This fear lay behind the U.S. proposal of 1946—the Baruch Plan —to establish a comprehensive supranational inspection and control apparatus with access to and authority over all relevant national facilities, including plants where raw materials could be converted into fissionable materials. The Soviet Union would have none of this, charging that the American proposal was a ruse to spy on Soviet capabilities and prevent the Russians from proceeding with their own weapons program. They put forward their own plan for the destruction of existing stockpiles of weapons *before* inspection and controls. But suspicions of Soviet postwar intentions were already high in the United States government. Under no circumstances, said President Truman, would we "throw away our gun" until we were sure that others could not arm against us.[1]

By narrowing expectations of what changes in the world's political system could be instituted after the Second World War, this early unsuccessful U.S.-Soviet dialogue over nuclear arms was probably more significant than the negotiations over the structure of the United Nations itself. After the rejection of its offer to transfer its most powerful weapons to a world authority, the United States government abandoned all hope not only of assuring peace through centralizing the control of military force but also of achieving substantial superpower disarmament. The Soviet Union was confronted with the need to open its closed society to international inspection if it was indeed serious about negotiating a disarmament agreement; in response Russia hardened its opposition to any kind of global supranationalism and became more than ever a champion in all UN forums of absolute national sovereignty.

Provisions for the buildup of UN military forces simultaneously with the reduction in national armaments would appear periodically in U.S. arms limitation proposals, mostly notably in the American general and comprehensive disarmament (GCD) plan of the early 1960s. Such proposals were put forward somewhat disingenuously, however, primarily in order to compel the Russians to reveal their objections to any realistic system of GCD and thereby demonstrate the lack of sin-

---

1. Harry S. Truman, *Memoirs: Years of Trial and Hope* (Doubleday, 1955), Vol. 2, p. 11.

cerity in the Kremlin's GCD proposals. The Russians continued to play the disarmament game by putting forward proposals for weapons dismantling or test cessation without any procedures for verification, knowing full well that the lack of reliable international enforcement would mean rejection by the United States.

The U.S.-Soviet arms limitation agreements actually negotiated, beginning with the nuclear weapons test ban of 1963, have been made possible through the dropping of U.S. demands for on-site inspection and the dropping of Soviet objections to being spied on from afar by technical means. Monitoring now was to be unilateral, by seismic and meteorological equipment for detecting the other party's weapons tests, and by aerospace photography and telemetry for detecting weapons deployment. Only in the nuclear nonproliferation treaty of 1968 has there been some authority given to a world body. In this case the International Atomic Energy Agency (IAEA) may determine by international inspection that ostensibly peaceful nuclear facilities are producing weapons in countries that have agreed not to. But there is nothing in the treaty that requires the Soviet Union to accept international inspectors on its own territory.

This is not to denigrate the importance of the mutual restraints thus far negotiated, in terms of stabilizing the U.S.-Soviet arms competition and contributing to the overall atmosphere of détente. The series of agreements emerging from the strategic arms limitation talks (SALT) of the early 1970s are of major significance in codifying the mutual recognition of certain facts: (1) Given the existing strategic balance, a thermonuclear war between the United States and the Soviet Union would destroy both societies no matter which one struck first. (2) It would be a more dangerous world if either side came to feel that it could in any way win or survive a thermonuclear war in a tolerable condition. (3) The weapons programs and developments on both sides should therefore be constrained by the overriding objective of preserving this situation of *mutual* "assured destruction."[2]

2. The Treaty between the United States of America and the Union of Soviet Socialist Republics on the Limitation of Antiballistic Missile Systems of May 26, 1972; the Interim Agreement and Protocol on strategic offensive weapons; and pertinent surrounding official statements appear in *Weekly Compilation of Presidential Documents*, Vol. 8, No. 23 (June 5, 1972), pp. 909–91.

Relying on mutual assured destruction to lessen the chances of nuclear Armageddon, however, is a far cry from the Baruch Plan's implications of world peace through world police and subsequent proposals, emanating mostly from nongovernmental groups, to centralize the control of the most lethal weapons in a global authority.[3] Since a full-blown world government is regarded as politically infeasible under contemporary conditions, arms control lobbies within and outside governments have focused their efforts for the most part on measures to stabilize the balance of terror.

For the time being at least, although the technological revolution in weapons has fashioned a global community of mutual vulnerability and fear, it has not stimulated a modification of the nation-state system. Mutual deterrence does nothing in itself to remedy the present lack of reliable community procedures that nations can employ to prevent their important interests from being violated. Consequently even mutual deterrence is inherently unstable if it relies only upon the existence of the weapons to uphold the strategic balance of terror.

Not all groups are willing to affirm that the common fear of another world war overrides all their deeply held values. Some groups continue to insist that to live under certain conditions is worse than death. Many would begrudge others the right to survive if their own way of life is denied. Indeed, the assumption that one's opponent will put survival of a way of life over simple physical survival is the underpinning of the balance of terror. The armed forces of today's superpowers give credence to the threat to destroy the world rather than surrender to the other's rule; the premise is that if either side were to suggest it might surrender in order to prevent further destruction, the opponent could be tempted to attack first.

To avoid Armageddon by threatening to participate in its unleashing is a brutalizing policy for those charged with its operation. There remain grounds for worry that, if the policy is frequently put to the test in crisis situations, it could erode the ethical sense that places a high value on human life. With reduced valuation on human life the costs of war itself might be discounted, with the result that military means would be more readily employed. Because of the risks of esca-

3. The most widely circulated proposal for a world authority to control the weapons of mass destruction appears as part of a new world constitution designed by Grenville Clark and Louis B. Sohn, *World Peace through World Law*, 2d ed. (Harvard University Press, 1960).

lation inherent in any war, this in turn raises the probabilities of the ultimate deterrent system eventually breaking down.

Even if mutual superpower deterrence does work according to its presumed inner logic and the United States and the Soviet Union appear absolutely dissuaded from launching a strategic nuclear first strike against the other, all types of war will not thereby be precluded. If it is generally assumed that nothing short of a strategic nuclear strike by one superpower against the territory of the other can provoke massive nuclear retaliation, the United States and the Soviet Union will not be reliably inhibited from fighting limited but nonetheless destructive wars against one another. Under some circumstances, particularly where there is a local imbalance of conventional forces, high confidence that neither side will initiate nuclear war might actually induce aggression in the hope of pulling off a fait accompli.

Moreover, assurances that the superpowers will not strike each other's territory can stimulate other than today's five nuclear-armed countries to acquire their own weapons of mass destruction. If the superpower alliance systems continue to disintegrate as contemplated in Part 1, lesser powers—no longer confident of the friendly superpower's nuclear protection and lacking their own capabilities for threatening effective reprisal—might fear being victims of nuclear blackmail by a hostile country already possessing nuclear weapons. As long as balances of military power remain the ubiquitous regulators of conflict, then the more "stable" the U.S.-Soviet balance of terror the weaker the constraints against the spread of nuclear weapons.

In sum, instead of generating a new world system of dispute settlement, with a central police force for suppressing violent interstate conflict, the threat of nuclear Armageddon has taken on itself the burden of conflict control but without any structural change in world politics. The threat of Armageddon is, however, a more or less dependable mechanism only for preventing rapid escalation to the highest levels of conflict, and then only on the part of countries who are fighting against a nuclear-armed nation. (But as the North Vietnamese showed throughout the 1960s, confrontation with a superpower adversary is not always a sufficient deterrent to belligerent action.) This leaves most interstate conflict situations outside the retaining wall of the balance of terror. And it is doubtful that the retaining wall itself has a reliable capacity to withstand the erosion of world order that could accrue from a series of limited wars. Contrary to early atomic age assumptions, the community of mutual danger has not been readily transmutable into a world political community.

Avoiding Biospheric Catastrophe

The incapacity of the world's fragmented political structure to provide adequately for the healthy survival of the human species has become evident of late in the environmental field. Here, too, critical functional incapacities result largely from the incongruity between the physical interdependence of peoples and the sovereign separateness of decision-making communities.

It has long been known that all human beings are ecologically linked to one another through their common dependence on the biosphere—the earth's envelope of air, water, and soil within which exist the only known living organisms in the universe. What is novel in the present period is a widespread awareness on the part of scientists, statesmen, and laymen that technological man's everyday activities, let alone thermonuclear warfare, could destabilize essential biospheric relationships in ways inimical to the healthy survival of life. As put by the official representatives of 113 countries meeting in Stockholm in June 1972:

We see around us growing evidence of man-made harm in many regions of the earth: dangerous levels of pollution in water, air, earth and living beings; major and undesirable disturbances to the ecological balance of the biosphere; destruction and depletion of irreplaceable resources; and gross deficiencies harmful to the physical, mental and social health of man in the man-made environment. . . .

A point has been reached in history when we must shape our actions throughout the world with a more prudent care for their environmental consequences. Through ignorance or indifference we can do massive and irreversible harm to the earthly environment on which our life and well-being depend.[4]

In contrast to the earlier conventional view that the immense biosphere would in time simply absorb man's alterations of nature, today many biologists, physicists, and chemists are concerned that the carrying capacity of the earth's life-support system not be exceeded. There is much disagreement among scientists over how sensitive the biospheric balance really is to various man-made disturbances, but few would assert that man yet knows enough about these critical relation-

4. *Declaration of the United Nations Conference on the Human Environment*, A/CONF. 48/14, July 3, 1972, pp. 2–3.

ships to warrant his continuing to assault the natural environment at the exponential rates characteristic of the last few decades. Those who express the greatest alarm, such as the Club of Rome in its sensational publication, *The Limits to Growth*,[5] and those who are more sanguine, such as the members of the M.I.T.-sponsored Study of Critical Environmental Problems (SCEP),[6] do agree that life on earth is supported by a complex feedback system—involving ocean and air currents, evaporation and precipitation, surface and cloud reflection and absorption —that keeps the global heat balance nearly constant. In the words of the SCEP group, "The delicacy of this balance and the consequences of disturbing it make very important that we attempt to assess the present and prospective impact of man's activities on this system."[7]

Great uncertainty, for example, surrounds the potential effects on the earth's heat balance of both the combustion of fossil fuels and deforestation. One concern is that perhaps before the end of the twenty-first century accumulation of carbon dioxide in the atmosphere resulting from industrialization could make the "greenhouse effect" of the earth's natural carbon dioxide belt *too* efficient. Instead of maintaining the current balance between incoming and outgoing radiation, a thickening belt of carbon dioxide might trap more and more heat close to the earth's surface; if this process were to raise average global temperatures by as little as two degrees centigrade, it could melt the polar ice caps. A substantial melting of polar ice, most climatologists agree, would be catastrophic. Some major land masses would be flooded; others would turn into deserts too hot for humans to bear.[8]

5. Donella H. and Dennis L. Meadows and others, *The Limits to Growth: A Report of the Club of Rome's Project on the Predicament of Mankind* (Potomac Associates, 1972).

6. Study of Critical Environmental Problems, *Man's Impact on the Global Environment: Assessments and Recommendations for Action* (M.I.T. Press, 1970).

7. Ibid, p. 10.

8. The current state of scientific knowledge about the potential effects of fossil fuel burning on the carbon dioxide belt is summarized in Sterling Brubaker, *To Live on Earth: Man and His Environment in Perspective* (New American Library, Mentor Books, 1972), pp. 91–94. See also SCEP, *Man's Impact on the Global Environment*, pp. 11–12; Barbara Ward and René Dubos, *Only One Earth: The Care and Maintenance of a Small Planet* (Norton, 1972), pp. 192–93; and Paul R. Ehrlich and Ann H. Ehrlich, *Population, Resources, and Environment: Issues in Human Ecology* (San Francisco: W. H. Freeman, 1970), p. 147.

Another concern—again surrounded by great uncertainty—is that large increases in airborne particulate matter might contribute to a destabilization of the earth's heat balance in the opposite direction, bringing on a new ice age or, short of that, severely affecting the supply of food. Most of the particles in the atmosphere that screen the earth from the heat of the sun are produced naturally from volcanoes, salt sea spray, dust storms, vegetation, and the like. But some airborne particles, such as sulfates, nitrates, and hydrocarbons, result from man's industrial processes. Clouds are another determinant of how much of the sun's heat gets through to ground level and how much is reflected back; and cloud formation might be affected significantly by high-flying subsonic and supersonic jet aircraft.[9]

Among the other human activities that could destabilize the climate of the globe are the diversion of rivers, deliberate attempts to modify snow and ice cover in the polar regions, projects to create new, very large bodies of water, land cultivation, and perhaps urbanization itself. "What needs to be clearly understood," stated the pertinent UN technical report prepared for the Stockholm conference, "is that the cooling and warming up of the earth has been experienced several times over geologic times and can be expected to occur again as a result of natural causes within times that we cannot determine. However, we now realize that man's activities may also add a powerful destabilizing factor to the interplay of the natural forces that determine the climate."[10]

The purpose here is not to support or attack doomsday prophecies but to observe that the need for remedial steps, let alone the implications of a failure to avoid catastrophe, would seem to require a sociopolitical capacity beyond that of the unmodified nation-state system to coordinate global action. As put by Ward and Dubos:

It is no use one nation checking its energy use to keep the ice caps in place if no other government joins in. It is no use the developed nations suggesting lower energy use just at the moment when the developing nations see increased use as their only exit from the trap of poverty. The global interdependence of man's airs and climates is such that local decisions are simply inadequate. Even the sum of all local separate decisions,

9. SCEP, *Man's Impact*, pp. 12–18, 82–107; Brubaker, *To Live on Earth*, pp. 61–63.

10. United Nations Conference on the Human Environment, *Identification and Control of Pollutants of Broad International Significance*, A/CONF. 48/8, Jan. 7, 1972, p. 21.

wisely made, may not be a sufficient safeguard. . . . Man's global interdependence begins to require, in these fields, a new capacity for global decisionmaking and global care.[11]

There is also uncertainty over the potential effects of supersonic air traffic on the ozone of the lower stratosphere which shields the earth from harmful ultraviolet radiation. Some scientists have suggested that the nitrogen oxides from supersonic transport (SST) exhausts could break down the ozone umbrella, allowing ultraviolet sunlight to penetrate to the earth's surface. Skin cancer, blindness, and the impairment of photosynthesis (the process whereby plants manufacture carbohydrates) are among the possible results.[12] As of this writing, the hypotheses underlying this prognosis are being intensively debated within the international scientific community. Meanwhile, however, the Soviet Union, France, and the United Kingdom are proceeding full speed ahead to deploy their SST fleets; and to keep other countries from cornering the market, aerospace interests are putting pressure on the United States to reconsider its decision not to build an American SST.

In short, as the biologist Garrett Hardin has pointed out, man's expanding technological prowess puts the separate nations in a relationship with the biosphere analogous to that of English herdsmen to the common grazing lands before the nineteenth century: The herdsmen's essential common resource would be destroyed in the long run by overgrazing as a result of increased herds. Nevertheless each herdsman felt constrained to add to his herd, fearing his competitors would best him in the very tangible short run if he held back. "Therein is the tragedy," observes Hardin. "Each man is locked into a system that compels him to increase his herd without limit—in a world that is limited. Ruin is the destination toward which all men rush, each pursuing his own best interests in a society that believes in the freedom of the commons. Freedom in a commons brings ruin to all."[13] The English avoided ruin, of course, by the so-called enclosure movement to

11. *Only One Earth*, p. 195.
12. Walter Sullivan, "Scientists Plan Series of Tests to Assess the Impact of Supersonic Air Traffic on Life and Climate," *New York Times*, Nov. 19, 1972.
13. Garrett Hardin, *Exploring New Ethics for Survival: The Voyage of the Spaceship Beagle* (Viking, 1972), p. 254. The original essay, "The Tragedy of the Commons," was published in *Science*, Vol. 162 (Dec. 13, 1968), pp. 1243–48.

carve up the commons into fenced-off parcels of private pasture. But the analogy with the biosphere is most instructive precisely because of this nonanalogous element: There is no reasonable way of parceling out the atmosphere. To avoid ruin the biosphere's common users must ultimately subordinate themselves to some mutually agreed-upon rules. Clearly the prevailing traditions of international relations do not augur well for the institution of such a regime.

Managing Other Common Resources

The incapacity of the nation-state system, as organized at present, to perform important new transnational management tasks is becoming increasingly evident with respect to other transnational "commons" —the oceans and smaller marine and river ecosystems, the weather, and outer space.

The decade of the 1960s may well be looked back on as the period when man experienced a "paradigmatic shift" in his view of the sea. Edward Wenk, Jr., has observed, "The Community of nations began to recognize that all peoples cluster on continental islands embedded in the vast ocean, that man's activities are intimately linked to the sea, and that the planet represents a closed ecological system wherein ostensible local events may have widely distributed effects."[14]

To be sure, for centuries the major powers have considered the great oceans as essential highways for commerce and war, and many populations have obtained important food and income from marine fishing. Clashes among nations over rights of passage in parts of the ocean (especially narrow straits) and over fishing grounds, and disputes over the jurisdiction of coastal waters have been a prominent feature of world politics. Naval encounters have often decisively altered the outcome of major wars. And maritime law is perhaps further advanced than any other field of international law. What is new in the current developing perspective is the awareness that: (1) the oceans and sea-beds beyond recognized national jurisdictions are wealthy in petroleum and hard minerals; (2) physically, not just politically, the vast oceans may not be able to accommodate all users; and (3) the maritime environment is a key component of the total biospheric ecosystem and of a number of very important subordinate ecosystems.

14. *The Politics of the Ocean* (University of Washington Press, 1972), p. 423.

The first modern offshore oil well was installed in 1948. By 1970 offshore deposits accounted for nearly 17 percent of the oil and 6 percent of the natural gas produced by the noncommunist countries. With rising demands and continued developments in drilling technology, according to most standard projections, by 1980 the offshore sources should account for more than a third of the noncommunist production of oil and a comparable rise in natural gas.[15] Increased demand and technological innovation are stimulating intensive drilling farther and farther off the coasts, raising complicated questions of national jurisdiction for which existing international treaties and precedents are of little help. The prevailing laissez-faire regime for the exploitation of ocean resources follows Garrett Hardin's archetype of the commons. Anyone may explore or exploit the area outside of recognized national jurisdictions as long as such activities do not interfere with freedom to navigate the high seas. No wonder that in the early 1970s many of the technologically lagging countries, fearing preemptive exploitation by industrial countries and multinational corporations, have been unilaterally extending their claims of national jurisdiction seaward. The Latin Americans, supported by China, have been asserting national ownership out to two hundred miles.

Man's view of the great oceans as lucrative sources of hard minerals is even more recent, and again there is no regime to regulate the prospecting and mining in ways that would be regarded as legitimate by most interested parties. Estimates of the economic returns to be expected from seabed mining still vary widely, but it is clear that, as the technology continues to develop, the mining industry will become progressively more active on the deep ocean floor where the manganese nodules are thought to be rich in copper, nickel, and cobalt. Much of this activity will be beyond the limits of national jurisdiction, even the maximal claims of the Latin Americans.[16] Does this mean that everyone has the right to the resources of this vast commons on a first come, first served basis? Should there be some form of registry or licensing by the international community to ensure that first exploiters act as trustees for the rest? Do the miners owe any portion of their

15. John A. Knauss, *Factors Influencing a U.S. Position in a Future Law of the Sea Conference*, Occasional Paper No. 10 (Kingston: Law of the Sea Institute, University of Rhode Island, April 1971), p. 12. See also Wenk, *Politics of the Ocean*, pp. 22–25.

16. Knauss, *Factors Influencing a U.S. Position*, pp. 15–16.

returns to the international community? Should countries whose live-lihoods depend on their ability to market land-mined hard minerals be protected from the potential trade-distorting effects of the new ocean mining?

As of this writing, the complex issues provoked by man's discovery of the oceans' vast reservoir of mineral wealth are nowhere near settle-ment, although a plethora of regime proposals are being prepared by dozens of countries for debate at the 1974 Law of the Sea Conference.

The Law of the Sea Conference will also try to come to grips with the problem of multiple and often incompatible uses of the oceans. The new "gold rush" in minerals might conflict with some of the seas' delicately balanced and still poorly understood relationships among plant and animal life. Oil spills, whether from underwater drilling, storage facilities, or tankers, have not only interfered with coastal recreation and tourism but have also been fatal to sea birds and some other marine species trapped in them. Fish and other seafood con-sumed by humans have been poisoned by pesticides and industrial effluents carried into the sea by rivers and sewer systems. More gen-erally, the sea as a major source of photosynthetic activity, carbon dioxide absorption, and climate control might, over the long run, be affected severely by man's increasing use of his water environment as a huge septic system. As Sterling Brubaker said in his survey of environmental problems for Resources for the Future, "We know all too little of how the sea and its biotic communities impinge on global ecology, but there is every reason to treat this relationship with great respect. Instead we utilize the sea thoughtlessly as the ultimate sink for all sorts of debris and chemicals generated on land and transported by air and water."[17]

Suppose the great oceans, which make up 70 percent of the globe's surface, were indeed regarded by most men to be the "common heritage of mankind" as many United Nations resolutions and docu-ments now assert. Does there exist today the requisite political and legal structure to give that concept operational meaning? The answer would appear to be no. The relevant question then becomes: What modifications in the existing international system would be required to give substance to the concept of common heritage? This question is discussed further in Chapter 10.

17. Brubaker, *To Live on Earth*, p. 148.

As with the great oceans, many large seas and rivers are being vic-
timized by a congestion of common users, some of whom are engaged
in inherently incompatible activities. Again existing international mechanisms appear to be ill-suited for making the authoritative allocations
required.

The Mediterranean—of direct importance to Spain, France, Monaco,
Italy, Yugoslavia, Albania, Greece, Turkey, Syria, Lebanon, Israel,
Egypt, Libya, Tunisia, Algeria, and Morocco—is practically choking
to death for want of multinational ecological care. The main culprit is
oil spillage from coastal refineries, terminal pipelines, and most of all
from ships cleaning their tanks at sea. Oil film on the water depletes
the sea of its oxygen and suffocates sea life. Nitrates and phosphates
from agricultural, residential, and industrial wastes flow down the
rivers into the sea where they overstimulate algae growth, further rob-
bing the sea of scarce oxygen and killing sea life. The human wastes
flushed in daily are not dangerous to the overall ecological balance of
the sea, which is poor in nutrients, but it is a major health problem to
humans and fish—especially in the resort areas of Spain, France, and
Italy. Finally, there are the pesticides that are consumed by the fish
and thereupon enter the human food chain. According to the director
of the National Research Center in Rome, "Nobody with any sense
would eat shellfish in Italy, and 70 per cent of our beaches are a health
hazard. It is not a question of *when* the sea will be dead; for the
Italian it has already happened. In other countries bordering the Mediterranean it is only a matter of time."[18]

The technical means exist for reducing the pollution and nursing
the Mediterranean back to health. Tens of millions who reside on or
visit the coastal areas would share in the social and economic benefits
which would surely exceed the cost of cleanup for every coastal country, provided most of them chipped in. But no effective multinational
process yet exists for allocating the burden, and in the meantime it
makes no substantial improvement for one or two countries to stop
using the sea as a toilet if the others continue.

Another notorious example of the mismanagement of common water

18. John Cornwall, "Is the Mediterranean Dying?" *New York Times
Magazine*, Feb. 21, 1971, pp. 24 ff. Jacques Piccard predicts life in the sea
will be dead within twenty-five years unless urgent remedies are taken; see
William Tuohy, "The Mediterranean Is Dying," *Washington Post*, March 5,
1972.

resources is the Rhine River–North Sea ecological system. The glacial waters that feed the Rhine's sources are contaminated with soot from the factories of Central Europe, which settles on the Alpine snow. The Alpine streams run into Lake Constance on the Swiss-German border, which suffers from eutrophication nearly as badly as Lake Erie. As the Rhine flows north along the French-German border, it receives heavy chlorides from the Alsatian potassium mines. Downstream it absorbs a variety of exotic effluents from the chemical complexes at Ludwigshafen, Germany, ingests the polluted air blowing over from the Ruhr industrial plants, and then meanders into Rotterdam, where it is both a source of drinking water and a sewer for port refuse. Loaded by now with tons of mercury, copper, and arsenic, it flows into the North Sea where it is imbibed by fish and other marine organisms. Despite local concern and embarrassing international publicity, France in 1972 was continuing its construction of a nuclear power station in Alsace, resisting the pressure of its neighbors to provide special devices against thermal pollution. (The French claimed the installation of cooling towers would be too costly.)[19] Food sources and recreational amenities of the North Sea are also under impending threat from oil pollution as drilling intensifies in its very rough waters.

Even in northwestern Europe, where regional multilateralism is farthest advanced, the need for developing a common approach to an important commons has not yet generated adequate innovations in political institutions. When the EC's commission in Brussels advocates rapid and concerted action to curb pollution on the Rhine, the countries largely ignore it. European Community member countries thus far have been unwilling to grant the commission directive authority for environmental coordination. They still pay more attention to the economic distortions that may result from different national regulations than to the health hazards of pollution.[20] Nor has the International Commission for the Protection of the Rhine against Pollution, set up

19. "Rhine Basin Countries Vow to Clean Up River," *Chemical and Engineering News* (Nov. 20, 1972), pp. 8, 11; John Tinker, "Europe's Majestic Sewer," *New Scientist*, Vol. 56, No. 817 (Oct. 26, 1972), pp. 194–99. See also *Business Week* (June 3, 1972), pp. 51–52; *Chemical and Engineering News* (Feb. 22, 1971), p. 28.

20. Dominique Verguèse, "Europe and the Environment: Cooperation a Distant Prospect," *Science*, Vol. 178, No. 4059 (Oct. 27, 1972), pp. 381–82.

in 1963, been granted any independent power.[21] This leaves antipollution measures pretty much up to the individual nations; but a self-help regime in the Rhine River–North Sea ecosystem is basically nonadaptive, given the clear pattern of upstream polluters and downstream consumers.

Technology's expansion of physical interdependencies across existing national jurisdictions is about to create new international problems in the field of weather modification. As techniques for suppressing storms or stimulating rainfall become operational, there will be substantial conflicts of interest among those in the paths of moving weather systems. A major concern will be where and when precipitation should occur, since more rain early in a weather path will usually mean less rain later in the path, and vice versa. All affected communities can be expected to insist—legitimately—that they play a part in the decisions to modify the weather and to allocate penalties and compensation for damage. This complex regulatory problem probably will not hit the international community full force until the 1980s, but a portent of the political turbulence that is bound to come can be seen already in the opposition of the Japanese to U.S. plans to move some of its experimental hurricane suppression programs from the Atlantic to the Pacific.[22]

Responding to Transnational Opportunities

Many of the scientific advances and new technological applications of the twentieth century have had their most dramatic cumulative or synergistic effects in the fields of transportation and communication, radically altering the role of location, distance, and topographic barriers in human affairs. From the standpoint of the physics of moving men,

21. Robert E. Stein, "The Potential of Regional Organizations in Managing Man's Environment" (Woodrow Wilson International Center for Scholars, 1972; processed).

22. Edith Brown Weiss, "The International Legal and Political Implications of Weather Modification," paper delivered at the Third Conference on Weather Modification, sponsored by the American Meteorological Society, Rapid City, South Dakota, June 26–29, 1972. See also Robert M. White of the National Oceanic and Atmospheric Administration, Department of Commerce, Statement to the Senate Foreign Relations Subcommittee on Oceans and International Environment, July 27, 1972, *Hearings: Prohibiting Military Weather Modification* (1972), pp. 62–70.

materials, and ideas the whole earth is already a community. The degree to which the earth community has been activated to form concrete cooperative relationships, however, is infinitesimal compared to what is now physically possible and rapidly becoming cost-effective in economic terms. The reasons for this sluggish response are almost all political, not physical.[23]

Despite energy shortages, intercontinental travel is becoming as easy and cheap as domestic intercity travel, sometimes even easier. This does not mean, however, that individuals can travel anywhere they want to or that men can ship any goods to whatever destination they wish. For the sovereign state, loss of control over who enters the realm or what is permitted in would be in effect loss of control over fundamental social and economic processes. The challenge of airline hijackings, narcotics smuggling, and other criminal uses of the global transportation network has therefore not elicited vigorous and concerted international action. (As the Americans saw in 1789, the need to regulate interstate commerce involves the enhancement of central law and order institutions.) Through standardization of air traffic and international airport procedures already existing, the means are technically at hand to develop effective international policing mechanisms. For such a development, however, the separate nations would be required to countenance a degree of supranational jurisdiction which some still consider threatening to their sovereign prerogatives.

Similarly, as more and more communications are handled by earth-orbiting satellites, there will be few if any purely technological barriers to linking the entire world in one comprehensive communications system. Such a system would probably be most efficient, costing consumers less and handling more traffic without message interference. But the political-economic questions are far from being solved, even in principle. The provision and maintenance of equipment for a global communications system involves very lucrative contracts. Who is to get these contracts? Who will let them? And by what criteria? As experience with the U.S.-dominated INTELSAT consortium shows, now that international satellite communications are no longer experimental, a pure efficiency standard for letting contracts is unacceptable to most

23. Lester R. Brown presents a rich menu of current and prospective opportunities for establishing transnational linkages in his *World without Borders* (Random House, 1972).

nations since it would perpetuate U.S. dominance.[24] A related set of questions concerns the allocation of preferred orbital positions and bands on the frequency spectrum. Should those who get up there first have the first claim to the preferred positions?

Probably the knottiest of all the political issues in the new era of communications is over the degree of freedom to broadcast directly to foreign populations. The technology for broadcasts by satellite relay to unaugmented home television receivers may be fully developed by the mid 1980s. Once this technology exists, should there be any legal regime to regulate program content? At one extreme is the United States, which now champions maximum freedom of international broadcasting; at the other extreme is the Soviet Union, which insists that each country have a veto on the programs beamed to it, and that the right to jam broadcasts or shoot down offending satellites be legitimized.

Another challenge to the meaning of national borders derives from the development of photographic and remote sensing systems, carried by spacecraft, which survey earth resources and activities on a continuing and global basis. The information gained from the observations of earth from space will facilitate the development of global models of the earth's natural ecosystems, climatic patterns, resources, and man-made alterations of the environment. This will make possible more effective local planning and, to the extent that it becomes feasible politically, global planning for the use of resources. This is the positive side of the coin. From the standpoint of some countries that expect to be technically ill-equipped for optimum use of the new information, the negative side is the loss of control over what some nations previously considered proprietary data important in negotiating terms of access to their resources by foreign entrepreneurs.[25] In this field too the questions of who owns, manufactures, maintains, and provides the various technical services are still handled essentially on the basis that capability makes right. If they continue to be handled unilaterally, however, optimal use of the technology is unlikely since fully elaborated and cooperating global networks, including ground stations, will be important for worldwide monitoring. Multilateral decision making and management of the technology, as already indicated,

24. Brenda Maddox, *Beyond Babel: New Directions in Communications* (London: André Deutsch, 1972), pp. 82–114.

25. Everly Driscoll, "ERTS and International Relations," *Science News*, Vol. 102 (Aug. 5, 1972), pp. 90–93.

would require a considerable reorientation toward international as opposed to purely national control on the part of the technologically advanced nations, particularly the United States.

The Problem of Institutional Lag

The incapacity of the existing world political system to respond adequately to the threat to man's security and well-being or to seize new opportunities for cooperation can be seen as an institutional lag—a relatively slow response at the political and governmental level to the rapid interlinking of human communities at the physical level. The spans of jurisdiction are being rapidly outgrown by transnational activity at the economic level too, a phenomenon to be described in more detail in the next chapter. The widening gap between the expanding material basis of community and the political structure of world society cannot, however, be bridged by legislative fiat—a kind of world constitutional convention to devise institutions congruent with the patterns of physical interdependence. The resulting structures would be flimsy legal artifices unless substantial groundwork were laid to expand community identity, especially among people who, except for familial attachments, still identify most strongly with a given nation-state. The problem is thus *institutional* in the broadest sense of the term and connotes the structuring of reliable patterns of responsibility and accountability among those whose actions affect one another (see Chapters 10 and 11).

CHAPTER EIGHT

Economic Transnationalism

The pursuit by each state of its own environmental interests, unaccountable to binding norms and structures designed to protect the world community, has been shown above to threaten the healthy survival of the human species. It has been suggested that nation-states may be accorded too *much* unilateral power under the existing system of world politics. This chapter will examine a set of economic developments that suggest the separate nation-states may have too *little* power over events within their jurisdictions. These environmental and economic developments are, however, both rooted in many of the same basic changes in the relationships between man, nature, and technology, and they may overlap when it comes to considering political solutions—namely, ways of ensuring that community organizations have the scope of authority adequate to serve the fundamental values of the community.

Economic Challenges to the Autonomy of the Nation-State

One of the major functions of the state, in addition to protecting a national community from external attack, economic exploitation, or cultural subjugation, has been to demarcate the boundaries of the national market and sustain the rules of access to and behavior within that market. In part this has meant the protection of privileged interests at the sacrifice of the general consumer's interest in being able to shop freely in the largest markets. But the other aspect of this function has been the redistribution of social benefits and obligations over and above those acquired through buying and selling in the open market.

144

Provision for the future, the care of the currently weak and needy, and a fair equalization of opportunity for the young—these highly valued goals have been increasingly implemented by the state in the twentieth century rather than by the family or other private institutions.

In the name of such market stabilization and social justice, national governments have carefully controlled foreign ingress and egress to the domestic market. Otherwise, it is claimed, those whose wealth or sources of income have been specially protected in the domestic economy could be overwhelmed by foreign competition; and some wealthy elements in the domestic economy could avoid heavy redistributive taxation by transferring their taxable assets out of the community.

Since economic protection and redistribution are primarily functions of the separate national governments, there is an inherent tension in world society between those who are sufficiently strong and mobile to compete in an open world market, unencumbered by redistributive regulations, and those who believe their well-being depends primarily upon the state-run mechanisms. It should not be surprising, therefore, that we are beginning to witness a revival of nationalistic economic protectionism, along with efforts by some of the weaker elements of the global economy to organize on a transnational basis, and a growing interest in strengthening multilateral governmental controls to catch up with the growing economic mobility. These different political responses to economic transnationalism and the prospects of one or some combination of them becoming dominant will be considered later in this chapter, after a brief survey of the economic phenomena causing the most concern.

The most prominent players in this game of eluding nation-state controls are corporate enterprises like General Motors, Royal-Dutch Shell, IBM, Michelin, Unilever, ITT, Sony—the so-called multinationals. Constituting a family of firms located in different countries and joined together by a parent corporation usually located in one of the advanced industrial countries, many a contemporary multinational enterprise has greater impact on the world economy than do some of the important nation-states themselves. Thus the value added by each of the ten largest multinational enterprises in 1971 was more than $3 billion—more than the gross national product of some eighty countries. The value added of all multinational corporations in 1971, estimated as roughly $500 billion, was about one-fifth of the combined

GNP of all the noncommunist countries.[1] Other major actors are banks and networks of private investors, which in tandem with corporate producers are responding to a number of reinforcing developments.

A major factor has been the application of high-speed communications and information processing systems to business management and actual production problems. The ability to transmit, receive, and store swiftly vast amounts of technical and accounting information has allowed for centralized, standardized, yet flexible direction of far-flung and diverse operations. Another closely related factor has been the revolution in high-speed transportation that shrinks distances and allows for the unprecedented transfer of personnel and product components among subsidiaries. A third factor has been the growing industrialization of many countries which, through the local manufacture of products otherwise imported, has stimulated big foreign sellers to invest in local subsidiary manufacturing plants rather than be displaced from their former markets. During the process of host country industrialization, tariff walls and other barriers to trade are likely to rise, which only add to the foreign seller's incentives to establish his own local manufacturing and marketing enterprises. The final factor is that worldwide differentials in the prices of labor, land, taxes and rents, and investment capital have induced large firms to locate or shift certain specialized plants to various foreign locations.[2]

Even where major barriers are erected around particular national or multinational markets to interfere with the circulation of material goods, modern communications and the evolution of business practices progressively put what are becoming the most important means of transferring assets—namely, visual or oral messages—beyond effective political control. The availability of "foreign" goods in national markets depends less on the ability of entrepreneurs to transport the goods across borders than on their ability to transmit and receive ideas and decisions rapidly, especially those that commit financial resources.

1. United Nations, Department of Economic and Social Affairs, *Multinational Corporations in World Development*, ST/ECA/190 (UN, 1973), p. 13.

2. Raymond Vernon, *Sovereignty at Bay: The Multinational Spread of U.S. Enterprises* (Basic Books, 1971); Louis T. Wells, Jr., "The Multinational Business Enterprise: What Kind of Organization," in Robert Keohane and Joseph Nye (eds.), *Transnational Relations and World Politics* (Harvard University Press, 1972), pp. 447–64.

American computers are sold in Europe or British tires in the United States, for example, not on the basis of their having been shipped across the ocean but on the basis of financial capital transfers that have allowed IBM to produce goods and services on the Continent and Dunlop to manufacture its products in the United States.

The extent to which such activities of multinational corporations have been overtaking international trade in goods as the dominant process in the world economy may be roughly conveyed by comparing the sales of foreign affiliates of U.S. firms with the value of U.S. exports. For 1970 the sales of U.S. foreign manufacturing subsidiaries were estimated to be $90.4 billion; exports of manufactured goods were $34.9 billion. The total sales of all U.S. multinational affiliates abroad were $108.7 billion in 1970, while total U.S. exports were $42.6 billion.[3] Another crude but significant indicator of the long-term secular expansion of the multinational economy is the growing "book value" of direct foreign investments (calculated from parent company entries in their balance sheets but normally underestimating the current value of their foreign assets). The pace and pattern of such investment for selected years from 1929 to 1970 are shown in Table 1. Direct foreign investments by the European Community (EC) countries and Japan, although still much smaller than those of the United States, have been growing at a faster rate since the late 1960s and also expanding more than exports.[4]

Some commentators see this phenomenon of transnational business as the means by which economic man creates the global city of abundance. By striving to maximize the returns on their investments, multinational enterprises presumably promote the growth of most of the national economies in which they function. Peter Drucker, a prominent management consultant and popular writer, portrays the multinational corporation as an institution which represents the interests of "the world economy ... against all the partial and particular interests of

3. *The Multinational Corporation and the World Economy*, report by the Senate Committee on Finance, 93 Cong. 1 sess. (1973), p. 11.

4. Lawrence B. Krause, "The International Economic System and the Multinational Corporation," in *Annals of the American Academy of Political and Social Science*, Vol. 403 (September 1972), pp. 95–96 (hereafter cited as *Annals*); Stefan H. Robock, "The Silent Invasion," *World*, Vol. 2, No. 2 (Jan. 16, 1973), pp. 26–30; John Diebold, "Multinational Corporations: Why Be Scared of Them?" *Foreign Policy*, No. 12 (Fall 1973), pp. 79–95.

TABLE 1. *U.S. Direct Investment Abroad, by Geographic Area, 1929, 1950, 1960, and 1970*

Billions of dollars

Country or area	Book value at year's end			
	1929	1950	1960	1970
Developed				
Canada	2.0	3.6	11.2	22.8
Europe	1.4	1.7	6.7	24.5
Japan	0.3	—	0.4	1.5
Other	—	0.4	1.3	4.4
Developing				
Latin America	3.5	4.4	8.4	14.7
Middle East	—	—	1.1	2.0
Other	—	—	1.4	4.6
Unallocated	0.3	1.7	1.5	3.6
Total	7.5	11.8	32.0	78.1

Source: *Implications of Multinational Firms for World Trade and Investment and on U.S. Trade and Labor*, U.S. Tariff Commission report to the Senate Committee on Finance, 93 Cong. 1 sess. (1973), p. 97.

the various members. It [is] . . . an institution that has a genuine self-interest in the welfare of the world economy, an institution that, in pursuing its own goals serves the world economy rather than any one of the individual national economies. . . . Its development during the last twenty years may well be the most significant event in the world economy, and the one that, in the long run, will bring the greatest benefits."[5] Similar optimism is expressed by many American businessmen, as exemplified by the vice-president of the Council of the Americas who asserted that "the fundamental and ultimate business of the world corporation is the people of the world, not the people of any one nation or any one political ideology. Its ideology is the provision of abundance."[6] Moreover it can be expected to operate as "a strong force for world peace," contends the president of the Bank of America. The large multinational firm, as he sees it, "has a direct, measurable, and potent interest in helping prevent wars and other serious

5. Peter F. Drucker, *The Age of Discontinuity: Guidelines to Our Changing Society* (Harper and Row, 1969), p. 91.
6. Enno Hobbing, "The World Corporation as Catalytic Agent," *Columbia Journal of World Business*, Vol. 6, No. 4 (August 1971), p. 51.

upheavals that cut off its resources, interrupt its communications, and kill its employees and customers."[7]

Over the long run, the most efficient allocation and management of the earth's resources probably would be best performed by those enterprises large enough and mobile enough to respond to technology-induced changes in the factors of production and consumer preferences on a worldwide basis. Free competition among such corporations, unencumbered by artificial national restraints on trade and investment, would allow for the location of production and service facilities close to markets, making needed goods available to more people at reduced costs. Capital markets would be linked, increasing the global availability of financial resources. The multinational enterprises would contribute to the transfer of technology from the highly industrialized to the less industrialized countries by training local citizens in new production techniques, creating new markets for local skills, and stimulating the growth of complementary or competitive local industries. Indeed, such effects can be pointed to in many places today, which explains the proliferation of direct foreign investments. The firms and funds would not gravitate to countries inhospitable to them.

But the uneven functioning of the world's political economy as structured at present cannot be ignored in either analysis or prescription. Disequilibria within and between countries can result from the self-serving approach of some multinationals. The beguiling picture of a providential harmony of economic interests without substantial governmental regulation of the market is a myth in the world economy no less than in domestic economies. As Lord Keynes observed, "In the long run we'll all be dead"; but in the short run one party's profit is often another party's loss. Some multinational producers conspire with particular national governments to keep competitors out of certain portions of the world market. Serious conflicts of interest often exist between internationally mobile top corporate structures and nonmobile subsidiary plants and labor, between middle classes of different nations competing for managerial positions, and between members of the labor force in national branches with high wages and their counterparts in other countries who will work for less at the same jobs. Some governments fear that the larger multinational firms, particu-

7. A. W. Clausen, "The International Corporation: An Executive's View," in *Annals*, pp. 12–21; quotation from p. 21.

larly those with worldwide assets exceeding those of the individual nations hosting their subsidiaries, are able to escape public interest controls on the national market.[8]

In the early 1970s multinational companies became notorious as vehicles for the transfer of funds between countries to avoid domestic monetary controls. There are numerous other channels, such as banks and investment brokers, that contribute to the transnational circulation of investment capital and can also integrate money and capital markets so as to bypass national economic policies. Domestic policies that regulate the interest rates charged to borrowers have become important in most industrial countries for moderating inflation and recession; and policies that alter or stabilize the international exchange value of a nation's currency may be used to overcome international trade or payments imbalances. But the massive amounts of liquid assets held by private institutions can now change national hands so fast that the whole thrust of a country's domestic economic policy can be overwhelmed by nongovernmental financial transactions.

Lawrence Krause explains the process by which the mobility of money and capital associated with multinational enterprises can undermine the autonomy of national monetary authorities:

Because the firms operate in many countries, they have knowledge of and financial ties to all major money markets and most smaller ones as well. Corporate treasurers will shift their liquid funds from country to country in response to interest rate incentives and will take positions in currencies in expectation of adjustments of exchange rates. Thus if the interest rate in one money market, for example, Frankfurt, is higher than another one, perhaps New York, then firms will shift funds from the United States to West Germany. Likewise, if one currency is thought to be a candidate for devaluation and another for revaluation, firms will move funds from the weaker to the stronger currency. . . .
If the national central bank tries to enforce tight money to fight inflation, firms borrow abroad and avoid restraint. If the authorities try to stimulate their economy through easy money policies, they may have their efforts

8. Charles Kindleberger (ed.), *The International Corporation* (M.I.T. Press, 1970). See also Stephen Hymer, "The Multinational Corporation and Uneven Development," testimony before the Subcommittee on Foreign Economic Policy of the Joint Economic Committee of the U.S. Congress, July 30, 1970 (processed); and Peter Evans, "National Autonomy and Economic Development: Critical Perspectives on Multinational Corporations in Poor Countries," in Keohane and Nye, *Transnational Relations and World Politics*, pp. 675–92.

frustrated as firms utilize their liquidity to invest abroad for higher rates of return. . . . Since the flows also affect the balance of payments to which governments respond, all governments have lost some of their sovereignty in economic policymaking to the private sector.[9]

Domestic taxation policies can also be overwhelmed. International bond and money markets have burgeoned partly to attract funds trying to escape the tax collector. Some countries deliberately avoid taxing interest earnings on foreign funds in order to attract financial business. The difficulty of enforcing tax laws on funds held abroad in effect encourages the wealthy residents of all nations to maintain such tax-free sources of interest income. These tax havens are models for "pollution havens," into which industries move production facilities from countries with strong ecology constituencies. Other domestic regulations— antitrust laws, capitalization requirements, and various trade restrictions—can be evaded by the transnational mobility of firms and funds. No less important, especially for the industrially lagging nations, is the so-called brain drain of technical personnel as well as the movement of skilled labor away from the countries where the social need for their skills may be the greatest but where their earning and advancement opportunities are limited. All in all, as Richard Cooper puts it, "as capital and skilled labor become less exclusively national in their orientations, countries desiring to pursue tax or regulatory policies that deviate widely from these policies in other countries will find themselves stimulating large inflows or outflows of funds, firms, or persons; these induced movements will in turn weaken the intended effect of the policies, or make them more costly."[10]

Alternative Political Responses

National Protectionism

Whatever worldwide benefits might be realized from giving economic transnationalism the freest play, domestic tensions would result from the high mobility of investment capital and advanced productive enterprises on the one hand and the comparative immobility of less de-

9. "International Economic System," p. 100.

10. Richard N. Cooper, "Economic Interdependence and Foreign Policy in the Seventies," *World Politics*, Vol. 24, No. 2 (January 1972), pp. 159– 81; quotation from pp. 165–66.

veloped segments of society on the other. These tensions are likely to stimulate considerable political agitation among the immobile segments to raise national barriers around the domestic market. Those who champion a more open world trading system, though often the most successful elements of the domestic economy, frequently have a smaller attentive constituency. In some cases they can create a larger coalition to prevent protectionist reactions, provided they can generate support for and confidence in domestic adjustment programs for economic interests that fear they will suffer in a more open transnational competition. Domestic adjustment mechanisms will not eliminate the grievances of the economically vulnerable, however, since appropriate government action requires taxation and regulatory regimes that are themselves capable of being bypassed by some of the financially mobile segments of the economy.

Even where transnational penetration of a domestic economy would contribute to its overall development through the transfer of resources and the creation of jobs (including gains for poorer segments of society, as might well be the case in many Third World countries), sociological and psychological sources of protectionism will often carry the day. "Dependencia" is frequently felt to be a worse condition than economic backwardness.[11] From the point of view of nationalists in a relatively poor country, substantial transnational economic penetration is seen as a postcolonial form of imperialism. Those citizens who get drawn into the transnational network often become responsible to superiors and stockholders of other countries. In the words of an empathetic U.S. sociologist, "If a similar chain of command existed in public organizations, the poor country would be deemed a colony."[12]

As of the early 1970s, in both the advanced industrial countries and those trying to industrialize, hostile attitudes toward multinational enterprises were on the increase, particularly on the part of organized labor, as were attempts to restrict the inward and outward flow of funds. Unless most countries coordinate their restrictive policies, however, protectionist actions of a given nation are likely to be economically self-defeating since mobile capital will locate in more hospitable environments.

11. Osvaldo Sunkel, "Big Business and 'Dependencia': A Latin American View," *Foreign Affairs*, Vol. 50, No. 3 (April 1972), pp. 515–31.
12. Evans, "National Autonomy and Economic Development," pp. 675–92.

Regional Integration

Political responses to economic transnationalism can also be organized regionally by a group of countries, to subject existing intraregional movements of capital and labor to public interest regulation and/or control economic access to the region. Intergovernmental accords need not merely impose constraints but can also stimulate the flow of economic factors across national lines within the region and sometimes attract new penetration of the region from the outside.

All of these political-economic interrelationships have been at work in the formation and elaboration of the European Community. Community-wide procedures are being established both to encourage the freer circulation of resources, people, and management among the member countries and to ensure that the socioeconomic effects of the enhanced mobility are consistent with the members' goals of social justice. The EC was in part designed to control penetration of its market by outsiders, but it is of more than one mind on the issue of restricting direct investment by foreigners. France has urged that all members of the Community adopt restraints as strict as its own against externally owned funds and firms. But other members, notably Belgium, the Federal Republic of Germany, and the United Kingdom, have not been quite as anxious to discourage the inflow of external risk capital, particularly from the United States. More likely are Community-wide discriminations against foreign-owned subsidiaries in the form of patent laws and other licensing arrangements that encourage the creation and expansion of Europe-owned multinationals.[13]

Regional integration as a way of developing intraregional economies of scale and restraining foreign domination of the regional market is also advocated by economists specializing in Third World problems. According to Joseph Grunwald and his associates in a Brookings Institution study on Latin American economic integration,

> Intraindustry agreements could provide for plants in the various member countries to specialize in particular products within an industry or—what requires more coordination—in different components of given products. Such complementarity arrangements would safeguard the interests of participating nations in a customs union and at the same time promote a better division of labor in the region.

13. Vernon, *Sovereignty at Bay*, pp. 241–47.

They see the region-based multinational corporation as probably the most efficient vehicle for implementing the principle of complementarity:

Existing companies in Latin American countries could join together to form multinational enterprises. The pooling of technical, managerial, and financial resources and production at high enough output levels to yield economies of scale would strengthen Latin American enterprises, making them more competitive with extraregional corporations.[14]

To date the Latin Americans have been more resourceful in attempting to regulate foreign investment on a regional basis than they have been in creating favorable opportunities for indigenous economic transnationalism. The Andean Common Market nations (Bolivia, Colombia, Ecuador, and Peru) have agreed on a common foreign investment code, stipulating percentages of capital that must be transferred within designated time frames by foreign companies to local investors in certain industries. But adequate legislation is lacking throughout the larger Latin American Free Trade Association (LAFTA) to encourage the formation of local transnational enterprises. Despite the regulations aimed at foreign firms, it is therefore the large foreign multinationals that have been the most active in spawning specialized subsidiaries within LAFTA. In the Central American Common Market a substantial part of foreign investment has gone to purchase existing local firms. As the study cited above points out, "This type of investment frequently fails to bring with it the traditional benefits of new capital or technology, and it may stifle local enterprise."[15]

Even in those regions in the less developed world where the greatest economic integration has been achieved, developed-country transnationals still have the advantage of entrepreneurial skills, extra pools of risk capital from outside the region, technological equipment, trained personnel, and overall mobility. This asymmetry frequently tends to confront the poorer countries with a major political dilemma: choosing the psychological pain of economic neocolonialism or the economic pain of real independence. It is a dilemma without apparent solution since powerful local constituencies are ready to toss out any regime

14. Joseph Grunwald, Miguel S. Wionczek, and Martin Carnoy, *Latin American Economic Integration and U.S. Policy* (Brookings Institution, 1972), pp. 120–22.
15. Ibid., p. 115.

that moves very far in either direction. Where regional movements are less far along and each poor country must face the world of affluent transnationalism on its own, the dilemma is usually just that much more constricting.

All in all, outside of Europe most regional polities, actual or potential (see Chapter 10), would seem to be too narrow in scope and their supranational powers too ineffective to rein in the most mobile elements of the transnational economy and subject them to public interest controls.

OPEC as a Special Case

The concerting of pressure against multinational oil companies by the Organization of Petroleum Exporting Countries (OPEC) provides another variant of political response, differing from the regional policies discussed above on two grounds: OPEC is a transregional organization, including Venezuela, Indonesia, and Nigeria as well as nine Middle Eastern states, and it is a product-specific organization rather than one governing issues of foreign investment generally.

As indicated in Chapter 5, OPEC's success in pressuring for an increase in oil prices and in the host countries' share in the petroleum companies is seen by some Third World leaders as a model for bargaining with other multinationals. But the conditions under which concerted pressure works in the oil field are rare elsewhere. Conducive to successful bargaining is a product in high demand, whose major sources are limited and controlled by a few countries which can threaten to take over the local multimillion-dollar assets of foreign companies. Nevertheless, as the competition among industrialized countries for raw material grows, Third World producers of copper, tin, rubber, and bauxite may well attempt to imitate OPEC tactics.[16]

The OPEC case also demonstrates the extent to which the public interest can be bypassed in the transnational economy—even when there is a two-sided bargaining game going on. The effect of the price rise on petroleum consumers was evidently not a crucial consideration for OPEC in the negotiations prior to the 1973 decision of Arab members to use oil as a political weapon. Nor were oil companies much concerned

16. C. Fred Bergsten, "The Threat from the Third World," *Foreign Policy*, No. 11 (Summer 1973), pp. 102–24.

before 1973 about the pricing aspect of their problems since they were bargaining as a group and were able to agree on how to pass these increases on to buyers in Western markets.[17]

The Transnational Mobilization of Labor

Another potential for bringing some international accountability to the multinational giants exists in the international labor unions. Most labor unions, heretofore international in name only, have been prone to agitate automatically for national protection when their industry's productivity in other countries lessened the demand for labor in their own country. Even when foreign goods are produced by a subsidiary of the firm with whom they are engaged in collective bargaining, by labor belonging to the same international union, the national unions have usually tried to protect themselves by pressuring their own government to keep out the products.[18] Some labor unions, however— frustrated by the ease with which the large multinational firm can close down a local subsidiary or transfer production and investments to other nations—finally are beginning to coordinate action with fellow workers in foreign subsidiaries of the same industry.

International trade union secretariats, traditionally serving mainly as information clearinghouses, are becoming more aggressive in sponsoring industrywide consultation and strategy planning on a transnational basis. Charles Levinson, the head of the Geneva-based International Federation of Chemical and General Workers Union (ICF), cites as an example of the new aggressiveness the role played by his federation in Turkey, where U.S. rubber companies were resisting unionization. "We got the parent union to intervene with parent companies in Akron. Management then realized they were no longer dealing with a small, powerless union in Turkey."[19]

Efforts are being made to harmonize demands with respect to job classification, work speeds, safety standards, and even wages and fringe benefits. In addition to the ICF, the most active unions on this front have been the International Conference of Free Trade Unions, the

17. William D. Smith, "Oil Replay," *New York Times*, Jan. 9, 1972.
18. Elizabeth Jager, "Multinationalism and Labor: For Whose Benefit?" *Columbia Journal of World Business*, Vol. 5, No. 1 (January–February 1970), pp. 57–64; David H. Blake, "Trade Unions and the Challenge of the Multinational Corporation," in *Annals*, pp. 34–45.
19. "Labor: The Global View," *Newsweek*, May 17, 1971.

International Metalworkers Federation, and the International Transport Workers Federation. Some international union officials are predicting that collective bargaining agreements on a world scale, backed by the sanction of coordinated transnational strikes, will be a normal feature of industrial relations within ten years. There already have been a few transnational strike threats, some of them partially successful. The most impressive precedent thus far was the common front of the Italian, French, German, and American unions against the French-controlled glass producer, St. Gobain, in 1969.[20] Robert Cox, director of the International Institute of Labor Studies in Geneva, catalogs the range of trade union strategies now being developed:

1) promoting contacts and working relations with existing trade unions of the same type in other countries in which the corporation has operations; 2) creating and sustaining unions in their own image in less developed countries; 3) applying pressure on corporation headquarters to recognize and bargain with unions in these other countries when corporations have been reluctant to do so; 4) banning overtime and other increases in work schedules in other countries in the event of a strike in any one country in which the corporation operates in order to prevent shifts in production; 5) organizing consumer boycotts of corporation products in case of employer intransigence; 6) coordinating the terminal dates of collective agreements in the various foreign operations of the corporation; and 7) coordinating bargaining ultimately on a worldwide corporation basis.[21]

To the extent that unions do indeed obtain collective bargaining clout on a transnational basis within certain industries, the effects can impinge on consumer interests and the general safety and welfare of various populations. Higher prices might result from successful bargaining or essential public services be disrupted during a bargaining impasse. It may well be, however, that this anarchistic potential of transnational labor-management strife will need to materialize in a number of large, socially disruptive crises before transnational legal

20. Charles Levinson, "International Collective Bargaining: Historic ICF Action on Saint-Gobain," *ICF Bulletin* (June–July 1969), pp. 9–23. See also I. A. Litvak and C. J. Maule, "The Union Response to International Corporations," *Industrial Relations*, Vol. 2, No. 1 (February 1972), pp. 62–71.

21. Robert W. Cox, "Labor and Transnational Relations," in Keohane and Nye, *Transnational Relations and World Politics*, pp. 554–84; quotation from p. 568. See also John Gennard, *Multinational Corporations and British Labour: A Review of Attitudes and Responses* (London: British–North American Committee, 1972).

structures for regulating the transnational economy in the public interest become politically salable.

Functional Supranationalism

In considering means to provide political communities with spans of control adequate to regulate the burgeoning transnational economy, analysts and statesmen come back to the question of the fundamental structure of world politics. In the words of Raymond Vernon:

> This is one of these areas of international tension . . . in which constructive international action may be called for on a more rapid timetable than [most] cautious proposals suggest. . . . The basic asymmetry between multinational enterprises and national governments may be tolerable up to a point, but beyond that point there is a need to reestablish balance. When this occurs, the response is bound to have some elements of the world corporation concept: accountability to some body, charged with weighing the activities of the multinational enterprise against a set of social yardsticks that are multinational in scope.
>
> If this does not happen, some of the apocalyptic projections of the future of multinational enterprise will grow more plausible.[22]

Former Undersecretary of State George Ball agrees, and advocates the establishment by treaty of an international companies law, administered by a supranational body, including representatives drawn from various countries, who would not only exercise normal domiciliary supervision but would also enforce antimonopoly laws and administer guarantees with regard to uncompensated expropriation. An international companies law could place limitations, for example, on the restrictions nation-states might be permitted to impose on companies established under its sanction. The operative standard defining these limitations might be the quality of freedom needed to preserve the central principle of assuring the most economical and efficient use of world resources.[23]

Some international economists, most notably Charles Kindleberger, suggest the creation of a permanent international forum on the model of the General Agreement on Tariffs and Trade (GATT) where governments can harmonize their policies for dealing with multinational corporations. Companies and countries could submit their grievances to the secretariat of the international forum, or perhaps to experts appointed by the forum, who would issue recommendations. Compliance

22. Vernon, *Sovereignty at Bay*, pp. 282, 284. See also Cooper, "Economic Interdependence," pp. 175–76.

23. George Ball, "Cosmocorp: The Importance of Being Stateless," in Courtney Brown (ed.), *World Business* (Macmillan, 1970), pp. 330–38; quotation from p. 337.

would be voluntary, but if the institution were widely used and its decisions respected over time, it might perform a very important role as international "ombudsman for corporations and countries seeking relief from oppressive policies."[24]

A spokesman for the International Federation of Free Trade Unions has proposed the international negotiation of a code of behavior binding on multinational firms, to be administered by an autonomous international center. The center would operate under the auspices of the International Labour Organisation, the World Bank, GATT, the International Monetary Fund, the United Nations Conference on Trade and Development, and the Organisation for Economic Co-operation and Development. A tripartite body of representatives of governments, multinational companies, and trade unions would hear complaints about the violation of the code. Exactly how the code or decisions of the tripartite body would be made binding is not spelled out.[25]

All of these suggestions assume that governments will be more willing to accord international institutions new authority than to allow the largely unfettered transnational economy to undermine the domestic policies. But the undermining effects of economic transnationalism are still too ambiguous (in many cases the relationships between the corporations and the governments remain close), the discipline of international economics still too wedded to neo-free-trade concepts, and the traditions of nation-state primacy too deeply ingrained in societal institutions and symbols for any meaningful pooling of sovereignty to be expected outside of the European Community in the near future. Groups disadvantaged under the present global political economy are likely to be suspicious—based on their experience with domestic and regional regulatory bodies to date—that the international institutions set up to harmonize rules of behavior for the transnationally mobile

24. Paul M. Goldberg and Charles P. Kindleberger, "Toward a GATT for Investment: A Proposal for Supervision of the International Corporation," *Law and Policy in International Business*, Vol. 2, No. 2 (Summer 1970), pp. 295–323; quotation from p. 323.

25. Herbert Maier in Subcommittee on Foreign Economic Policy, *A Foreign Economic Policy for the 1970's*, Hearings, 91 Cong. 2 sess. (1970), pp. 833–34. For summaries of these and related international proposals see Chadwick F. Alger, "The Multinational Corporation and the Future International System," in *Annals*, pp. 104–15; and Robert S. Walters, "International Organizations and the Multinational Corporation: An Overview and Observations," in *Annals*, pp. 127–38.

are likely to be dominated by the most mobile economic interests themselves. To relieve these suspicions and mobilize popular demand for the transfer of substantial public interest powers to supranational bodies, it would be necessary for the crisis of the nation-state to become much more acute; concepts of equity and world public interest would have to be more widely disseminated and shared, and more coherent designs for restructuring the world's political economy would have to capture the popular imagination.

CHAPTER NINE

Cultural Pressures on the Nation-State

The authority of nation-states in managing the long-distance inter-actions of peoples rests on more than the congruence of state jurisdic-tions and organized clusters of economic activity. Even if the nation-state system adapts to the challenge of economic transnationalism—by strengthening national government controls over the mobility of capi-tal and intergovernmental regulation of the destructive economic com-petition between nations or trading blocs—the ability of nation-state institutions and symbols to command the loyalty and affection of their citizenry probably will continue to erode. This cultural crisis of the nation-state is unevenly distributed and finds varied expression among countries with different domestic political systems and levels of socio-economic development. It is doubtless becoming a global phenomenon in the last decades of the twentieth century, however, and probably cannot be reversed without coercively preventing large masses of people from utilizing the fruits of the contemporary technological and scientific revolutions.

The various cultural pressures eroding the authority of the nation-state can be grouped, for purposes of exposition, under the headings of cosmopolitanism, the affluent counterculture, and ethnicity.

Cosmopolitanism

Cosmopolitanism is restricted here not to any purposefully sys-tematic philosophy but rather to an *attitude* characterized by rela-tively low emotional or affective identification with particular national or local political jurisdictions, institutions, and symbols, and relatively intense identification with worldwide, or potentially worldwide, associations and symbols. Thus cosmopolitanism includes ecumenical philosophies such as those propounded by Pierre Teilhard de Chardin, Julian Huxley, Sarvepalli Radhakrishnan, and William Ernest Hocking; the societal analysis in the writings of Arnold Toynbee, Andrei Sakharov, Lord Ritchie-Calder, Margaret Mead, Lewis Mumford, F. S. C. Northrop, Kenneth Boulding, Jan Tinbergen, Gunnar Myrdal, Barbara Ward, R. Buckminster Fuller, Erik Erikson, and Richard Falk; the proposals for world law and order of activist-intellectuals such as Robert M. Hutchins, Louis B. Sohn, Elizabeth Mann Borghese, and Norman Cousins; the social orientation expressed in the work and utterances of men of public affairs such as Maurice Strong, Edwin Reischauer, Sicco Mansholt, Lester Pearson, Arthur K. Watson of IBM, R. Kingman Brewster of Yale University, and the members of the Club of Rome; and also the attitudes, sometimes only implied and often unarticulated, of thousands of scientists, businessmen, journalists, electronic media people, academics, artists, athletes, and other professionally mobile men and women in virtually every country.

These people are usually a part of the constituencies favoring the kind of strengthened multilateral institutions to be discussed in Chapter 10. They also tend to be in favor of arms limitation agreements, low defense budgets, and many are protesters against the use of coercive foreign policies by their countries. In contrast to the alienated affluent elements to be discussed below, most cosmopolitans tend to feel very much a part of the modern technological society—as though riding the crest of the wave of the future. They support proposals and promulgate world views that will help put the earth-shrinking techniques of the twentieth-century scientific and technological revolutions to the service of an integrated and peaceful world community. Cosmopolitans agree with the alienated affluent in regarding the institutions and symbols of the nation-state as inadequate for protecting and advancing human welfare.

Although there are no good estimates of the amount or distribution of people who share the cosmopolitan frame of reference, they can be expected to be most prevalent in those cultural classes and regions that experience the greatest transnational mobility. To be sure, mobility per se or contact with foreigners does not always create transnational fellow-feeling; indeed, where there are already deep cultural dissonance and jealousies contact will frequently exacerbate hostility (see the discussion of ethnicity below). But the data available on those classes and professions that often travel or change domicile support, in the aggregate, the proposition that frequent exposure to other cultures breaks down preexisting parochialisms and creates new transnational emotional bonds.[1]

In the mobile social strata, particularly the upper middle classes in highly industrialized societies of the noncommunist West, self-identification and loyalties are more and more in terms of one's profession rather than race, religion, nationality, or domicile. Transnational mobility and communication within the profession, as well as protecting the rights and status of the profession and advancing its values, become goals which claim stronger emotion commitment than do national security or national welfare. There is a corollary tendency to transfer larger extraprofessional community obligations to the transnational society within which one now functions.[2]

The Affluent Counterculture

The scientific and technological revolutions to which cosmopolitanism is a response have sprung from modern Western industrial civilization, whose culture is characterized by (1) rationalistic analysis; (2) work mores which encourage the postponement of sensate gratification while energies are put to work to maximize future returns; and (3) standards of individual and social worth which determine one's value largely by one's contribution to the material well-being of the family or larger social unit.

Now, however, the most fully ripened varieties of Western society, called "postindustrial" by Daniel Bell[3] or "technetronic" by Zbigniew Brzezinski,[4] are producing some traits which seem antithetical to the

1. See Robert Cooley Angell, *Peace on the March: Transnational Participation* (Van Nostrand Reinhold, 1969).

2. See John Gardner, *Self Renewal* (Harper, 1963), p. 83; Alvin Toffler, *Future Shock* (Random House, 1970), pp. 83–85, 131–32; Eugene Jennings, "Mobicentric Men," *Psychology Today*, Vol. 4, No. 2 (July 1970), pp. 34 ff.

3. "Notes on the Post-Industrial Society (I)," *The Public Interest*, No. 6 (Winter 1967), pp. 24–35: "Notes on the Post-Industrial Society (II)," *The Public Interest*, No. 7 (Spring 1967), pp. 102–18.

4. *Between Two Ages: America's Role in the Technetronic Era* (Viking, 1970).

basic culture. Many of technology's most favored children are turning against more than technology itself, expressing an alienation from the sociological relationships and values which are the preconditions of advanced industrialism. As observed by the distinguished French sociologist Raymond Aron:

they denounce bureaucracy, Soviet as well as capitalist, they want participatory democracy, they are opposed to the values of the business bourgeoisie, work or money, they rail against specialization and want to give free rein to emotions and creativity. Thus they seem to be rebelling against the exigencies of the scientific culture and to be nostalgic for the culture of the past or already anticipating a postscientific culture beyond the productivist obsession and the reign of computers.[5]

In the process the authority of all large-scale institutions—corporate, national, and international—has become a primary target for animosity.

In the United States, data for the 1968–71 period, the high point of opposition to the Vietnam war, suggest that about 10 percent of the eighteen- to thirty-year-old population consciously felt at odds with the dominant mores and institutions of the society. Most of the disaffected youth were university students, primarily in the social sciences and humanities. Although overt protests, particularly violent demonstrations, declined after 1969, reliable attitude surveys showed the proportion of university students who believed the United States was "a sick society" had risen from 40 percent in 1968 to 45 percent in 1971. In 1971 three out of ten students indicated they would prefer to live in some other country, and 15 percent found "the prospect of accepting a conventional way of life in the society as it now exists intolerable." Opinion analyst Daniel Yankelovich estimated at the end of 1971 that "about 30 per cent of the student body is alienated to some degree, and ... from a third to a half of this group is deeply alienated."[6]

Data on youth dissidence in Western Europe and Japan for the same period indicated a similar pattern of alienation from the dominant culture. Smaller proportions of university populations were involved than in the United States, and there was less radicalism in lifestyle as distinct from politics. But the numbers were increasing, and the generalized counterculture posture was becoming more evident

5. "Student Rebellion: Vision of the Future or Echo from the Past," *Political Science Quarterly*, Vol. 84, No. 2 (June 1969), pp. 289–310.

6. Daniel Yankelovich, Inc., *The Changing Values on Campus: Political and Personal Attitudes of Today's College Students* (Washington Square Press, 1972), p. 83, and data throughout.

in most industrial countries, especially in France, the Netherlands, West Germany, and Scandinavia.[7]

The particular grievances of politically radicalized students—the Vietnam war, racial conflict, and environmental pollution in the United States; the Okinawa issue in Japan; university reform in France—have been taken at face value by some commentators as the *causes* of youth alienation.[8] The overt issues seized upon by the activist New Left are equated with the reasons underlying their opposition to "the system" in much of the polemical literature on youth protest produced by its political champions as well as its detractors.

Some sociologists and psychologists see the dissidence of contemporary youth as merely the current expression of the unavoidable psychological conflict between generations. According to this school of thought each historical period will be catalyzed by a different set of issues, which shapes the particular generational conflict of the time; but the essential psychological ingredients are always present in the youth of every period. Which young people become active combatants in the instant generational conflict, and with what degree of intensity, is determined for the most part by their individual psychological histories, especially their early relationship with their parents. The basic thesis is that the tendency of sons to become alienated from their fathers is part of the human condition and, consequently, so is the tendency of most youth to project this alienation onto their relationships with society's institutions of authority. From this point of view, both the political and cultural radicalism of the young is motivated by the

7. See Ronald Inglehart, "The Silent Revolution in Europe: Intergenerational Change in Post Industrial Societies," *American Political Science Review*, Vol. 65, No. 4 (December 1971), pp. 991–1017. See also Joachim Fest, "The Romantic Counter-Revolution of Our Time: Letter from Germany," *Encounter*, Vol. 36, No. 6 (June 1971), pp. 58–61; Hans Heigert, "Germany's Restive Students," *Interplay* (March 1970), pp. 35–41.

8. Samuel Lubell, for example, has contended that the "failure to adjust the draft in 1963 can be said to mark the beginning of our youth crisis. The absence of draft reform would mean that when our involvement in Vietnam deepened, for every young man taken into the service, three or four times as many would feel they had to find ways of evading the draft, postponing career decisions, and building up resentments against society.

"The grievances would enable tiny minorities of student agitators, often fewer than a hundred on a campus, to radicalize a sizeable part of all college students across the country." *The Hidden Crisis in American Politics* (Norton, 1970), pp. 182–219; quotation from p. 184.

desire to confront the older generation with behavior shockingly at variance with its expectations. Hair styles and dress challenge prevailing norms of male-female differentiation; art forms, drugs, and sexual relationships are characterized by immediate gratification of impulse in opposition to the mastery of impulse which is associated with effective competition in the achievement-oriented adult society. These countercultural challenges are designed (often unconsciously) to provoke the wrath of the older generation, to trap it into brutal or stupid responses which then provide the youth with self-justification for its final emotional separation and entry into independent adulthood.[9]

Fads and fashions in particular grievances and protests are equaled in their fickleness by the fads and fashions of commentators on the affluent counterculture. Some observers, especially in the popular media, will announce the long-term "cooling" or "heating up" of radical dissent merely on the basis of seasonal levels of overt protest. Others attempt to correlate each rise or fall in the temperature of dissent with foreign policy crises or domestic cycles of inflation and recession.

But none of this adequately explains the data that is now available on the socioeconomic characteristics of various youth groups and general changes in their bases of recruitment and behavior patterns over the past decade:

1. Alienation from the dominant cultural mores of industrialism and postindustrialism has been most evident among university youth in the advanced Western democracies and Japan, and it is concentrated largely in the humanities and the social sciences.

2. Whereas in the 1960s counterculture attitudes seemed to be concentrated among upper middle-class sons and daughters of liberal or "Old Left" parents, in the early 1970s similar attitudes were expressed by increasing numbers of students who came from "mainstream" American homes.[10]

9. See Lewis S. Feuer, *The Conflict of Generations: The Character and Significance of Student Movements* (Basic Books, 1969), pp. 514–15; see also Bruno Bettelheim, "Obsolete Youth: Towards a Psychograph of Adolescent Rebellion," *Encounter*, Vol. 33, No. 3 (September 1969), pp. 29–42; quotation from p. 35.

10. See Milton Mankoff and Richard Flacks, "The Changing Base of the Student Movement," *Annals of the American Academy of Political and Social Sciences*, Vol. 395 (May 1971), pp. 54–67; see also Herbert Gold, "A

3. The range of counterculture targets has widened to include not just foreign policy and military and educational establishments but also institutions of law and order, patriotic symbols generally, financial institutions, the Protestant work ethic, traditional sexual mores and roles, and the family unit.

4. The means of expressing disaffection have broadened from the organized disobedience of the 1960s to encompass social behavior antipathetic to the "straight" middle classes, including drug use, unfamiliar hairstyles, nudity, public sex, and other verbal and physical acts conventionally defined as "obscene."[11]

5. The extremist fringes of the counterculture have been falling apart while its nonviolent core appears to have been expanding. "Extremist" includes here those who advocate violent revolution and/or engage in acts of physical destruction to vent their grievances; "nonviolent" includes members of the drug culture, the apathetic, and the dropouts, those who outwardly conform but feel alienated from the dominant culture, those who engage in the more conventional forms of direct action such as marching and sit-ins, those involved in constructive political participation, and some of the new religious fanatics.[12]

6. The manifestations of the counterculture life-style have been spreading to the countries of Eastern Europe. Students have long been in the forefront of antiregime political agitation in Hungary, Poland, and Czechoslovakia. Since the Soviet suppression in 1968 of Czechoslovakia, Western fads in dress, hairstyle, popular music, literary forms, and even attitudes toward work appear to have become substitute means of expressing disaffection toward the communist party establishment.[13]

Season at Middle America U.," *Atlantic Monthly*, Vol. 229, No. 5 (May 1972), pp. 48–53.

11. John R. Seeley, "Stances and Substances," *Annals of the American Academy of Political and Social Sciences*, Vol. 395 (May 1971), pp. 95–104; Barbara G. Meyerhoff, "The Revolution as a Trip: Symbol and Paradox," in ibid., pp. 105–16; Yankelovich, *Changing Values on Campus*.

12. Yankelovich, *Changing Values on Campus*; and Kenneth Kenniston, "A Second Look at the Uncommitted," *Social Policy*, August 1971, pp. 7–19.

13. Translation of Radio Warsaw broadcast in *Atlas* (March 1971), p. 39; and "Ukraine Leader Urges Soviet to Get Rid of 'Khippis'," *New York Times*, June 30, 1971. For a review of the relevant data from the Soviet Union see Walter D. Connor, "Juvenile Delinquency in the USSR: Some Quantitative and Qualitative Indicators," *American Sociological Review*, Vol. 35, No. 2 (April 1970), pp. 294–95.

Today's diffuse counterculture phenomena can only be explained by the changes cutting deeply into the social structure of advanced industrial societies—changes to which affluent youth, especially those oriented toward the humanities, arts, and social sciences, are most sensitive but to which other classes are also reacting.

First and foremost is the dwarfing of the individual human being by the scale of institutions required to keep advanced industrial societies running. The physical and emotional separation of decision makers from the effects of their particular acts is dramatized most starkly in the computerization of mass-destruction warfare and in the lack of identifiable responsibility for the contamination of the environment. It is compounded by the sparse opportunities for meaningful personal contact even between members of the same institution outside of specialized subcompartments. Students in the huge multiversity, taught and counseled by closed-circuit television and identified by IBM card numbers, have been the first to react openly to the depersonalization of institutional relationships, but manifestations of this alienation are also growing within labor unions, government bureaucracies, and large commercial enterprises.

Second, economies of scale in advanced industrial society coupled with increased utilization of automation has changed the kinds of skills needed at the top rungs of the occupational ladder. Management of the dominant culture requires systems analysts, scientists, and technically oriented executives who can direct large-scale private and public organizations based more and more on high technology and electronic information and decision systems.

These central functional roles of advanced industrialism are filled increasingly from the "knowledge industry" of the universities. Many students in the humanities and more traditional social sciences, however, perceive that what they have to contribute is valued less and less by the dominant culture, and that their prospects for status and meaningful employment are bleak unless they get in harness with the technetronic age. For some of these students their postbourgeois values preclude their choosing to conform to the patterns of high achievement and self-discipline required to succeed in the scientific-rationalistic culture; they are consequently now inclined to oppose that culture, often by confrontation or dropping out.[14] University officials

14. Bell, "Notes on the Post-Industrial Society (I) and (II)"; Robert Liebert, *Radical and Militant Youth: A Psychoanalytical Inquiry* (Praeger,

report a general quieting of the campus scene since 1971, and there is evidence of more serious attitudes toward studies and career; but at the same time there is an unusually large proportion of bright high school seniors exhibiting counterculture life-styles who choose not to go on to college.

Third, in many postindustrial societies, authority—the capacity to influence others by virtue of their recognition of the authority's special command over knowledge, resources, or people—is disintegrating in numerous fields simultaneously.[15] The accelerating rate of scientific, technological, and socioeconomic change, extensively cataloged in a growing popular literature, is disrupting allegiance to traditional influences; and faith is waning that the traditional authority does indeed retain command of significant knowledge, resources, and groups of people. When doubts are exacerbated by evidence of moral culpability in high places, as revealed most dramatically by the Watergate episode in the United States, disrespect for all establishments tends to spread.

Concurrently, the impermanence of residence, job, friendships, and even familial obligations—the culture of mobility and transience—is destroying the cohesion of community structures through which authorities are given their legitimate power and by which they are held accountable to the general public interest.

The operators and guardians of the established structures of society are themselves transients and unsure of their ability to command respect by virtue of their social, professional, or political positions. The young, anxious to discover any weakness in authority, are bound to sense such confusion in their elders, their teachers, their bosses in the bureaucracy, and their commanding officers in the military, and take considerable delight in provoking a "crisis of legitimacy" wherever this can be done. Even the ad hoc structures of participatory democracy, formed to bypass regular governmental structures by creating local institutions responsive to grass-roots groups, frequently meet indifference or animosity from those who do not have the same primary community identifications.

Margaret Mead's thesis that all of this reflects the emergence of a

1971), p. 81; Edward Shils, "Plenitude and Scarcity: The Anatomy of International Cultural Crisis," *Encounter* (May 1969), pp. 37–57.

15. "The Gallup Poll: Confidence in Key Institutions Shaken," *Washington Post*, July 1, 1973.

"prefigurative culture"—one in which the children teach their parents what the future holds in store—need not be accepted completely to agree with her that

a profound disturbance is occurring in the relationships between the strong and the weak, the possessors and the dispossessed, elder and younger, and those who have knowledge and skill and those who lack them. The secure belief that those who knew had authority over those who did not has been shaken.[16]

To the extent that deauthorization of established institutions spreads throughout a society, it undermines the capability of the national government to speak for the people within its territorial jurisdiction or to commit the nation to major, particularly long-term, international undertakings. No democracy, certainly, could hope to mobilize its population to fight on behalf of others if close to half of its educated youth had no confidence in the judgments exercised by the nation's official leadership or in the legitimacy of their offices.

It is highly unlikely, however, that the affluent, antibourgeois counterculture will become the *dominant* culture in any major country in the foreseeable future, despite the prophecies of Charles Reich and others.[17] In an advanced industrial or postindustrial society a resourceful technocratic managerial class, loyal civil servants, and reliable skilled labor who will dependably report to work each day are critical to basic public health and security. A set of social mores that failed to recognize these functional needs could not survive as an official public ethos. Any sign that such a counterculture was gaining in ascendancy would probably bring on a conservative reaction, demanding reeducation of all citizens in their social responsibilities and insisting on enhanced rewards for middle-class virtues through changes in taxation and welfare programs. This kind of backlash against New Left romanti-

16. Margaret Mead, *Culture and Commitment: A Study of the Generation Gap* (Natural History Press, 1970); quotation from p. xvii.
17. Charles A. Reich, *The Greening of America* (Random House, 1970); Herbert A. Marcuse, *An Essay on Liberation* (Beacon, 1969); Jean-François Revel, *Without Marx or Jesus: The New American Revolution Has Begun* (Doubleday, 1971); Theodore Roszak, *The Making of a Counterculture* (Doubleday, Anchor Books, 1969); Jerry Rubin, *Do It! Scenarios of the Revolution* (Ballantine Books, 1970); Abbie Hoffman [Free], *Revolution for the Hell of It* (Pocket Books, 1970); and Abbie Hoffman, *Steal this Book* (Pirate Editions, 1971).

cism is already augured to some degree by the repressive attitudes of right-wing politicians in all the advanced Western countries.[18]

More likely than the extreme of either a full counterculture paralysis of society or a neofascist takeover is a growing preoccupation by most industrial countries with a major internal conflict of values among various social and professional classes. Stable authority structures and moral codes are bound to be increasingly difficult to sustain throughout a society in the decades ahead. Bases of community other than the nation-state will vie with one another for the affection and loyalty of intersecting populations. To the extent that this cultural pluralism exists in many countries simultaneously, transnational bonds between peoples who share the same values are likely to thicken as the authority of nation-state institutions weakens.

Ethnicity

Paradoxically, the nation-state system is being undermined from within by the concept of nationhood itself: In the seventeenth century this concept provided a foundation for legitimizing territorial jurisdictions in Europe. It was strengthened in the eighteenth and nineteenth centuries by the French revolutionary ideal that governments derive their just powers from the consent of the governed, and in the twentieth century Wilsonian concepts of self-determination expanded nationhood into a universal principle that all nations ought to have the right to their own states.

There is, however, no objective or permanent basis for categorizing the peoples of the world into nations. New subjective definitions of national community may gain prominence among some groups, making them intensely uncomfortable with an existing government premised on older definitions. Groups who feel themselves to be culturally unique by virtue of their particular set of ethnic traits—whether language, religion, physical characteristics, or other emanations of shared historical evolution—have chronically threatened international and domestic stability since medieval times. In the contemporary post-

18. See Seymour Martin Lipset, *Passion and Politics: Student Activism in America* (Little, Brown, 1971), pp. 249–63; and Inglehart, "The Silent Revolution in Europe."

colonial period it has been an acute problem for most of the new states, which have themselves gained independence under the banner of national self-determination.

Even so most social analysts and philosophers expected a decrease in the volatile formation of nations with the maturing of the modern highly industrialized state. Consolidation of the polity was thought to be a necessary condition for modern industrialization, which in turn would reinforce the homogenization of populations within the nation-state, as transportation and communication networks made for a rapid interchange of goods and ideas.

In the free-enterprise societies, it was supposed, the expanding economy and the desire for jobs in the technological sectors would encourage integration by stimulating internal migrations to the urban centers, demands from all segments of society for education in the new knowledge and skills, and attempts by ethnic subcultures to assimilate the general culture of the dominant society. In more authoritarian societies, where human and material resources can be commandeered, it was expected that the assimilation process would be accelerated by compulsory language and literacy programs and sometimes by the direct suppression of subcultural and religious institutions and mores that might interfere with complete loyalty to the central state. Once industrialization had proceeded beyond a certain point, however, cultural integration was supposed to proceed on its own momentum.

Neither of these variants of the assimilation process has worked out according to expectations. The increased mobility of men and messages has indeed given the technological centers of society greater potential attraction and control. But the same developments have enabled special cultural elites to mobilize sentiment and support in their own communities, especially when their communities feel discriminated against by the central state apparatus.

Relatively underprivileged ethnic groups become more receptive to the idea that they are indeed victims of unjust discrimination when they are daily exposed via the mass media to the apparent privileges of the majority. The fact that industrialization has raised the absolute level of goods and services available to all groups in the society does little to relieve this sense of injustice and often only exacerbates it. It is the perception of *relative* deprivation that is crucial to the mobilization of group jealousies; and the realization that, even in an economy of abundance, the room at the top is limited, and that competition for status and power increases the higher one climbs, engenders intense bitterness among cultural groups that are upwardly mobile. Often their bitterness is reflected in systematic discrimination against those on the status rungs just below.[19]

When grievances against the material and status privileges of others emanate from a group which is differentiated by a number of cultural factors—say, language, religion, and concentration in certain occupations; or physiological traits and geographic clustering—the situation is ripe for the ethnic group to be politicized and demand greater autonomy or even full independence.

The militant Catholic minority in Northern Ireland have used religion, their ghettoized distribution, economic class consciousness, and more than eight centuries of Celtic and Catholic grievances against Anglo-Scotch colonization and religious discrimination to mobilize the movement against the prevailing constitutional structure. The Protestants, 65 percent of the population, have had more than proportionate control over the area's wealth, schools, police forces, local government, and seats in the British Parliament. The Catholic minority in Northern Ireland view as most unjust the artificially gerrymandered political system which gives the Protestants this majority; if Northern Ireland were united with the independent Republic of Ireland to the south, the Catholics would be in the majority. From the point of view of the Protestants, however, the 1921 partition that left Protestant Ulster a province of Britain and gave the Catholics autonomous control of the twenty-six southern counties was a more than fair resolution of the otherwise interminable civil war.[20] Given the past six years of intercommunal violence over these issues, the British government's rather futile attempts to maintain civil peace with British troops, and the imposition of direct rule from London in 1972, the ultimate acquiescence of the British to the militant Catholic demands for separation from Britain and some sort of federation with the South seems at this writing to be the only way to avoid a continued rupturing of the political fabric of the United Kingdom. But even such an ultimate

19. For a trenchant analysis of the gap between actual ethnic conflict and recent theoretical scholarship on nationalism, see Walker Connor, "Nation-Building or Nation-Destroying?" *World Politics*, Vol. 24, No. 3 (April 1972), pp. 319–55.

20. J. C. Beckett, "Northern Ireland," *Journal of Contemporary History*, Vol. 6, No. 1 (1971), pp. 121–34.

"solution" would not eliminate the bitter communal strife, since it would transform Ulster's current Protestant majority into a disaffected minority within the larger Irish union.

The United States, the prototypical melting pot of diverse cultures, has been attempting to adapt its institutions to the discovery in the latter 1960s that a growing proportion of its 22 million Negroes did not want to be fully assimilated into American white society after all but preferred to be regarded as part of a worldwide black nation whose polar center was Africa. Recent opinion surveys show impressive percentages of blacks nationwide affirming the new signs of black and African cultural identity rather than deprecating them.[21] In 1970 nearly one-third of American blacks maintained that the community would "probably have to resort to violence" to gain their rights; and the percentage of adherents to this belief tended to rise among those with rising incomes and professional status as well as more contact with whites, and among younger segments of the community.[22] Although the blacks are too dispersed throughout the United States to make serious demands for statehood, de facto black city-states are beginning to result from the politicizing of the community and the fact that urban migration leaves blacks the dominant ethnic group in major central cities. They are dependent on the larger multinational American society for much of their security and welfare, yet often act as if they were involved in "international" negotiations vis-à-vis the larger society.

In Belgium a bitter polarization of society along cultural and linguistic lines periodically threatens to overwhelm other bases of political alignment which sustain the authority of the unified nation-state. The 5.5 million Dutch-speaking Flemings in the north want greater autonomy from the traditionally dominant 4 million French-speaking Walloons of the south. The animosity between the two groups comes to a head in the French enclaves within Flanders, which have been growing as the Walloons move north to escape the economic decline

21. A Harris poll of March 1970 revealed that 47 percent of all blacks in the United States viewed the growing interest in Swahili and other aspects of African culture as "important and a permanent sign of black identity and pride," and 84 percent felt this way about black studies in high schools. The Harris Survey, *Yearbook of Public Opinion 1970* (Louis Harris and Associates, 1971), p. 262.

22. Ibid., p. 252. Over 60 percent of all blacks agreed that "the system is rotten and has to be changed completely for blacks to be free" (p. 254).

in the coal-mining industries of the south. The Flemings have been demanding a restriction on bilingualism in education and other public institutions in an effort to make life intolerable for the French in the north.[23]

The French Catholics of Quebec are agitating for a separate nation since in religion, language, geography, and life-style they are distinctive from English-speaking Canadians, who dominate the country's political and economic structures. (Six million Canadians out of a total population of 21 million are French-speaking, and 5 million of these live in Quebec, whose total population is 6 million.) Economic modernization has only aggravated and spread the perception of relative deprivation. Urbanization and education may have made the French-Canadians less religious, but they have also become more nationalistic. As more French-Canadians have assumed the urban professional roles they have become more militant in their demands for increased occupational opportunities and are angrier than ever that two-thirds of the good business jobs in Montreal still are held by the city's English-speaking minority.[24]

The traditional resistance to assimilation by the linguistically and culturally distinct Basques has flared into a full-blown nationalist movement demanding that the four Spanish and three French Basque provinces be formed into a separate sovereign state. Modernization and increased literacy in the Basque areas have brought the middle classes into contact with the outside world and exposed them to the stimulating example of Irish, Flemish, Quebec, and other nationalist movements; it also has exposed the Basque cause to the world and provided a rallying point for anti-Franco Spaniards.[25]

The survival of Yugoslavia as a multinational state is jeopardized by the Croats and Slovenes agitating for national autonomy against the champions of a strong federal center led by Serbia. The richer northern regions, Croatia and Slovenia, are separatist, not wanting to

23. Derek W. Urwin, "Social Cleavages and Political Parties in Belgium: Problems of Institutionalization," *Political Studies*, Vol. 18, No. 3 (September 1970), pp. 320–40; Boris Kidel, "The Flemings and Walloons: Belgium's Nightmare," *Washington Post*, July 25, 1971.
24. Hugh Seton-Watson, "Unsatisfied Nationalisms," *Journal of Contemporary History*, Vol. 6, No. 1 (1971), pp. 11–12.
25. Stanley Payne, "Catalan and Basque Nationalism," *Journal of Contemporary History*, Vol. 6, No. 1 (1971), pp. 15–51.

share their wealth with their historic rival Serbia and the poorer regions to the south. Facing increasing paralysis of central decision-making institutions as a result of these bitter ethnic animosities, President Tito in 1971 devolved considerable authority over economic policies to the regions and provided for a "collective presidency" of regional representatives to run the country after his death. Renewed interethnic violence and economic troubles in 1972, however, prompted him to reconsider this move. The prospects are chancy that a post-Tito collective presidency would be able to function in such important areas as resource allocation and dispute resolution, in which case the breakup of Yugoslavia into autonomous republics would be a real possibility. Such disintegration probably would be accompanied by major interethnic conflict between and within the regions (none of which are completely homogeneous), with the attendant danger that other Eastern European countries and the Soviet Union would attempt to intervene in the struggles.[26]

Within the current Soviet sphere of influence in Eastern Europe, ethnic rivalries seethe beneath brittle political structures—a deep historic legacy of the area which communist state authoritarianism has been unable to dissipate. The greatest eruptive potentials, which the USSR is tempted to exploit to maintain its hegemonial control, are found in Czechoslovakia and Rumania. In Czechoslovakia Slovak animosities against the more modernized and urbanized Czechs have produced a succession of vitriolic Slovak independence movements since these two peoples were amalgamated, for the first time in history, by the peace settlement after World War I.[27] In Rumanian Transylvania the ethnically distinct Magyars are highly susceptible to appeals for national autonomy or irredentist demands that Transylvania be detached from Rumania and joined to Hungary.[28]

The Soviet Union is itself a conglomeration of about one hundred linguistically distinct ethnic groups, most of whom harbor historical

26. A comprehensive discussion of the current political meaning of the ethnic regional rivalries in Yuogslavia is provided by Paul Shoup, "The National Question in Yugoslavia," *Problems of Communism*, Vol. 21, No. 1 (January–February 1972), pp. 18–29.

27. H. Gordon Skilling, "Communism and Czechoslovak Traditions," *Journal of International Affairs*, Vol. 20, No. 1 (1966), pp. 118–36.

28. Paul Lendvai, "The Possibilities of Social Tensions and Upheavals in Eastern Europe and Their Possible Effects on European Security," *Europe and America in the 1970s: II: Society and Power*, Adelphi Paper No. 71 (London: Institute for Strategic Studies, November 1970).

grievances against domination by greater Russia. The USSR is therefore especially vulnerable to and anxious about the global recrudescence of ethnic nationalism. Lenin proclaimed the right to national self-determination, and in the 1920s the Soviet regime granted formal autonomy to the major national minorities, creating constituent republics. The Bolsheviks, of course, viewed self-determination as detrimental to socialism. Formal national autonomy was merely a characteristic Leninist stratagem of co-optation. In each case, in strict interpretation of Marxist-Leninist orthodoxy, the language, symbols, and folk art of the nationality were brought into the service of the communist party, which remained highly centralized and uniform through the USSR.

In reality the policy was one of russification and compulsory assimilation where the Marxist believes it counts: the socioeconomic infrastructure. The constitutional recognition of cultural differences, however, has allowed the regime to excuse uneven development of the various regions on the grounds that they are incompletely assimilated. This has always been a transparent formula to the non-Russians and has been a target of periodic discontent. Fanned by knowledge of events in the noncommunist world, ethnic ferment appears to be on the rise once again, not only among Jews who identify with Israel but also among the 40 million Ukrainians, the Latvians, the Lithuanians, the Estonians, the Soviet Moslem peoples, and the Crimean Tatars.[29]

The situations briefly described above are only a sampling of the politicizing of ethnicity that has become a worldwide challenge to the authority of existing nation-states. We need only mention the increasing militancy of the Palestinians for a state of their own; the unhappiness of South Tyrol with Italian rule; the agitation of the French-speaking population in Berne, Switzerland, for autonomy from the German-speaking population; the resentment of Bretons at being a part of France; the upsurge of Welsh and Scottish nationalism; or the emergence of a militant black power movement among the aborigines of Australia. The secessionist or irredentist movements in the Third World —most prominently the successful Bangladesh independence movement, the unsuccessful Biafran secession, the chronic Turko-Grecian conflict, and the potentially explosive Tamil Nad movement in South

29. Harry Schwartz, "Tensions in Brezhnev's Realm," *New York Times*, March 29, 1971; "The Ukraine Stirs," *The Economist*, Feb. 26, 1972. See also "Special Issue: Nationalities and Nationalism in the USSR," *Problems of Communism*, Vol. 16, No. 5 (September–October 1967); and Erich Goldhagen (ed.), *Ethnic Minorities in the Soviet Union* (Praeger, 1968).

India—are too numerous to catalog and in any case have not been unexpected. It is the worldwide scope of the rising ethnic militancy and its tendency to increase with modernization that is of concern here— especially in light of the fact that less than 10 percent of the some 135 contemporary states are essentially homogeneous ethnically.[30]

In almost every modern nation-state industrialization and economic development have visibly benefited some regions, ethnic groups, or classes more than others. In the early postwar period the promise of equalization—leveling up through universal education and leveling down through progressive taxation and other redistributive policies— was still fresh, and temporary inequalities could be accepted as part of the process of equalization itself. But with each passing year the failure to realize the promise results in greater impatience by the relatively disadvantaged, and it then becomes subjectively valid for them to see themselves as victims of systematic discrimination by the privileged groups. The situation thus ripens for indigenous regional, ethnic, or class leaders to step forward and demand power in addition to programs, and to promote the heady notion that things would be better if the distinctive group, even with more limited material resources, designed and operated its own sociopolitical system. In countries where the poorer ethnic elements are in the majority or are special beneficiaries of redistributional programs, the better-off ethnic groups can be aroused to agitate for their own autonomy.

Few of the would-be separate nations, however, are strong enough in numbers or command enough resources to carry through a full-blown secessionist revolution on their own. Consequently, although ethnic self-reliance is the ideal that holds them together, many militant vanguards are tempted to seek allies among other aggrieved groups at home or abroad that are severely alienated from the dominant culture, with separatist movements in other countries, or sometimes with foreign nation-states that also oppose the existing national government.

The Intersection of Countercultures

Cosmopolitanism, affluent alienation, and ethnicity, the three types of pressures against the existing nation-state structure of world poli-

30. Connor, "Nation-Building or Nation-Destroying?" p. 320.

tics discussed in this chapter, all emanate from different cores of grievances and have different sets of demands. The cosmopolitans are primarily interested in loosening the territorial jurisdictions which inhibit the processes of global integration. The alienated affluent, though largely of the same socioeconomic strata as the cosmopolitans (often the alienated are children of cosmopolitan parents), are first and foremost angry at the authority structures and large impersonal institutions that seem to them to inhibit their spontaneous enjoyments. The autonomy-demanding ethnic groups are mainly interested in running their own political and civic institutions, free from the interference of those who do not appreciate their cultural idiosyncrasies.

Thus there are many respects in which the three types of counterculture are antithetical to one another. The alienated youth oppose the rationalistic, technocratic aspects of cosmopolitanism; and they resist what they view as cosmopolitan efforts toward a global expansion of the dehumanized institutions that now pervade the modern social-service state. The ethnic liberation movements often clamor for *smaller* political sovereignties than now exist, and are wary that the multilateral, supranational authorities championed by some cosmopolitans may have even fewer lines of accountability to local culture. Most of the militant subnational groups hope to attain for their own people the very fruits of modernist civilization that the alienated affluent now deprecate; and in their own political organizations they often stress the same virtues that the youth counterculture considers obsolete: subordination of the individual to the solidarity of the group, hierarchy, and self-disciplined, gratification-delaying life-styles.

Yet there are important areas in which these diverse constituencies reinforce one another.

The cosmopolitans, by and large, tend to be very sympathetic to the grievances of alienated youth and the ethnic minorities. They often contribute financially to the dissident movements; and, through their representatives in the media and among intellectuals, they attempt to explain to less sympathetic groups in the population the reasons for the alienation of affluent youth and the anger of the disadvantaged. The cosmopolitans object only to the parochialism and romanticism of the typical youth and subnational movements, not to the depth of their grievances; and some cosmopolitan analyses and solutions seem to be showing real concessions to the dissident points of view. World-order activists in the advanced industrial countries have become concerned with the ecological consequences of technologically generated economic growth, and some of them are taking a fresh look at the antitechnocracy of the youth counterculture. And the emotional steam behind the demands for ethnic self-determination is causing those who shape global institutions to reexamine the concept of political community in some of their grand designs.

The more politically active portions of the affluent counterculture, in taking up the causes of the world's politically disenfranchised and materially deprived, disseminate the view of many cosmopolitans that wealth and power must be redistributed on a global basis and that the existing nation-state structure of the world is inadequate for this task. Moreover it is to these elements of the youth counterculture, who consider themselves a transnational community though linked more by common generational sentiment than by organization, that the cosmopolitans look for the source of future adult constituencies for constructive world community projects.

Although there are few tangible links in organization or program among the various ethnic liberation movements in different countries or between these movements and the affluent counterculture, all are obviously stimulated and inspired by one another's exploits. The simultaneous flare-up of insurrectionary movements in the late 1960s and early 1970s was more than coincidental. The leaders of the disparate groups were well aware of the techniques being used by their counterparts in other countries. The ease of rapid international travel had fashioned a "global city" not merely among the advanced sectors of the industrialized world. The Irish militant Bernadette Devlin was able to drum up support for her cause among disaffected university youth in Boston. Black Panther leaders could do the Havana-Algiers-Hanoi-Peking-Pyongyang grand tour. Satellite-relayed television brought the same fires, tear gas, and rifle reports into living rooms from Harlem to Tokyo. Finally, the repressive reactions of established regimes to the real or imagined conspiracy of antistate groups within or across existing territorial jurisdictions stimulated bonds among disparate movements which might otherwise have had little in common save their opposition to the powers that be.

Implications for the Established Political Order

The cultural crisis of the nation-state is regarded by the ruling parties of Eastern Europe and the USSR as a potential threat to their survival as much as is any aggression by Western countries. It is likely to reinforce the communists' reluctance to welcome the extension of Western networks of open communications into the East. But news of turbulent events in the West cannot be completely suppressed, and knowledge of such suppression is bound to undermine further the authority of these regimes with their peoples.

Third World governments are also wary of the dissemination of the anarchistic ideologies and dropout life-styles of the affluent radicals and the stimulating sights and sounds of the insurrectionary activities of deprived minorities in the developed nations. For a few years Fidel Castro provided some hospitality to black-power leaders, but shrill talk of racial self-determination was not particularly welcome in multiracial Cuba. The nihilistic behavior of American Black Panther exiles soon began to irritate the authoritarian Algerian regime, which had welcomed them in the late 1960s. And it is difficult to imagine the government of India facilitating a direct television broadcast of the demands of Quebec separatists directly into home or community receivers in linguistically chauvinistic Madras.

In the advanced Western democracies, where existing political systems have much greater capacity to absorb domestic dissent without collapsing, there is greater ambivalence among established elite groups concerning the proper response to movements whose express purpose is to undermine the nation-state. On the one hand, the majority of the middle-class population is still loyal to national institutions and symbols and willing to support repressive measures if government leaders claim they are needed to protect national security or even only public order and morality. On the other hand, the growing obsolescence of the nation-state is proclaimed by respected industrial, intellectual, and artistic leaders—most of whom also champion the values of cultural pluralism and local self-determination, limited only by larger community requirements of public health, safety, and distributive justice.

On the one side are loyalists to the traditional nation-state structures and supportive moralities, and on the other side is a loose coalition of those who feel the nation-state has become a straitjacket. This axis of polarization could well emerge as the most salient political division in world politics by the twenty-first century, both within countries and across existing national boundaries.

PART THREE

Prognosis and Prescription

CHAPTER TEN

The Transformation of World Politics

Part 1 described the tendencies associated with the fragmenting of the cold war coalitions—namely, the erosion of the geopolitical and ideological foundations of the cold war, the rise of new issues, and a diversification of international friendships and adversary relations. The system of international politics which appeared to be emerging featured multiple and crosscutting coalitions formed around a variety of issues, which eventually could develop into either a paranoid world of many nuclear-armed countries or a more benign system where power was based on the ability to cooperate in constructive projects.

Part 2 described processes below or above the interstate level that were complicating the problem of maintaining a viable world order—namely, the technological revolution which created physical communities irrespective of political borders; economic transnationalism, often too dynamic to be controlled by either separate nation-states or regional coalitions; and the growth of transnational and subnational social relationships and loyalties. The networks of nongovernmental relationships were most evident in the relatively open societies of the noncommunist industrialized world, with their fullest flowering in the so-called postindustrial areas: the United States and Northwestern Europe. But some transnational movements and corporate structures with a global scope of operations were seen as knocking at the doors of the more self-protective nation-states to the south and east.

If these two sets of trends continue, a major transformation of the international political order is bound to result.

The Evolving Polyarchy

The forces now ascendant appear to be leading toward a global society without a dominant structure of cooperation and conflict—a *polyarchy* in which nation-states, subnational groups, and transnational special interests and communities would all be vying for the support and loyalty of individuals, and conflicts would have to be resolved primarily on the basis of ad hoc bargaining in a shifting context of power relationships.

Such a system of world politics could evolve in either peaceful or dangerous directions. It could well be that, as important economic segments, technologists, scientists, and other professional elite get drawn more deeply into webs of transnational association, many of them would develop vested interests in the maintenance of nonhostile relations with their commercial or professional partners in various nations. They thus would not want to see specific clashes of interests inflated into national or multinational causes célèbres. Some of the transnational groups could be expected to mobilize resources across national jurisdictional lines to pressure domestic parliaments and bureaucracies against such an escalation of conflict.[1]

Modern history, of course, gives little ground for confidence that the emerging transnational relationships alone could *prevent* the exacerbation of international differences to levels of extreme hostility and open warfare. The primary adversaries in both world wars of the twentieth century were major trading partners before and between the wars. And transnational communities have at times agitated to make one government coerce another to secure the "human rights" of their brothers and sisters abroad. But if the interpenetration of societies now taking place were to proceed without severe nationalist backlashes, a transnational sector could eventually develop that was more organically a part of the constituent national socioeconomic systems than was possible under the traditional pattern of commercial interdependence. Such an interpenetration of societies could delay or dissuade resort to war-provoking actions by providing an alternative arena for conflict—

1. For an elaborate statement of the view that nongovernmental links across borders will reduce the chances of war see Robert Cooley Angell, *Peace on the March: Transnational Participation* (Van Nostrand Reinhold, 1969).

namely, a rich web of interaction for bargaining, registering grievances, and threatening sanctions *before* total nation-to-nation hostility develops. The art of diplomacy in such a system would require an understanding of the structure of this web and its interconnections with public authorities and special interest groups, and a knowledge of how to press upon its sensitive nodes to bring about desired community responses. Since there would be more pressure points, there would be less reason to jump from specific grievance to military threat. To wield effective power one would have to be well connected with the various transnational sectors.

In this polyarchic system, however, many of the power holders would be largely unaccountable to the wishes of the less developed, less mobile elements of a society. The upper transnational tier would probably comprise corporations and professionals in the high technology fields, and bargaining among these corporate elites would determine the social order. In some fields these elites may operate within an institutional setting that gives voice to the wishes of the "stockholders" or immediately affected populations. But with few, if any, multinational public structures to ensure general public-interest accountability, the public at large would lose the political power it has slowly acquired through national parliaments, and those corporate entities able to survive the transnational competition would largely run the show. Moreover there would be no effective institutional framework for settling disagreements among the corporate sectors, as in national parliaments, with intersectoral bargaining put in the hands of representatives of the general public.

In short the transnational power structures would lack legitimated authority coextensive with their scope of operation, and if opposed they might need to resort to coercion or else give up some of their power. Widespread discontent among disadvantaged groups would increase the prospects of active conflict, including physical combat, among would-be authorities, and contracts and other intergroup commitments would lack stability. Some individuals might be tempted to rely on small tribal or family protective societies for minimal physical and psychological security; some might accept the protection of the powerful corporate groups; others might try to form local leagues of mutual assistance. Polyarchy could turn into anarchy, where raw power is the only social arbiter.

There are, of course, too many diverse trends and countertrends at work in contemporary world politics for a consistent pattern of either cooperation or anarchy to evolve over the next few decades. The most plausible forecast would envision the continued emergence of an increasingly complex, polyarchic system, with persistent tension among the various bases of community:

1. There would be no division of the globe into dominant blocs, as with the ideological and geopolitical bipolarity of the cold war period, though ideology would remain a basis of coalition formation on certain issues, especially in the field of human rights. North-South tensions, though prominent and periodically taking the form of coercive confrontations, would not be sufficiently coherent to sustain polarized global alignments. Countries in the same trade or currency areas would be expected to concert their economic policies. Such coalitions, however, would be crosscut by other cooperative relationships based on technology-sharing or environmental management needs, and by conflicts of national interest between members of the trade or monetary zones.

2. Nation-states would remain the most powerful class of actors in world politics, but not all nation-states would be as powerful as the largest multinational corporations in terms of their ability to mobilize resources and affect the lives of people. Characteristically, those nation-states whose socioeconomic systems were most vulnerable to the actions of more powerful countries, multinational corporations, or other transnational forces would be the most rigid defenders of the principle of national sovereignty and unfettered domestic jurisdiction. Within their own societies they would exhibit the least tolerance for subnational or transnational political movements. The most determined strongholds of nation-statism would be found among the new nations of the Third World and the communist countries.

3. Transnational activity and cosmopolitan life-styles would be concentrated among the highly industrialized countries, since the patterns of behavior require developed transportation and communication networks, literacy in international languages, and personal incomes consistent with participation in the culture of mobility. Political tension between the affluent transnational strata and nationalist elements of society would also be greatest in the highly industrialized societies, where the transnationals could convincingly claim to be the modernizers. In less developed societies the modernizers usually would be nationalists as well, and the transnationals would have to tread lightly lest they be persecuted as neocolonialists.

4. Challenges from ethnic communities to the authority of nation-state institutions would be unevenly distributed and often express markedly different social phenomena. In some countries—especially in South Asia, Southeast Asia, and Africa—the revival of traditional identifications would mark the wane of unifying anticolonialist movements and the inability of regimes in power to substitute sufficiently compelling nation-building myths in the postcolonial period. In the command economies, particularly in Eastern Europe and the Soviet Union, subnationalist flare-ups would be primarily delayed reactions to enforced modernization and compulsory assimilation of ethnolinguistic communities. In the industrialized countries of Western Europe and North America the political mobilization of ethnic, linguistic, and religious communities would be expressions of rising discontent with the unequal distribution of life's amenities under pluralistic democracy.

Such a complex system of world politics, involving many crosscutting coalitions between and within countries and lacking a dominant worldwide axis of conflict, might appear to be much safer than either the cold war system organized around two hostile blocs or previous balance-of-power systems. Its very complexity and lack of coherence might appear to be the best guarantee of stability, since without salient focuses for systemwide polarization, local wars could not easily draw in all major powers. In this respect global society would begin to resemble the most developed domestic societies where elaborate patterns of interlinked individual and group interest restrain militants who would polarize the society.

But no functioning domestic society relies entirely on the factors of complexity and interlinked groups to sustain a peaceful and just order. Conflicts of interest arise which cannot be resolved simply by bargaining between powerful interests. Antisocial or criminal behavior is contained by communitywide rules which have some central application and enforcement. The use of violence to enforce community standards is considered legitimate only if performed by those vested with the authority to act for the entire community. Large projects serving broad public interests might not be constructed and maintained if left to individual or decentralized action, for they often require communitywide financing and management by officials responsible to the community at large.

As shown in Chapter 7, the impact of technology makes it imperative for nation-states to perform certain functions in cooperation with one another if elementary needs of security, health, and welfare are to be adequately tended, let alone considerations of social justice. War anywhere, even though few countries participated directly, could spread lethal substances to nonparticipants if some of the newest technological devices were employed. Nonrenewable resources could be depleted. Local assaults on shared ecosystems could spread to other nations, and some cumulative effects on the natural environment could endanger the healthy survival of the human species itself. Users of common or as yet unallocated resources—rivers, fisheries, sea lanes, air corridors, broadcasting frequencies, satellite orbits, the weather itself—cannot avoid getting in one another's way. Advanced industries capable of exploiting the ocean's mineral wealth, supposedly the "common heritage of mankind," are pressuring their governments to authorize unilateral exploitation to get the jump on competitors from other countries. And, finally, large segments of the human race, now exposed to the gap between their standard of living and that of the privileged minority, are growing increasingly bitter and capable of irrational destructive attacks on those better off.

Thus while the complexity of the emerging world political system and its lack of coherent political structures may preserve a stability of sorts by containing traditional conflicts below the level of major interstate violence, the lack of adequate mechanisms for transnational community action where required does not augur well for system stability over the long run. The projected complexity and lack of coherence rather portend a failure to adapt to changing human needs.

Regionalism as an Alternative

One potential response to the new requirements of world order would be the development of processes and institutions to reflect and promote the interdependence of nation-states within the same geographic portion of the globe. At its most modest, such structural innovation would merely facilitate interaction within particular regions through the removal of trade barriers and other inhibitions to the free circulation of goods, people, and ideas. At its most ambitious it would divide the world into eight to a dozen regional federations, each maintaining order and welfare within its realm. This continuum from intensified intraregional interaction to political union appears to constitute the most desirable and feasible path to world order in the minds of many statesmen and analysts who have become attracted to the regional concept. There is little consensus over the timing and details of the processes in various regions but a wide implicit agreement that the evolution of the world political system in this direction is historically necessary.[2]

Part of the difficulty with the regionalist approach is that there is neither a natural basis for deciding in which region some important countries fall nor a convincing subjective definition. This is not an academic question of defining terms but a political problem which affects the self-definition of various populations and the privileges and obligations governing their daily lives. Should the Turks expect to be considered a part of the European community or the Middle East? Is Mexico primarily North American, Central American, or Latin American? Is Australia part of Southeast Asia? Is Pakistan part of the same region as China, as India, or as Iran? Is Yugoslavia part of Western Europe, Eastern Europe, or another grouping defined as the Mediterranean region? Up to a point there may be no necessity to choose. Multiple memberships can of course coexist. But when membership involves a commitment to trade freely with and accept the investments of one's regional partners and to discriminate against the goods of nonmembers, the threshold separating innocent pluralism from primary obligation has been crossed.

There are stages in the integration process when a country's identification with one regional grouping at the expense of other relationships raises sharply the issue of which considerations have priority—historical-cultural ties, ideology, military security, or economics. Thus the British government's decision to enter the European Community (EC)

2. Diverse regional paths to world order have been championed by many personages of the contemporary period, including Jean Monnet, Walter Hallstein, George Ball, Amitai Etzioni, Zbigniew Brzezinski, Raúl Prebisch, Felipe Herrera, Franz Josef Strauss, Julius Nyerere, J. J. Servan-Schreiber, and Lord Gladwyn. Much of the enthusiasm for regionalism, prominent in Western policy circles and international relations scholarship during the 1960s, appears in retrospect to have derived from an infatuation with rather simplistic models of the integration process and from insufficient consideration of the global context of alignments and adversary relations. A refreshingly skeptical second look at this earlier enthusiasm for regionalism is found in Joseph S. Nye, *Peace in Parts: Integration and Conflict in Regional Organization* (Little, Brown, 1971). Much of the discussion in this section is informed by Nye's work.

was fraught with massive implications for both the international and the domestic politics of the United Kingdom. England's inability to avoid being pulled painfully in many directions is a compelling reason why it is likely to resist efforts to transform the limited, functionally specific European Community into a full-blown, multipurpose political union, though it can support common action short of federation. France's upper limit of integration into the Community is also rather low, determined in part by a romantic desire to cut a wide swath in global diplomacy, in part by its special relationships with the francophone states of Africa, and in part by the hope of making its own deals with Arab oil producers. West Germany's threshold of political integration into Western Europe is probably higher, but not so high as to foreclose its ultimate reunification with East Germany nor to undermine U.S. strategic guarantees. And of course neither Norway nor Denmark would want their membership in the Community to mean a substantial reduction in their ties to Sweden and Finland.

Ten years ago champions of regional integration tended to believe that those nations in Europe that had chosen (and been chosen) to participate in the Community would rather neatly harmonize their conflicting commitments. It was thought that each would subordinate extra-Community obligations in order to extend Community-wide consensus to fields beyond the narrow sector of economic agreements that brought them together in the first instance. A decade's experience has shown, however, that there is as much contrapuntal dissonance as harmony. One careful student of the intricacies of institution-building in Europe speculates:

There may well emerge several functionally specific international organizations, or less formal groupings, with overlapping memberships. Each grouping will act collaboratively in a policy or problem area delimited by the range of convergence of its members' interests. Hence the economic organization of Europe will differ from, but overlap, the military organization of Europe, and the political organization of Europe—which may be simple bilateral coordination—will overlap both the economic and military organization.[3]

Europe has many favorable preconditions for unity: Its states have been subordinated to a succession of imperialisms in common (Rome,

3. Donald J. Puchala, "The International Political Future of Europe," in William D. Coplin and Charles W. Kegley, Jr. (eds.), A Multi-method Introduction to International Politics (Markham, 1971), pp. 381–401; quotation from p. 387.

Napoleonic France, Hitler Germany, the threat of Soviet domination, and the actuality of a hegemonic American presence); they have experienced similar religious conflicts among two strains of Western Christianity and had to work out a pluralist religious modus vivendi between them under secular national roofs; all have highly mobile elite groups with frequent intermarriage; their economies were industrialized and their politics democratized within roughly the same one-hundred-year period, and they thus experienced similar class conflicts, at times organized by transnational political parties; all participated in a common balance-of-power system with highly ritualized rules of diplomatic interaction; they divested themselves of overseas colonies within the same fifteen-year period. Still and all the political integration of Western Europe, even to the point of having a common foreign and defense policy, remains highly problematical, although the EC has shown impressive unity in negotiating with the United States on economic issues.

The enlargement of the Community to include the United Kingdom and Scandinavia and to provide various kinds of associate memberships to former colonies in the Mediterranean, African, and Asian regions is already diluting the politico-cultural homogeneity of the original continental core and encouraging the intensification of cross-pressures such as those alluded to above. The most optimistic and realistic prognosis for the next two or three decades foresees a loose confederacy with minimal supranational functions, primarily for managing the compensatory internal subsidies that would need to accompany monetary union and a tight coordination of external trade policies. This prognosis would be modified only if some exciting new personalities arose to give fresh emotional embodiment to the idea of Europe or if the revival of a security threat from the East coupled with an American disengagement made political unity a practical imperative.

Elsewhere the preconditions for voluntary regional integration are less favorable and the cross-pressures often more intense.

In Eastern Europe all tendencies to define the region as separate from the USSR have been squelched. The Soviet coalition would have to loosen substantially before a regional unity movement in Eastern Europe would have the antisuperpower implications of the unity movement in Western Europe. Except for the bloc defectors, Yugoslavia and Albania, Rumania is the only country *openly* to reject the supranationalism of the Council for Mutual Economic Assistance (COMECON) as being little more than an arm lock of the Soviet empire (see Chapter 4, above), but other nations in the area are also not particularly enthusiastic about increased regional integration. Nationalism is still the major means for limiting superpower hegemony in Eastern Europe.[4]

Nor is there any basis for substantially integrating the Northeast Asian region, containing as it does the two rival Oriental superpowers, Japan and China, and a divided Korea. Compared with the period between 1949 and 1972, the present decade can be expected to show a major increase in interaction among the countries in the area, due to the lowering of barriers to economic intercourse, and perhaps even some multilateral projects. But there is no reason to expect this new interaction to generate pressures for a common market, let alone political integration.

Southeast Asia will resist absorption into a community with either of its powerful northern neighbors. The emerging relationship of the smaller Asian nations to China and Japan is analogous to the relationship of the nations of Europe to the Soviet Union and the United States—their natural inclination is to be independent of both giants. For the United States actively to sponsor Asian regional integration that would include Japan but not China could only incite China to exploit its local hegemony in order to prevent nations from joining, and the results would be resented by all the nations of Southeast Asia.

Even Southeast Asia itself provides a problematical base for significant regional integration. The area's principal intergovernmental organization, the Association of Southeast Asian Nations (ASEAN), is composed of all the important maritime states in the region (Indonesia, the Philippines, Malaysia, and Singapore) but only one of the six mainland countries (Thailand). Its progressive development into a common market, let alone a community integrated for political security, is premised on Thailand's continuing to put a higher priority on close association with the maritime states of the region than with its mainland neighbors. Merely to state this condition is to underline the fact that ASEAN, while a successor to the cold war alignment

---

4. Membership of the smaller countries in transideological regional organizations such as the Danube Commission or the Economic Commission of Europe (and eventually perhaps some all-European security commissions) also limits Soviet regional hegemony, as does participation in such global organizations as the United Nations, the General Agreement on Tariffs and Trade, and so forth.

system of the area (oriented around the Southeast Asia Treaty Organization), still constitutes too restrictive a base for community-building. For example, if there should be a development of the greater Mekong basin which includes the communist nations in the area, the amount of economic and cultural intercourse between Thailand and its maritime partners is unlikely to be reduced in absolute terms, but the primacy given to the ASEAN relationships is virtually certain to be reduced.

Many of the factors complicating the processes of regional integration in Southeast Asia are also evident in the other Third World areas —South Asia, the Middle East, Africa, and Latin America. Although these factors have unique manifestations in each region, they can be grouped as follows:

Reactions to intrusive superpowers. Alliances or special economic relationships of a superpower with particular countries or sets of countries within a region can easily polarize the region into adversary coalitions. When nationalist politicians perceive the virtues of nonalignment, however, the intrusion of a superpower can be a powerful spur to all-regional unity.

The existence of marginal countries. Some countries within each region, often those most advanced industrially, have major commercial and modernist-sector ties to countries in other regions. (See the discussion of such North-South relations in Chapter 5). Others have strong religious or ethnic ties to neighboring nations outside the region. These extraregional associations can be of equal or greater importance to these countries than their intraregional ties, and in such cases the cross-pressured countries will work against all but the most minimal integration of the region.

Subregional cultural or economic groupings. Religious and ethnic transnational communities within a region sometimes will form into tightly integrated subsystems. This can set the ball of integration rolling by stimulating other groups within the region to integrate, and, where there are good bases for cooperation among these subregional groups, the foundations for confederal institutions will be laid. But if the cultural cleavages are reinforced by economic rivalries within the region, the effects of subregional integration are likely to be just the opposite—tempting militants to escalate specific grievances to generalized intercommunity conflict, and producing intraregional polarization, even opposing military alliances.

Development gaps within regions. The poorer nations within a region are likely to resist regionwide economic integration unless they are given reasonable assurance that: (1) they are accorded guaranteed access to the other national markets in the region; (2) the goods they will be purchasing from within the region are not overpriced in comparison with what is available to them in the global market; (3) they would not suffer a net loss in export earnings by possible retaliation from extraregional customers; (4) they would be given a better opportunity to develop and diversify their own economies by concentrating their commerce within the region; and (5) intraregional adjustment assistance and other welfare-equalization measures would be available to compensate for dislocations and shortfalls attributable to intraregional disparities. The small likelihood that all of these conditions can be fulfilled leads to the conclusion that a rather low degree of integration is politically sustainable among neighboring nations of varied economic power.

Domestic political instabilities. The gap between the ruling elite and the masses in many of these countries, combined with the vulnerability of regimes in power to deposition by competing elite groups, on the one hand allows greater leeway for governments to enter into cooperative agreements with one another, but on the other hand makes for less confidence that a multilateral agreement negotiated today will be honored tomorrow by a successor regime. Consequently, while there may be a lot of surface multilateral activity in a region, few statesmen are likely to invest a great deal of their own prestige or their nation's resources in multilateral regional projects, whose functioning can be paralyzed by the noncompliance of one or more of the regional partners. In-country projects supported by UN agencies or developed industrial countries are likely to be better bets.

None of this is meant to disparage increased cooperation on a regional basis or its political institutionalization such as in the EC and even COMECON. Wherever the intermeshing of societies across nation-state lines occurs without coercion, it is likely that disputes between the involved nations will be inhibited from escalating to war and that the productive capacities of the whole area will be more effectively utilized. Moreover, attempts to keep and resolve intraregional disputes within the region can be beneficial to overall objectives of world order if they reduce incentives for superpower intervention and confrontation. Nor should a listing of the factors frustrating further integration be interpreted as a lack of recognition of the important efforts to foster regional approaches to common problems in the Central American Common Market, the Latin American Free Trade Association, the East African Federation, the Organization of African Unity, the Arab League, and the Association of Southeast Asian Nations.

The main point of this discussion is to put these efforts in perspective and scale down to realistic size the expectation that regional political integration is likely to be an adequate response to the global conflicts *and* agreements that are developing in the last quarter of the twentieth century.

Constructing a Political Framework for World Community

If the attempt to build political community on the basis of geographically defined regions is a helpful but largely inadequate response to twentieth-century requirements for collaboration and conflict resolution, where does this leave us? There is still a large gap between the de jure fragmentation of the globe and the de facto communities of mutual vulnerability and potential cooperation created by the contemporary scientific and technological revolutions. Some of the de facto communities are regional, such as the countries bordering the Arctic; some are transregional but subglobal, such as the populations dependent upon imported sources of energy; but the physical interdependence of intersecting communities can only be adequately perceived as a global pattern.

The global perspective is becoming available to more people as a result of developments in the fields of transportation, communications, and information processing. Through pictures transmitted from earth-orbiting satellites the layman can easily comprehend some of the complicated ecological interdependencies that were accessible previously only to rare imaginations. The average citizen is now exposed through popular books and other media to the consequences of his local community's or country's actions upon others, and vice versa. The Club of Rome's 1972 publication, *The Limits to Growth*, whatever its methodological shortcomings, was indisputably a harbinger of this coming level of discourse. The realities of increasing interdependence were brought home to many people around the globe in the winter of 1973–74 by the shortfall in normal fuel supplies. The critical question is whether man can take the necessary steps toward consciousness of and commitment to world community to bring his political arrangements into line with his new perspective on the nature of his physical habitat.

Some Preliminary Scaffolding

The wide gap between the physical fact of global community and its political realization is being spanned in a few fields, but the planks are as yet very sparsely laid and very thin.

In the peace and security field the most important political innovation thus far is contained in the Nuclear Nonproliferation Treaty (NPT) of 1968. With respect to the structure of world politics the NPT is perhaps of greater significance than the bilateral agreements between the United States and the Soviet Union in the strategic arms limitation talks (SALT), which can only codify and reinforce the military dimensions of the superpower standoff. The NPT is the renewal of an attempt (started in 1946 and dropped with the failure of the Baruch Plan) to adapt the world political system to meet the threat of thermonuclear weapons.

The greatest departures from the traditional principles of the nation-state system are found in the treaty's so-called safeguard provisions, designed to ensure that nuclear facilities in the nonweapons countries are not converted to weapons purposes. The significance of these provisions will become of greater moment during the next few decades as nuclear energy becomes more widely used for industrial power. Articles III, IV, and V of the NPT provide for a supranational inspectorate, recruited by and responsible to the International Atomic Energy Agency, to intrude beyond the traditional confines of national jurisdiction.[5] Guidelines approved by IAEA members in 1971 would station inspectors permanently at important nuclear facilities of nonweapons countries, with the right to make spot checks of the nuclear materials entering and leaving each stage of the production process.

The negotiation of the nuclear safeguard procedures with individual nations continues to be a long and arduous process, and in some cases is being hedged with so many qualifications that what amounts to national self-inspection is disguised in an international mantle. But it is of major significance that both the Soviet Union and the United States

5. United States Arms Control and Disarmament Agency, *Documents on Disarmament 1968* (Government Printing Office, 1969), pp. 461–65.

have agreed that world security from the spread of nuclear weapons requires an impartial international inspectorate with real power to intrude into the domestic affairs of nations.[6]

Other nations are not entirely happy with the oligopolistic assumptions perpetuated in the NPT, especially its safeguard provisions; but most of them, often under considerable prodding by the superpowers, have accepted the self-denying ordinances and supranational intrusions as a necessary means of preventing their rivals from building nuclear weapons. The United States and the Soviet Union still seem some way off, however, from subordinating themselves to supranational control for whatever mutual strategic arms limitations they might negotiate.

Meanwhile with the disintegration of cold war coalitions it is feared that some smaller nations, previously restrained by superpower ties, might now be inclined to escalate their conflicts with one another and, as in the Middle East, sorely tempt superpower interventions and counterinterventions. Consequently there is new interest in a beefed-up UN peacekeeping system. Building on the partially successful, partially frustrating experience with UN forces in the Middle East, Cyprus, and the Congo, a prominent panel of experts assembled by the United Nations Association in 1969 recommended "a major initiative by the United States . . . to reach an understanding with the Soviet Union and other key members of the Security Council on the principles that would underlie the development and use of greatly strengthened United Nations forces."[7]

Similarly, in 1971 President Nixon's Commission for the Observance of the Twenty-fifth Anniversary of the United Nations, under the chairmanship of Henry Cabot Lodge, recommended "drastic steps by the

6. For details and difficulties in connection with the NPT safeguards system see Mason Willrich, *Global Politics of Nuclear Energy* (Praeger, 1971), especially pp. 85–96.

7. UNA-USA National Policy Panel on Multilateral Alternatives to Unilateral Intervention, *Controlling Conflict in the 1970s* (United Nations Association, April 1969), p. 40. The twenty-six-member panel was chaired by Kingman Brewster, Jr. (president of Yale University), and included Harding F. Bancroft (executive vice-president of the *New York Times*), Najeeb Halaby (president of Pan American World Airways), General Matthew B. Ridgeway, Cyrus R. Vance (former deputy secretary of defense), Jerome B. Wiesner (provost of M.I.T.), and Charles W. Yost (who became the U.S. ambassador to the United Nations before the final report was drafted).

world community, especially by the great powers . . . to revitalize the peacekeeping and peacemaking capabilities of the U.N." As the American people became reluctant to countenance any direct U.S. involvement in overseas conflicts, the commission advised the President that "multilateral substitutes to defuse dangerous situations and keep local conflicts from escalating to wider war become an urgent necessity rather than a luxury." Specifically the commission recommended that the United States pledge air and sealift facilities for immediate transport of UN peace troops, the latter to be drawn from a "Peace Reserve" of 25,000 trained troops earmarked by countries in various parts of the world.[8]

Prior to the Arab-Israeli war of 1973, however, the actual institution of standby UN peacekeeping forces of substantial strength was regarded as politically infeasible by most students of the problem and also by diplomats with experience in past UN peacekeeping efforts. The emerging international consensus on the dangers of big-power involvement in local conflicts was far from a consensus on rules governing the future involvement of the United Nations and the capabilities to be placed at its disposal.[9] But it turned out to be fortunate in October 1973 that the United Nations already had experience at putting together truce supervision forces and that units in Cyprus were ready for instantaneous dispatch to the Suez area and could become the embryo for larger truce supervision units. Man learns slowly.

In the international monetary and trade fields a growing number of economists, public officials, and concerned citizens are searching for stronger international and possibly supranational measures to avoid the prospect of anarchy and economic warfare. In the wake of the 1971 international payments and currency crisis, the food shortages of 1972–73, and the embargoes and cartel-imposed oil price rises of 1973–74, more substantial alterations of the international economic order are being contemplated than is usual among non-Marxist economists. Reforms now under serious international consideration include: a stronger role by the International Monetary Fund (IMF) in setting the size of international reserves and allocating them to member nations; clarifica-

8. *Report of the President's Commission for the Observance of the Twenty-fifth Anniversary of the United Nations* (Government Printing Office, 1971), pp. 4–7.

9. Larry L. Fabian, *Soldiers without Enemies: Preparing the United Nations for Peacekeeping* (Brookings Institution, 1971).

tion of international ground rules outlining permissible and impermissible national policies to restrict free international trade and enabling nations to call each other to account before international bodies, such as the negotiating forums of the General Agreement on Tariffs and Trade (GATT); and a world food bank that would build up reserves in times of surplus and allocate them in times of scarcity.[10]

Gradually more economists are coming around to the view expressed by Richard Cooper that

the model regime which we implicitly use at present—autonomous and purposeful nation-states in harmonious and unrestricted economic intercourse, through the competitive market place . . . governed by occasional treaties and conventions to assure good conduct and to iron out modest problems of overlapping jurisdiction, leaving virtually all economic decisions to national governments—is simply not viable in the long run.[11]

Yet Cooper and his fellow economists are virtually unanimous in regarding the world as *politically* unready for the supranational institutions needed to share in the performance of functions now primarily under the authority of the nation-state—namely, economic stabilization, taxation to provide public goods and services, regulatory policies concerning business and unions, and redistributional policies.[12] Even the industrialized nations, as Miriam Camps points out, "are not yet ready—intellectually, psychologically, bureaucratically—for the radical course of much more integration of their economies, much more coordination of policy, and much more collective management."[13]

Such international economic management is difficult to achieve even among countries with similar social and political systems. The difficulties are compounded now that the communist countries, in their effort to participate more fully in the global economy, are pressuring institutions like GATT, the IMF, and the World Bank to alter some of their rules so as to make it easier for the communists to join. Given the persistence of cold war legacies, increasing the membership of international

10. See *Reshaping the International Economic Order* (Brookings Institution, 1972); and James P. Grant, "A World Food Bank?" *Washington Post*, Aug. 16, 1973.

11. Richard N. Cooper, "Economic Interdependence and Foreign Policy in the Seventies," *World Politics*, Vol. 24, No. 2 (January 1972), pp. 159–81; quotation from p. 175.

12. Ibid., p. 174.

13. "Sources of Strain in Transatlantic Relations," *International Affairs*, Vol. 48, No. 4 (October 1972), p. 572.

institutions in the direction of universality is clearly at odds with the aim of strengthening their ability to penetrate the crust of national economic sovereignty.

Pressures are also rising to give the existing network of international institutions a larger role in economic development programs. A shift from a predominantly bilateral to a largely multilateral mode has been vigorously urged by champions of development assistance;[14] but the consensus forming in the United States around the multilateral approach in the late 1960s and early 1970s, as shown in Chapter 5, was more a product of disillusionment with Third World foreign entanglements than a sign of growing international sentiment.

If the World Bank and its sister agencies assume a greater role in the transfer of development resources to the poor countries while the rich countries fail to increase their contributions to these agencies, then the international institutions would be serving primarily as lightning rods to deflect the hostility of the Third World away from particular rich countries. Many developing countries in the United Nations Conference on Trade and Development (UNCTAD) Group of Seventy-seven, therefore, are not at all sanguine about the assumed benefits of multilateralism. Even so, the developing countries have no desire to revive the demeaning relationships of benefactor and client characteristic of the cold war, and generally favor the decline of bilateralism and a shift to international forums where they have more control and where coalitions can be formed more easily on North-South issues.

Multilateralism has made the most impressive—though still marginal—progress recently in oceans management and pollution control. The Law of the Sea Conference scheduled to convene in 1974 was mandated by near unanimous United Nations resolutions to assure that: (1) beyond established national jurisdictions the oceans and seabed resources are the "common heritage of mankind"; (2) any exploitation within the still unallocated areas should be for the "benefit of mankind"; (3) exploitation within the common heritage area should be only in accordance with procedures of an "international regime" to be set up. But on the eve of the conference the prospects appeared dim that

14. For example, Lester B. Pearson, *Partners in Development: Report of the Commission on International Development* (Praeger, 1969); see also Robert E. Asher, *Development Assistance in the Seventies: Alternatives for the United States* (Brookings Institution, 1970).

the policies and institutions produced would be comprehensive enough to deal with the complex and interrelated problems of the ocean.[15]

In the early 1970s in response to the growing recognition of transnational ecological interdependencies there was an earnest effort to develop reliable procedures to ensure that those responsible for each other's welfare *in fact* are responsible *in law*. The United Nations Conference on the Human Environment which convened at Stockholm in June 1972 did much to stimulate awareness. It hatched no treaties, but it did produce declarations of deep concern, a menu of subjects for subsequent negotiations, and a recommendation—subsequently implemented by the UN General Assembly—for a permanent world environment agency. The new agency, a 58-nation Council for Environmental Programs, came into being in 1973 with modest funds and a mandate to study, monitor, and report on threats to the environment of broad international significance. It would also have some authority to initiate its own environmental programs and to finance and review those of specialized UN agencies such as the Food and Agriculture Organization, the International Maritime Consultative Organization, the World Meteorological Organization, and the International Atomic Energy Agency.[16]

The grant of authority to the UN environmental agency was hardly supranational, and its ability to act significantly as a catalyst and coordinator of multilateral action would depend to a great extent on two factors: the cooperation it would receive from the specialized agencies, traditionally very jealous of any encroachment on their niches; and the bargains that would be struck between the affluent industrial countries and the poor industrializing ones, perhaps in the form of compensatory financing or subsidized technical assistance, to

15. See Seyom Brown and Larry L. Fabian, "Diplomats at Sea," *Foreign Affairs*, Vol. 52, No. 2 (January 1974), pp. 301–21 (Brookings Reprint 282). See also Evan Luard, "Who Gets What on the Seabed?" *Foreign Policy*, No. 9 (Winter 1972–73), pp. 132–47; Terese Sulikowski, "The International Seabed: Prospects and Proposals," *SAIS Review*, Vol. 17, No. 1 (Fall 1972), pp. 12–19.

16. Maurice Strong, "One Year after Stockholm: An Ecological Approach to Management," *Foreign Affairs*, Vol. 51, No. 4 (July 1973), pp. 690–707; "World Environment Newsletter," *World* (Aug. 1, 1972), pp. 37–40; John Tinker, "Stockholm: Success or Failure?" *New Scientist*, Vol. 54, No. 802 (June 29, 1972), pp. 754–55.

induce the latter to accept environmental constraints on their own programs for economic growth.[17]

Desiderata for More Effective World Community Institutions

The preceding section pointed to a few signs of international political responsiveness to the ever-increasing physical connections between the peoples of the world, but these responses thus far lack coherence in concept and in structure. The existing pattern of functionally specific international institutions fails to come to grips with both the growing vertical interdependence of various sectors of activity and the expanding horizontal interdependence of geographically separate communities. A viable response to the underlying secular trends and emerging world community needs would seem to require leading statesmen to make stronger commitments and give higher priority to policies that would implement the following desiderata:

Multilateral capabilities for resolving disputes should be enhanced. Treaties and declarations renouncing the resort to force may be useful evidence of aspiration for self-control, but they fail to provide the structural reform essential to the reliance on peaceful means in a world where conflict itself has not been eradicated. There is no avoiding the need to legitimate and substantially expand the powers of multicountry institutions—some functionally specific, some regional, some global—for dispute resolution and resource allocation. States that anticipate they will be serious antagonists in particular fields will need to agree in advance to rely on third parties, international organizations, and supranational mechanisms to mediate, arbitrate, adjudicate, or otherwise provide a basis for the resolution of conflict before the resort to military or economic coercion. In the same vein, major international forums and organizations should include in their membership those who are antagonists on issues in which the institution has competence.

International activities and projects with highly interdependent effects should be brought under common institutional roofs (for example, licensing exploitation of oil and seabeds and ecosystem management). Relatively specialized bodies could still perform certain functions, but they should be accountable to general policy directives and

17. Nigel Hawks, "Stockholm: Politicking, Confusion, but Some Agreements Reached," *Science*, Vol. 176, No. 4041 (June 23, 1972), pp. 1308–10; "Specialized Agencies Jockey for Position," *World* (Oct. 24, 1972), p. 44.

guidelines set by umbrella institutions. Where interdependent effects are direct and substantial, the specialized agencies might be made more accountable to the affected public interests if their budgets were subject to review and final approval by the supervisory bodies.

Populations substantially affected by the actions of others should be participants in the decision processes that authorize those actions. In negative terms this means that international actions, whether by non-governmental groups, national governments, or regional and international institutions, are illegitimate to the extent that they lack the consent of those affected by them. This desideratum, of course, begs the following questions: How is the relevant unit of population defined for purposes of the international decision structures in the various fields of action? (Is the relevant population a nation-state, a nation without a state, a subnational or transnational community, an industry or labor association?) On what basis are populations to be represented in the decision-making forums? (Are democratic principles of selecting representatives to be insisted upon, or should each population group be permitted its own system of selection?) Which populations are indeed likely to be "substantially affected" and therefore legitimate consent groups in particular fields of activity? (Are all consumers of fish, for example, or just the fishing states to be represented in the bodies that regulate fisheries?) The fact that these questions are highly complex and that the answers cannot be derived directly from first principles in political or legal philosophy is no argument against giving weight to the desideratum. It only means that these perennial questions of political order and justice need to be raised freshly in the context of today's trends, and faced explicitly in redesigning world community institutions.

Criteria of distributive justice, analogous to those prevailing in developed domestic societies, should be applied internationally when allocating burdens and benefits. The objective should be to erode the distinctions between equity standards that are supposed to govern allocation decisions within national communities and those that prevail between countries. It is part and parcel of the difficult process of extending man's definition of his moral community from the nation to all inhabitants of the globe. This is probably the most controversial of the desiderata, especially since it might be interpreted as legitimizing the global redistribution of existing assets, thereby requiring relatively well-off societies to accept a worse condition for themselves. In addition, some economists would argue that redistribution of assets would be a highly inefficient means of improving the lot of the disadvantaged in that it would reduce productive capacity worldwide. Perhaps a prudent compromise would be to attempt to institute on the world scene a standard akin to the "Difference Principle" formulated by the philosopher John Rawls—namely, that community-imposed inequalities, especially in new projects, are to be regarded as illegitimate unless it can be convincingly demonstrated that the inequalities benefit everyone, in particular the least privileged populations.[18] (Opportunities to apply such a principle internationally are likely to be plentiful over the next few decades in ocean management and ecology control.)

Suppose much of the world's international and transnational activity were indeed to become subject to review and "steering" by multifunctional institutions of virtually universal membership, structured and mandated to apply distributive justice criteria.[19] Would this not degrade the efficiency of those institutions, more restricted in mandate and sometimes in membership, which still perform needed international functions?

This is precisely the issue that, more and more, the world's most powerful actors will need to face. In many areas of world politics unavoidable trade-offs will have to be made between functional efficiency and broad political acceptability, between effectiveness in accomplishing current technical tasks with the least material sacrifice and effectiveness in the long-term building of world community structures.

One central conclusion of this book's analysis is that, given the disintegration of the cold war structures, a substantial expansion and strengthening of world community structures is required for man to make an adaptive evolutionary response to his newly developed powers for altering nature. Where choices have to be made between narrow-gauged task efficiency and the broader objectives of world order,

18. John Rawls, A Theory of Justice (Harvard University Press, 1971), pp. 75–83.

19. I borrow from Miriam Camps in using the notion of "steering" to describe the role of world community institutions. Steering suggests governance rather than government by the world institutions, which after all will remain less powerful (that is, less able to command resources and apply sanctions) than many of their constituent members. Steering connotes setting guidelines and mobilizing political pressures—sometimes through an international secretariat which can provide member nations with technical and not unattractive options for negotiating their differences—as contrasted with the kinds of authoritative command decisions made by national governments.

the latter often will need to be given more priority than has been the case heretofore. As the world becomes in fact a global city, as a result of the increased physical interdependence of nations, an accountability in law to the peoples of the global city becomes a precondition for voluntary compliance with international programs, and therefore ultimately for the effectiveness of such programs as well. Although those who already understand a problem may easily reach agreement and get a multilateral program going (especially in some of the new technology fields), bypassing those whose future cooperation will be important may well prove to be efficiency-wise but effectiveness-foolish.

Another central conclusion is that a decisive shift in basic sociopolitical attitudes toward community—who is responsible for whom, who is accountable to whom—is required for any move toward pooling national sovereignty in global institutions. The new transnational and subnational forces which make for a confusion of attachments and loyalties may expedite this shift in attitudes and present statesmen with opportunities for forging a new constituency, one willing to support institutional innovations of the kind called for by the desiderata outlined above.

Perhaps the foundations of a new American statesmanship should be laid here, in the conjunction of rising needs for institutional innovation to meet new tasks of world order and the waning legitimacy of cold war and traditional structures of political authority. How the United States can make the most of these opportunities is the subject of the final chapter.

CHAPTER ELEVEN

Policy Opportunities for the United States

The main trends analyzed in this book point to the conclusion that if the major world actors merely drift on the rising but often contradictory currents loosed by the breakup of the cold war coalitions and the weakening of national authority structures, the chances are high that a dangerously incoherent pattern would evolve over the next few decades. One could even envision a semifeudal world of societies huddled insecurely under the protective umbrella of local potentates, many of whom would have little authority save that extorted through their control over nuclear or other mass-destruction capabilities. It would be a Hobbesian world of "the war of each against all," compounded by the maddening realization that many local groups had in their hands the wherewithal to start a general conflagration.

Of course there are good grounds for hoping that the drift toward such an anarchic world would be arrested by prudent statesmanship and arrested early enough to avoid the drastic Hobbesian alternative of a global Leviathan: a centralized authoritarian system of law and order imposed on the world by those with coercive power sufficient to overwhelm all opponents. It takes little imagination to recognize that any attempt to impose such a system probably could not be undertaken without provoking a world war. But the farther the drift toward incoherence and anarchy, the dimmer are the prospects for a peaceful transformation of world politics into a just and uncoercive system of world order.

208

Constructive Statesmanship for the Last Quarter of the Twentieth Century

What then is required to promote the world's political development in the more constructive directions outlined in Chapter 10: toward cooperative interdependence at the interstate level and toward responsive and representative political community structures at the transnational and global level?

First of all, a special responsibility falls on the existing nuclear-armed countries, particularly the two superpowers, to refrain from invoking their military superiority, even implicitly, in order to gain compliance with their demands. If such self-restraint is not exercised other countries—most prominently Japan, but also India, Brazil, and others—will be compelled to conclude that an essential factor in one's bargaining position is status as a nuclear-armed country.

Second, the largest, strongest, and wealthiest countries should refrain from attempting to maintain or establish spheres of dominance or even permanent extended alliance systems. Such hegemonial relationships are inherently unstable since they cut against the drive for greater autonomy on the part of smaller nations, tempting them to seek partnerships with extraregional superpowers in order to retain bargaining leverage against the dominant regional country. Moreover there are certain to be overlapping, and thus contested, areas in the would-be spheres—dangerous enough in the bipolar system, the danger would be compounded in a multipolar system.

Third, the leading economic and technological countries should allow substantial lines of interdependence between countries within and those outside of their own geographic regions. They also need actively to encourage the elaboration of multiple and intersecting webs of interdependence between countries formerly in rival ideological blocs and between historically rival nations. The objective should be to create on the world scene the dense interlinking and crosscutting of communities that prevents extreme polarization and civil war within the more stable domestic societies. This interpenetration of societies also needs to be encouraged among subnational and transnational communities as well as among multistate blocs and nation-states.

Fourth, it is imperative to counter the growing alienation between the more affluent, mobile elements of world society and those whose relative poverty and vulnerability to competition make them despair of cooperation with those who could help them. A global system of open access and interdependence would have to be regulated by institutions and policies designed to redress this felt asymmetry. If political borders between countries become significantly more porous, those weaker elements of society who now are protected (however imperfectly) by national social welfare policies and progressive taxation systems might indeed be effectively disenfranchised. To protect and reassure the weaker elements the world's political economy would have to be structured to implement equity and social justice in the global market in ways analogous to those within the advanced democracies—with special subsidies and credits to the disadvantaged and multinational regulation of multinational firms.

Finally, to prevent the misuse of the world's common resources, resolve conflicts over them, and circumvent a new stage of dangerously competitive empire-building in newly exploitable environments—the oceans and outer space—new sets of representative institutions need to be elaborated and empowered on regional and global bases. The structure of these institutions should give all the communities affected a fair say over how the common goods of mankind are used.

The Role of the United States

The requirements of constructive statesmanship for the last quarter of the twentieth century again point up the incongruence between the political behavior of man—whose characteristic initial response is to the demands of constituencies and power structures close at hand—and the increasing physical and economic interdependence of various communities. Only occasionally have the demands of national constituencies and the requirements of national power allowed political leaders to embrace larger objectives of world order and justice as part of the national interest. Outstanding examples are Great Britain's practice of enlightened self-interest at various periods in its history and the role of the United States in the formation of the United Nations and the Bretton Woods system and in the reconstruction of postwar Europe and Japan.

Does the post–cold war pattern of world politics now emerging permit the United States to pursue its interests in a new context and respond freshly to world community needs? This is the central question raised here. If the ingredients of national power are indeed changing in the ways indicated in Chapter 6,[1] and if countries with the most influence are likely to be those which are active in the widest range of coalitions and partnerships, then the power-maximizing statesman should want to help in the depolarization and demilitarization of international politics. At the same time he should seek out opportunities for strengthening and participating in world institutions for allocating resources and resolving disputes.

To be sure, there are reasons to doubt that the American electorate will support this kind of statesmanship, particularly if it means sharing resources with others. New domestic instabilities and economic problems associated with postindustrialism have risen concurrently with the apparent obsolescence of the cold war; the newspapers report former allies turning against the United States and show this country's government and corporations to be highly unpopular in the Third World. In the wake of the tragedy in Vietnam even those segments of the policy community and the public which had been most internationalist were disposed to question whether the United States has the surplus wealth or wisdom to tend to the well-being of the world—unilaterally or multilaterally. In early 1973 public opinion analysts William Watts and Lloyd A. Free reported a decline in American internationalism since the beginning of the Johnson presidency. Whereas in 1964 the statement that "the U.S. should mind its own business and let other countries get along as best they can" was opposed by 70 percent of a representative sample of Americans eighteen years of age and older, in 1972 only 56 percent opposed this statement. Similarly, those who agreed with the statement that "we shouldn't think so much in international terms but concentrate more on national problems here at home" rose from 55 percent to 73 percent over the same period.[2]

But perhaps the most significant feature of American opinion in the early 1970s was the degree to which it continued to be internationalist, despite all the frustrations the country had suffered in its foreign rela-

1. See also Seyom Brown, "The Changing Essence of Power," *Foreign Affairs*, Vol. 51, No. 2 (January 1973), pp. 286–99.
2. William Watts and Lloyd A. Free (eds.), *State of the Nation* (Universe Books for Potomac Associates, 1973), pp. 203–04. See also Albert H. Cantril and Charles W. Roll, Jr., *Hopes and Fears of the American People* (Universe Books, for Potomac Associates, 1971).

tions in recent years. The 1972 polls registered 63 percent agreeing with the proposition that "the United States should cooperate fully with the United Nations" (down only nine percentage points since 1964)—this in the face of begrudging administration and congressional support for the organization and a reduction in the U.S. contribution to its budget. Analyzing the responses to a variety of opinion polls on foreign aid, "going it alone," and the like, Watts and Free found that more than half the American people remained predominantly internationalist in their attitudes toward the role of the United States, about 10 percent were predominantly isolationist, and about a third had very mixed attitudes. Compared with 1964 there were fewer in the predominantly internationalist category, and more in the mixed category, but there had been no discernible growth in outright isolationism.[3]

Recent surveys of American opinion also show a surprising survival of altruism and generosity toward the less fortunate countries. The Overseas Development Council found in 1972 that, contrary to the impressions voiced by timorous public officials, "public support for the idea of giving U.S. assistance to underdeveloped countries is at an historic high of 68 per cent . . . and . . . appears to be quite independent of attitudes about the Vietnam war."[4]

This phenomenon of persisting internationalism and altruism cannot be adequately explained without reference to the deep strain of idealism in the American political character which continually seeks universal expression. The country sees itself at its best as a place where people of all cultures, religions, and nationalities share domicile and power—a model, perhaps, for fashioning the polity of the globe. And in the twentieth century at least the country also views itself as a catalytic participant in the construction of a just and noncoercive world order—the popularity of Henry Kissinger's peacemaking role in the Middle East being the most recent case in point. Wise foreign and domestic observers, from Tocqueville on, have noted that when this part of the American identity is suppressed, when the country turns inward to become totally preoccupied with its own maladies, it loses an essential part of its purpose. Apparently the majority of Americans continue to hold similar views about the broader world role of the United States.

3. Watts and Free, *State of the Nation*, pp. 199–204.
4. Paul A. Laudicina, *World Poverty and Development: A Survey of American Opinion* (Overseas Development Council, October 1973).

Clearly, it is none too early to start laying the groundwork for a renaissance of a vigorous and generous American internationalism consistent with the needs for world order in the remainder of the century. At a minimum, initiatives could be taken along the following lines:

1. The United States, by its own example, could play down the use of force as a sanction behind diplomacy and encourage the dismantling of permanent military coalitions premised on the prospect of an international clash of arms between major ideological groupings. This would not preclude the maintenance of the minimal military forces necessary to assure the Soviet Union or any other potential adversary that it would be futile for them to resolve their disputes with the United States by force. And to dissuade the powerful nations from picking on the weak, it may be necessary occasionally to underline the fact that the United States reserves the right to help the victims of military attack. Meanwhile the United States could support neutralism and arms limitation in areas previously the scene of great power confrontation. It might encourage the development of institutions for regional multilateral security in such neutralized arenas, to be administered by the local nations, with the United Nations involved in dispute-resolution and peacekeeping in case of a breakdown of regional mechanisms, and with a superpower concert operating as the ultimate backup. At a minimum, the restricted role of the military strength of the superpowers could be conveyed by demilitarizing the vocabulary of power that has been featured in U.S. foreign policy pronouncements since World War II.

2. The United States could seek out increased opportunities for cooperating on practical projects with ideological opponents. This would involve resisting temptations to mobilize cold war allies to speak in concert on new issues or to rely on alliance structures as the scaffolding for new institutions. It might require more work and some sacrifice of efficiency to put together new functionally specific coalitions that cut across the preexisting military alliances. Without such initiatives by the United States an open world of interdependent and mutually respectful communities has little chance of evolving. A necessary corollary to such initiatives, however, is self-restraint against inflating particular conflicts of interest into ideological conflicts over ways of life.

3. The United States could vigorously resume its role of champion of a more open global market in natural resources, industrial products,

investment, and monetary transactions—again, more by example than by preaching to others. This would probably require a substantial program of adjustment assistance at home and a willingness to negotiate systems of reasonable international safeguards and compensations for those societies less well equipped to take their chances in the free market. A corollary would be U.S. support for preferential access by poor Third World countries to the markets of industrial countries without requiring the poor to grant preferential or even free access to their markets in return.

4. The United States could cooperate in funneling capital and other resources from the rich to the poor countries through international institutions. If such North-South resource transfers are to help significantly in bettering the lives of the world's poor and alleviating their growing hostility toward the affluent minority, the people of well-endowed countries, particularly the United States, eventually will need to share substantial parts of their wealth with those less fortunate on grounds other than economic self-interest or military security. In response to the prospect of global shortages of food, energy, or other essential goods, the United States should visibly and credibly support equitable sharing arrangements and refrain from touting its ability to be self-sufficient.

5. As the world's leading center of technological innovation, the United States could make it attractive to others to share in the opportunities now arising to develop global systems for exploiting the earth's wealth for the benefit of mankind. If U.S. scientists and technologists are to be granted access to coastal and seabed areas containing sources of new mineral wealth, if preferred frequencies and orbital slots for space satellite systems are to be granted willingly to the United States, and if other nations are to cooperate with the United States and other advanced industrial nations in constructing global networks for monitoring and regulating the use of the globe's atmospheric, water, and terrestrial resources to ensure that essential ecosystems are not dangerously abused—then the United States will have to stimulate other countries, including the technological have-nots, to cooperate with U.S. nationals in these ventures. This probably means that equity criteria will have to be significantly applied not only to the responsibilities for funding the new multilateral ventures but also to the distribution of benefits.

6. In promoting greater reliance on multilateral institutions, the United States could support principles of representation that would give voice, insofar as possible, to all communities affected by the multilateral activities. International lending institutions, for example, might give the recipient countries more responsibility than at present for allocating the money and setting the conditions of repayment. The design of maritime regimes will also offer opportunities to give the consumers of the various resources of the sea as well as their producers and marketers a fair say in how the ocean commons is administered. The same holds for other transnationally used environments and resources, some traditionally considered subject only to domestic jurisdiction. The shared participation should be on more than a token basis and should include decision-making functions as well as technical tasks. In short the people of the United States would have to be more willing than they have been to dispense with some of the traditional trappings of national sovereignty.

7. Finally, the United States could support the quest for status and even juridical recognition by transnational and subnational organizations and movements, whether based on ethnic, religious, generational, or other cultural or class grounds. Americans would be encouraged to experiment with forms of association and community that cut across the nation-state structure of world politics. In upholding the principles of freedom of information, personal mobility, and association for all members of the world community, the United States government would mainly work through international forums rather than unilaterally demand such behavior from other states.

These U.S. policy suggestions assume a continuing increase in the centrifugal forces disintegrating the cold war coalitions simultaneously with the growth of crosscutting coalitions. They assume further increases in the transnational mobility of people, goods, and information—compromising the ability of national governments, in the absence of substantial multilateral cooperation, to implement social justice and other public interest objectives. They assume a continued worldwide growth of feelings of relative deprivation on the part of the less affluent countries and the less affluent social strata within countries. Finally, they assume that the current complex field of interacting social forces can be significantly shaped by U.S. foreign policy in the next few years.

It is doubtful that, given the current volatility of world politics, any alternative U.S. foreign policy orientation could be less provisional or speculative, *even* if premised on the conservative notion that "things only seem to change, but everywhere they remain the same." The question for American readers is this: With the vast uncertainties ahead, what possibilities for change in the international system would be most consistent with the essential spirit of this country? One set of answers has been attempted here, not in certitude but in the spirit of dialogue.

Index

Acheson, Dean 12n
Africa, 104, 106, 114, 189, 192
Albania, 50, 138, 193
Alger, Chadwick F., 159n
Algeria, 138, 181
Alienation, 164–70, 178–79
Alliance for Progress, 94, 96
Alsace, 139
American Institute of Public Opinion, 26–27
Andean Common Market, 154
Angell, Robert Cooley, 163n, 186n
Anticommunist coalition: and domestic problems, 42–44; economic interdependence in, 36–42; foundations of, 8–28; international pressures, 109–19; nonmilitary issues, 31–33; security issues, 29–31, 43; transforming of, 44
Arab oil embargo, 18, 35
Arabs, 23, 96, 105, 106, 119
Aron, Raymond, 164
Asher, Robert E., 202n
Association of Southeast Asian Nations (ASEAN), 194–95
Atlantic community, 43. See also North Atlantic Treaty Organization
Australia, 50, 177, 191
Austria, 84

Ball, George, 158, 191n
Baltic Sea, 11
Bancroft, Harding F., 199n
Bandung conference (1955), 52, 98
Bangladesh, 100, 177
Bank of America, 74, 148–49
Barnett, A. Doak, 78n, 79n
Baruch Plan, 127, 129, 198
Basques, 175
Becker, A. S., 100n

Beckett, J. C., 173n
Belgium, 153, 174–75
Bell, Daniel, 163, 168n
Bender, Peter, 55n, 64n
Berenyi, Ivan, 68n
Bergsten, C. Fred, 37n, 39n, 41, 105, 155n
Berlin, 90
Berlin agreement, 55
Berne, Switzerland, 177
Bettelheim, Bruno, 166n
Biafra, 177
Biosphere, 131–35
Black Panthers, 180, 181
Black Sea, 11, 23
Blake, David H., 156n
Blechman, Barry M., 19n
Bolivia, 154
Borghese, Elizabeth Mann, 162
Boulding, Kenneth, 162
Brandt, Willy, 87–88, 91
Brazil, 101, 107
Bretons, 177
Bretton Woods agreements, 41
Brewster, R. Kingman, Jr., 162, 199n
Brezhnev, Leonid I., 7n, 15, 49, 52, 62, 64, 69–70, 71, 88n, 99
Brinton, Crane C., 24n
British navy, 11
Bromke, Adam, 49, 64, 65n
Bronfenbrenner, Martin, 40n
Brown, Courtney, 158n
Brown, Lester R., 141n
Brown, Neville, 18n
Brown, Seyom, 12n, 15n, 112n, 203n, 211n
Brubaker, Sterling, 132n, 133n, 137
Brzezinski, Zbigniew, 15n, 21n, 42n, 163, 191n
Burks, Richard V., 67n

Camps, Miriam, 41, 201, 206n
Canada, 43, 74, 79, 81, 90
Cantril, Albert H., 27n, 211n
Caribbean Sea, 11, 23
Carman, E. Day, 12n
Carnoy, Martin, 154n
Castro, Fidel, 23, 96, 181
Central American Common Market, 154
Central Europe, 94
Chardin, Pierre Teilhard de, 162
Chase Manhattan Bank, 74
Chiang Kai-shek, 51
China, 28, 32, 50. See also Peoples Republic of China; Sino-Soviet split
Chossudovsky, Evgeny, 69n
Chou En-lai, 51, 52, 80–81
Clark, Grenville, 129n
Clausen, A. W., 148
Clubb, O. Edmund, 51n
Club of Rome, 132, 162, 197
Cohen, Paul, 17n
Colombia, 154
COMECON. See Council for Mutual Economic Assistance
Common Agricultural Policy of (EC), 39
Common Market. See European Community
Communications, 17, 107, 112, 141–42, 146, 180, 181
Communist China. See Peoples Republic of China
Communist Party of the Soviet Union (CPSU), 46, 47–49, 50, 55, 60, 62; Party Congresses, 47, 68, 69–70
Comte, G., 106n
Connor, Walker, 173n, 178n
Connor, Walter D., 167n
Cooper, Richard N., 31n, 36n, 151, 158n, 201
Coplin, William D., 192n
Cornwall, John, 138n
Cosmopolitanism, 161–63, 179, 188
Council for Environmental Programs, 203
Council for Mutual Economic Assistance (COMECON), 56–59, 65, 74, 84, 88, 117, 126, 193–94
Council of Europe, 88, 89
Council of the Americas, 148
Cousins, Norman, 162
Cox, Robert W., 157
CPSU. See Communist Party of the Soviet Union
Crimean Tatars, 177
Croatia, 175
Cuba, 50, 67, 113; missile crisis in, 15, 23

Czechoslovakia, 25, 48–49, 52, 55, 56, 57, 61, 64, 89, 119, 176

Dallin, Alexander, 50n
Danube Commission, 59
Danube Iron Works (Hungary), 84
de Gaulle, Charles, 14, 30, 88
Denmark, 192
Devlin, Bernadette, 180
Diebold, John, 147n
Diebold, William, Jr., 30n, 34n
Dinerstein, Herbert, 97n
Driscoll, Everly, 142n
Drucker, Peter F., 147–48
Dubcek, Alexander, 48–49
Dubos, René, 132n, 133–34
Dunlop, 147
Durdin, Tillman, 80n

Eastern Europe, 54–65, 176, 189, 193–94. See also Czechoslovakia; Hungary; Poland; Rumania
East Germany, 55, 67, 192
East-West Conference on European Security and Cooperation, 59
EC. See European Community
Eckstein, Alexander, 81n
Economic policy: in anticommunist coalition, 34–42; new importance of, 29–30, 110–17; in regions, 153–56; toward Third World, 93–108; and U.S.–Soviet relations, 67–78; world integration of 200–02
Economic Policy Committee (AFL-CIO), 37
Ecuador, 154
Egypt, 18, 107, 111, 138
Ehrlich, Ann H., 132n
Ehrlich, Paul R., 132n
Environment: dangers to, 123, 131–40, 168; UN protection of, 202–04
Erikson, Erik, 162
Ermath, Fritz, 59n
Estonians, 177
Ethnicity, 171–78, 179, 189
Etzioni, Amitai, 191n
Europe, 84–87, 106. See also Eastern Europe; Western Europe
European Community (EC), 30, 31, 38, 39, 44, 70, 104, 114, 123, 139, 159; agricultural policy, 40; and domestic interests, 43; and economic transnationalism, 153; and foreign investments, 147; new economic relations with U.S., 35; and regional integration, 192–93; and Third World, 115; and USSR, 88

European Free Trade Association, 43
Evans, Peter, 150n, 152n

Fabian, Larry L., 200n, 203n
Fairhall, David, 19n
Falk, Richard, 162
Farlow, Robert, 59n
Faupl, Rudolph, 38n
Federal Republic of Germany, 30, 31, 43, 55, 63, 67, 81, 84, 91, 153, 165
Feron, James, 62n
Fest, Joachim, 165n
Feuer, Lewis S., 166n
Fiat, 85
Finland, 192
First Development Decade, 94, 101
First National City Bank, 74
Flacks, Richard, 166n
Flemings, 174–75
Food and Agriculture Organization (UN), 203
Ford Motor Company, 70
France, 11, 15, 43, 69, 79n, 114, 138, 153, 165, 192
Free, Lloyd A., 211, 212
French-Canadians, 175
Fuller, R. Buckminster, 162

Galtung, Johan, 88–90
Gardner, John, 163n
GATT. See General Agreement on Tariffs and Trade
Gelb, Leslie H., 27n
General Agreement on Tariffs and Trade (GATT), 39, 40, 60, 104, 158, 159, 201
General and comprehensive disarmament plan (GCD), 127
General Motors Corporation, 145
Gennard, John, 157n
Germany, 10, 57, 64, 86, 90. See also East Germany; Federal Republic of Germany
Gierek, Edward, 64
Gilpin, Robert L., 30n
Gladwyn, Lord, 191n
Goldberg, Paul M., 159n
Goldhagen, Erich, 177n
Gold, Herbert, 166n
Gomulka, Wladislaw, 47, 63, 64
Good, Robert C., 95n
Gosovic, Branislav, 104n
Grant, James P., 101n, 201n
Great Britain, 10, 11–12, 15, 43, 50, 79n, 153, 191–92, 193
Greece, 138, 177
Griffith, William E., 14n, 58n

Grossman, Bernhard, 81n
Group of Seventy-seven, 103–04, 202
Grunwald, Joseph, 153–54
Gulf of Finland, 11
Gupta, Sisir, 100–01
Gwertzman, Bernard, 73n

Haiphong harbor, 15, 71
Halaby, Najeeb, 199n
Halle, Louis J., 12n
Hallstein, Walter, 191n
Halperin, Morton H., 74n
Hannigan, Thomas, 38n
Hardin, Garrett, 134, 136
Hardt, John P., 73n
Harrison, Selig S., 33n, 74n
Hawks, Nigel, 204n
Heigert, Hans, 165n
Helsinki conference (1973), 91–92
Herrera, Felipe, 191n
Hijazi, Isham A., 106n
Hobbing, Enno, 148n
Ho Chi Minh, 46
Hocking, William Ernest, 162
Hoffman, Abbie, 170n
Hong Kong, 81
Horelick, A. L., 100n
Hungary, 25, 56, 84, 176; economic modernization in, 60–61; nationalism in, 61–62; and USSR, 47–48, 60–62
Hunter, Robert E., 31n, 101n
Husak, Gustav, 49
Hutchins, Robert M., 162
Huxley, Julian, 162
Hymer, Stephen, 150n

IAEA. See International Atomic Energy Agency
IBM. See International Business Machines
IBRD. See World Bank
Ideology, and determination of foreign policy, 21–23
IMF. See International Monetary Fund
India, 15, 98, 99, 100, 105–06, 107, 111, 177–78
Indian Ocean, 19
Indochina, 22
Indonesia, 50, 95, 107, 111, 194
Inglehart, Ronald, 165n, 171n
INTELSAT, 141
Intercontinental missiles. See Nuclear weapons
International Atomic Energy Agency (IAEA), 128, 198, 203
International Bank for Reconstruction and Development. See World Bank

International Business Machines (IBM), 145, 147, 162
International Commission for the Protection of the Rhine against Pollution, 139–40
International Conference of Communist and Workers' Parties (1969), 50
International Conference of Free Trade Unions, 156–57
International Federation of Chemical and General Workers Union, 156
International Federation of Free Trade Unions, 159
International Institute of Applied Systems Analysis, 72
International Institute of Labor Studies, 157
International Labour Organisation, 159
International Maritime Consultative Organization, 203
International Metalworkers Federation, 157
International Monetary Fund (IMF), 40, 41, 103, 104, 159, 200–02
International power, changing character of, 112–17
International Telephone and Telegraph Corporation (ITT), 145
International Transport Workers Federation, 157
Iran, 18, 97
Iraq, 18, 100
Israel, 15, 18, 23, 98, 99, 119, 138
Italy, 50, 69, 79, 85, 138

Jager, Elizabeth, 156n
Japan, 10, 15, 30, 42, 70, 74, 81, 94, 194; and balance of military power, 116; and China, 82–84; communist party of, 50; domestic problems, 43; and economic power, 34, 116–17; and foreign investments, 147; and new international system, 114–15; and Third World, 115; and U.S., 32–33, 40, 82, 83; and USSR, 73–74, 82–84
Jennings, Eugene, 163n
Jews, 77, 177
Joint U.S.-Soviet Commercial Commission, 72
Jones, Joseph M., 12n
Jones, Stephen B., 10n
Judy, Richard W., 68n

Kadar, Janos, 47, 61, 62
Kaiser, Robert G., 85n
Kama River project, 70
Karnow, Stanley, 81n

Kauanda, Kenneth, 98
Kegley, Charles W., 192n
Kennedy John F., 22, 23, 26, 30n
Kennedy Round, 34, 37
Kenniston, Kenneth, 167n
Keohane, Robert O., 30n, 146n, 150n, 157n
Keynes, John Maynard, 149
Khrushchev, Nikita, 23, 48, 52, 94; and destalinization program, 46–47; and Poland, 63; and Sino-Soviet split, 51
Kidel, Boris, 175n
Kindleberger, Charles P., 150n, 158–59
Kissinger, Henry A., 35, 36, 76, 77, 212
Knauss, John A., 136n
Korea, 194
Korvig, Bennet, 61n
Kosygin, Aleksei N., 68
Kotz, Nick, 73n
Krause, Lawrence B., 34n, 147n, 150–51
Kremlin. See Union of Soviet Socialist Republics

Lake Constance, 139
Laqueur, Walter, 7n
Latin America, 97, 104, 106, 136, 154
Latin American Free Trade Association (LAFTA), 154
Latvians, 177
Laudicina, Paul A., 212n
Law of the Sea Conference (1974), 137, 202–03
Lebanon, 138
Lendvai, Paul, 176n
Lenin, Nikolai, 69, 177. See also Marxism-Leninism
Levinson, Charles, 156, 157n
Lewis, Flora, 35n
Libya, 138
Lieberman, Herman, 68n
Liebert, Robert, 168n
Lippmann, Walter, 11n
Lipset, Seymour Martin, 171n
Lithuanians, 177
Litvak, I. A., 157n
Lodge, Henry Cabot, 199
Lowenthal, Richard, 53n
Luard, Evan, 203n
Lubell, Samuel, 165n
Lubman, Stanley B., 82n
Ludwigshafen, 139
Lusaka conference, 98

MacKinder, Halford J., 10
Macmillan, Harold, 30n
McNamara, Robert S., 13–14, 101, 102, 107

Maddox, Brenda, 142n
Madras, 181
Magyars, 176
Mahan, Alfred Thayer, 10
Maier, Herbert, 159n
Malaysia, 50, 194
Malmgren, Harold B., 34n, 37n
Management, 38–39, 156
Mankoff, Milton, 166n
Mansholt, Sicco, 162
Mao Tse-tung, 46, 51, 52, 53, 80
Marcuse, Herbert A., 170n
Marshall Plan, 33, 34
Martin, Lawrence E., 95n
Marxism-Leninism, 24, 25, 47, 50–51, 177
Maule, C. J., 157n
Maurer, Ion Gheorghe, 58
Mazour, Anatole, 12n
Mead, Margaret, 162, 169–70
Meadows, Dennis L., 132n
Meadows, Donella H., 132n
Mediterranean Sea, 11, 19, 23, 138
Mekong basin, 195
Mexico, 101, 191
Meyerhoff, Barbara G., 167n
Michelin Company, 145
Middle East, 18–19, 23, 77, 98, 99–100, 115, 118–19
Military power, 9–20, 54–55, 110–11, 113, 116, 118. See also Nuclear weapons
Monaco, 138
Mongolia, 11
Monnet, Jean, 191n
Monroe Doctrine, 11
Morgan, Dan, 85n
Morocco, 138
Morse, Edward L., 31n
Multinational corporations, 145–52, 154, 156
Multipolarity, 7, 33, 117–18
Mumford, Lewis, 162
Mutual deterrence, 129, 130
Myrdal, Gunnar, 162

Nagy, Imre, 47
Nasser, Gamal Abdel, 52, 98
Nationalism, in Hungary, 44, 61–62; in Poland, 47, 63–64. See also Ethnicity
Nationalist China, 96. See also Taiwan
National Research Center (Rome), 138
Nation-state system, 3; adequacy of, 123–24; and alienation, 163–71; and communications, 141–42; and cosmopolitanism, 161–63; and domestic economic policy, 144–45, 150–52; domi-nance of, 124–25; ethnicity, 171–78; incapacities of, 125–42; and multina-tional corporations, 145–52; and nu-clear weapons, 129–31; and pollution, 133–35; in a polyarchy, 188; and pres-ervation of natural resources, 135–40; and space technology, 142–43
NATO. See North Atlantic Treaty Or-ganization
Natural resources, 18–19, 124, 135–40, 149
Negroes, 174
Nehru, Jawaharlal, 52, 95, 98
Netherlands, 50, 165
New Economic Mechanism (NEM), 60, 62
New Left, 165
New Zealand, 50
Nigeria, 106
Nixon, Richard M., 15, 28, 32, 33, 71, 72, 199, 200; Foreign Policy Message, 79; and China, 79, 80–81; and Third World, 96–97
Nkrumah, Kwame, 95
North America, 11, 42, 189
North Atlantic Treaty Organization (NATO), 20, 30, 31–32, 35, 87, 88, 90–91, 119
Northeast Asia, 194
Northern Ireland, 173–74
North Korea, 50
North, Robert, 52n
Northrop, F. S. C., 162
North Sea, 139
North Vietnam, 50, 67, 70, 71, 130
Norway, 50, 192
Nuclear Nonproliferation Treaty (NPT) (1968), 128, 198–99
Nuclear weapons, 13–18, 118, 123, 127–31, 198–99, 209
Nye, Joseph S., Jr., 30n, 146n, 150n, 157n, 191n
Nyerere, Julius, 98, 191n

Oberdorfer, Don, 33n, 79n
Oceans, 135, 136–37
Oder-Neisse River, 63
OECD. See Organisation for Economic Co-operation and Development
Official Development Assistance, 102
Ohira, Masoyoshi, 84n
Okinawa, 32n, 82
OPEC. See Organization of Petroleum Exporting Countries
Organisation for Economic Co-operation and Development (OECD), 123, 159

Organization of Petroleum Exporting Countries (OPEC), 105, 155–56
Organized labor, 37–38, 156–58
Osgood, Robert E., 11n
Ostpolitik. See Brandt, Willy
O'Toole, Thomas, 73n
Overseas Development Council, 212

Pakistan, 100, 191
Palestinians, 177
Palmer, Michael, 91n
Pan-Europeanism, 88–90
Pares, Bernard, 12n
Patolichev, N., 69
Payne, Stanley, 175n
Pearson, Lester B., 162, 202n
Peoples Republic of China, 59, 67, 73, 94, 96, 112, 136, 194; and balance of military power, 116; and economic power, 117; and Eastern Europe, 52, 53; and foreign trade, 81; and Japan, 82–84; and Third World, 106, 115; and U.S., 78–81; and USSR, 50–54, 78, 80–81, 82, 96
Persian Gulf, 19, 23
Peru, 154
Peterson, Peter G., 67n, 70, 75, 76
Philippines, 194
Piccard, Jacques, 138n
Pisar, Samuel J., 68–69, 85n
Pluralism, 45, 64, 65
Poland, 47, 48, 52, 56, 63–65
Polyarchy, 186–90
Portugal, 98
Postindustrialism, 43, 163–71
Prague, 48, 57
Prebisch, Raúl, 103, 191n
Protectionism, 37–38, 151–52
Protestants, 173–74
Puchala, Donald J., 192n

Quebec, 175, 181

Radhakrishnan, Sarvepalli, 162
Rakowska-Harmstone, Teresa, 49n
Ramsey, James A., 85n
Rawls, John, 206
Ray, George F., 61n
Ray, Hemen, 52n
Regionalism, 190–97
Reich, Charles A., 170
Reischauer, Edwin, 162
Reistrup, J. V., 70n
Republic of Ireland, 173
Resources for the Future, 137
Revel, Jean-François, 170n
Rheinstahl, 84

Rhine River-North Sea ecosystem, 139–40
Ridgeway, Matthew B., 199n
Ritchie-Calder, Lord, 162
Robock, Stefan H., 147n
Rockefeller, David, 74n
Rogers, William P., 91
Roll, Charles W., Jr., 27n, 211n
Roman Catholics, 173–74
Romulo, Carlos P., 98n
Roszak, Theodore, 170n
Rotterdam, 139
Royal-Dutch Shell Corporation, 145
Rubin, Jerry, 170n
Ruhr industrial plants, 139
Rumania, 52, 57–59, 85, 176, 193
Rusk, Dean, 22, 26
Russia, 10, 11–12. See also Union of Soviet Socialist Republics

Sadat, Anwar, 100
St. Gobain, 157
Sakharov, Andrei, 162
SALT. See Strategic arms limitation talks
Samuel, Howard, 38n
Saudia Arabia, 18, 106, 115
Scandinavia, 165, 193
Schwartz, Harry, 177n
Schwartz, Morton, 97n
Scotland, 177
SEATO. See Southeast Asia Treaty Organization
Second Development Decade, 102
Seeley, John, 167n
Serbia, 175, 176
Servan-Schreiber, J. J., 191n
Seton-Watson, Hugh, 175
Shils, Edward, 169n
Shoup, Paul, 176n
Shub, Anatole, 58n, 79n
Shulman, Marshall D., 25
Shultz, George P., 41
Shuster, Alvin, 35n
Siberia, 71, 73, 82
Singapore, 81, 101, 194
Sinkiang, 11
Sino-Soviet split, 50–54
Skilling, H. Gordon, 49n, 176n
Slovaks, 176
Slovenia, 175
Smith, Hedrick, 75n
Smith, William D., 156n
Smolansky, Oles M., 100n
Sohn, Louis B., 129n, 162
Sony Corporation, 145
South Africa, 98
South America, 11

South Asia, 106, 189
Southeast Asia, 106, 189, 194–97
Southeast Asia Treaty Organization (SEATO), 195
South Korea, 96, 101
South Tyrol, 177
South Vietnam, 96
Soviet Moslems, 177
Soviet Union. *See* Union of Soviet Socialist Republics
Spain, 138, 175
Special Drawing Rights, 103
Spykman, Nicholas, 10n
Stalinism, 48, 62
Stalin, Joseph, 10, 41
Stein, Robert E., 140n
Steyr-Daimler-Puch, 84
Stockholm conference. *See* United Nations Conference on the Human Environment
Strange, Susan, 31n
Strategic arms limitation talks (SALT), 14, 15, 128, 198
Strauss, Franz Joseph, 191n
Strong, John W., 50n, 51n
Strong, Maurice, 162, 203n
Study of Critical Environmental Problems (SCEP), 132
Sukarno, 52, 95
Sulikowski, Terese, 203n
Sullivan, Walter, 134n
Sunkel, Osvaldo, 152n
Supersonic transports, 134
Supranationalism, 158–60
Sweden, 192
Syria, 138
Szulc, Tad, 62n, 106n

Taiwan, 79, 80, 81, 83, 101
Tamil Nad movement, 177
Tanaka, Kakuei, 83
Tanganyika, 98
Tanzania, 97
Thailand, 50, 194, 195
Third World, 59, 177, 202; China as potential leader of, 115; demands on industrialized countries, 103; efforts at coalition in, 98–99; GNP and income growth in, 101–02; lack of unity in, 104; leverage with developed countries, 104–06; new approaches to, 96–102; and OPEC, 155; and polarization, 93–96; in a polyarchy, 188; prospects of, 106–08; and protectionism, 152; and regional integration, 153–55, 195–96; and threat from countercultures, 181. *See also* Group of Seventy-seven
Tinbergen, Jan, 162
Tinker, John, 139n, 203n
Tito, 46, 176
Tocqueville, Alexis de, 10
Toffler, Alvin, 163n
Toma, Peter A., 61n
Touré, Sékou, 95
Toynbee, Arnold, 162
Transnationalism: emerging, 126; and environmental control, 131–35; multinational corporations and economic, 145–51; and natural resources, 135–40; and nuclear arms control, 126–31; political responses to economic, 151–60; and polyarchy, 186–87, 188. *See also* World community
Transportation, 17, 19, 107, 134, 140–41, 146, 180
Transylvania, 176
Treaties of Peace, Friendship, and Cooperation, 100
Truman, Harry S., 127
Tunisia, 138
Tuohy, William, 138n
Turkey, 97, 138, 156, 177, 191

Ukrainians, 52, 177
Ulam, Adam B., 12n, 48n
Ulster, 173, 174
UN. *See* United Nations
UNCTAD. *See* United Nations Conference on Trade and Development
Unilever Corporation, 145
Union of Soviet Socialist Republics, 28, 106, 112, 189; and arms limitation treaty, 14; and balance of military power, 116; and Brandt, 87; and China, 30, 50–54, 78, 80–81, 82, 96; and coercive use of power, 119; and cold war coalitions, 8–9; and COMECON, 56; and commercial relations with Japan, 73–74; and commercial relations with U.S., 70–76; and control of nuclear weapons, 127–28, 198–99; and controversy within communist party, 50; and Czechoslovakia, 48–49; and détente, 86–87, 91; and Eastern Europe, 54–65; and East-West economic relations, 84, 85; and EC, 88; and economic power, 116–17; and ethnic nationalism, 176–77; and geopolitical strategy, 12–13; and Helsinki conference, 91–92; and Hungary, 47–48, 60–62; ideology, 21–26; and India, 99, 100; and international broadcasting,

142; and legitimacy of authority, 46–50; and limited war doctrine, 16–17; and Middle East, 18–19, 99–100; and multiple coalitions, 114; and mutual deterrence, 130; naval power, 19; new relations with allies, 110; and Poland, 47, 48, 63–65; and Rumania, 57–59; and Siberian pipeline, 73; and Third World, 94–96, 97, 106, 115; and threat from countercultures, 181. *See also* Communist Party of the Soviet Union

United Kingdom. *See* Great Britain

United Nations (UN), 97, 102, 126, 127, 199–200, 202–04

United Nations Association, 199

United Nations Conference on the Human Environment (1972), 106, 131, 203

United Nations Conference on Trade and Development (UNCTAD), 59, 103, 106, 159, 202

United States, 10, 48, 59, 67, 90; anticommunist policy, 26–28; and arms limitation treaty, 14; and balance of military power, 116; black alienation in, 174; and China, 78–81; and coercive use of power, 119; and cold war coalitions, 8–9, 10; commercial relations with USSR, 70–76; and control of nuclear weapons, 127–28, 198–99; and détente, 91; and EC, 153; economic policy, 33–34, 41; initiatives to be taken by, 213–16; and international broadcasting, 142; and Japan, 32–33, 40, 82, 83; and limited war doctrine, 16–17; and Middle East, 18–19, 99; and military intervention, 26–27; and military security, 11–20; and multinational corporations, 147; and multiple coalitions, 114; and mutual deterrence, 130; and NATO countries, 32; new relations with allies, 110–12; opposition to Vietnam war in, 164; popular opinion in, 211–12; and Siberian pipeline, 73; and Sino-Japanese relations, 82; and Third World, 94–97, 115; trade policies, 36–40; and UN, 200. *See also* Anticommunist coalition

Uren, Philip E., 56n, 85n

Urwin, Derek W., 175n

U.S.-Soviet space flight, 72

U.S. Defense Department, 70

U.S. Export-Import Bank, 71, 72

U.S. navy, 11

USSR. *See* Union of Soviet Socialist Republics

U.S. State Department, 70–71

U.S. Trade Expansion Act (1962), 34

Valkenier, Elizabeth Kridl, 97n

Vance, Cyrus R., 199n

Verguèse, Dominique, 139n

Vernon, Raymond, 146n, 153n, 158

Vietnam war, 22–23, 27, 77, 96, 119, 164

Wakaizumi, Kei, 84n

Wales, 177

Walker-Leigh, Vanya, 104n

Walloons, 174–75

Walters, Robert S., 104n, 159n

Waltz, Jay, 79n

Ward, Barbara, 132n, 133–34, 162

Warsaw Pact, 47, 57, 63, 64, 87

Wasowski, Stanislaw, 68n

Watergate, 169

Watson, Arthur K., 162

Watts, William, 211, 212

Weather, 140

Weiss, Edith Brown, 140n

Wells, Louis T., Jr., 146n

Wenk, Edward, Jr., 135, 136n

Werth, Alexander, 12n

Western Europe, 30–32, 42, 125, 189; alienation in, 164–65; and economic power, 116–17; preconditions for regional integration of, 192–93

West Germany. *See* Federal Republic of Germany

White, Robert M., 140n

Wiesner, Jerome B., 199n

Willrich, Mason, 199n

Wilson, George C., 19n

Wionczek, Miguel S., 154n

Wohlstetter, Albert, 17n

Wolfe, Thomas W., 16n, 19n, 57n

World Bank (IBRD), 41, 101, 102, 126, 159, 201, 202

World community: desiderata for effective, 204–07; initiatives for U.S., 213–16; organizations tending to, 198–204; steps toward, 209–10

World Meteorological Organization, 203

Wriggins, W. Howard, 95n

Yankelovich, Daniel, 167n

Yost, Charles W., 199n

Yugoslavia, 25, 50, 60, 138, 175–76, 191, 193

Zambia, 98

Zimmerman, William, 25n, 59n, 60n